TWENTIETH CENTURY VIEWS

The aim of this series is to present the best in contemporary critical opinion on major authors, providing a twentieth century perspective on their changing status in an era of profound revaluation.

Maynard Mack, *Series Editor*
Yale University

HOMER

HOMER

A COLLECTION OF CRITICAL ESSAYS

Edited by
George Steiner
and
Robert Fagles

Prentice-Hall, Inc., *Englewood Cliffs, N.J.*

ENGLEWOOD CLIFFS, N.J.

LIBRARY OF CONGRESS CATALOG CARD NO.: 62-16890

Printed in the United States of America

39457-C

Current printing (last digit):

13 12 11 10 9 8 7 6 5 4

Foreword

What we offer here is not intended as a manual of critical governance. It is a book based entirely on the principle of delight. It seeks to conjoin the reader to the great company of those who, like himself, have found in Homer one of the prime mirrors and windows of the soul. It is a collection of lively encounters between Homer and some of the more perceptive and articulate of his modern readers.

We make no claim to inclusiveness. In particular, we have made no attempt to offer a representative selection of Homeric scholarship. (Any such would have to include large sections on Homeric archeology and philology. These vital topics, moreover, are dealt with, in the light of the best modern scholarship, in the long-awaited and recently published *Companion to Homer,* edited by F. H. Stubbings and the late Professor A. J. B. Wace.)

We have, however, tried to exemplify the startling diversity of modern critical methods. And while restrictions in length have forced us to omit the famous, controversial essay by Simone Weil, the reader will find here many modes of approach ranging from the Marxist to the philosophic and the allegoric. He will see the artist, the scholar, the anthropologist, the critic, each seeking his own path to the fact of Homer. None has a monopoly of truth or insight. Criticism is always partial; only the work of art is whole. But the variousness of critical effort points to the greater miracle—to the truth that Homer, after some twenty-seven hundred years, continues to be as alive, as challenging, and as crucial to our imaginings as he was to the ancient Greeks. Even as he will continue to invite criticism, so he will survive it.

G. S., R. F.

Table of Contents

HOMER

Introduction: Homer and the Scholars

by George Steiner

When a small boy, I was confronted with one of those questionnaires inquiring what personages of history I should most like to have met. I answered Homer, Christ, and Shakespeare. Not out of any precocious sublimity, but because I was resolved to discover from each whether he had, in fact, existed and whether he had spoken the marvelous words attributed to him. Unaware, I had struck upon the great triple theme of what the nineteenth century called the higher criticism.

On these deep waters scholarship had launched its grand armadas. The discovery of the nature of Homeric composition, the analytic study of the Gospels and of the historical Jesus, and the quest for the identity of Shakespeare were the three classic mysteries toward which scholarship directed its modern weapons: archaeology, linguistics, bibliographic recension. But in the wake of the great galleons of erudition there has always swarmed a motley host of amateurs, mystics, and inspired cranks. The Homeric question, scriptural exegesis, and the problem of the authorship of Shakespeare's plays have long been regarded by the layman as fair game. Here everyman has his persuasion, and no decade passes without its new theory. Of late, we have been assured that the *Odyssey* was written by a young woman, that Christ survived Calvary and lies buried in Northern India, and that the manuscripts of Shakespeare are to be found in Marlowe's tomb.

Professional scholars react to such beliefs with bitter scorn. But they are haunted by a curious fact: in each of these three pre-eminent riddles of literary and historical criticism, it is the outsider who has made some of the most brilliant and decisive discoveries. An obsessed amateur dug up Troy, and a young architect with a passion for cryptography broke the secret of the Minoan script. A journalist—admittedly, an Edmund Wilson—was perhaps the first to realize the implications of the Dead Sea scrolls. An eighteenth century civil servant, Maurice Morgann, was the first to

"Homer and the Scholars." From *The Atlantic Monthly,* Vol. 208, No. 2 (August 1961), 77-84.

bring to bear on a Shakespearean text modern psychological and historical insights.

Homeric scholars, Semitic philologists, and professional students of Shakespeare, moreover, are themselves creatures of passion and fanatic conviction. No areas of humane learning solicit more ferocious controversy. There is something in philology that appeals to the worst in man. A. E. Housman's reviews were founded on the axiom that a false emendation is a far worse crime than murder. But behind the brutality and pontifications in high academic places, we hear a whistling in the dark. No one would deny the extraordinary accomplishments of historians, comparative linguists, and archaeologists. Yet the stubborn truth remains: today the Homeric Question is not much nearer solution than it was in 1795, when Wolf published his *Prolegomena ad Homerum*. The historical person of Christ and the composition of the Gospels are matters for conjecture no less than when Renan wrote the *Vie de Jésus* (1863). And there are numerous puzzles regarding Shakespeare's plays and the range of reference in them baffling enough to convert sane men to Baconianism even now.

But, though the problems remain, our methods of approach to them change. And the fascinating aspect is this: in each case—Homer, Christ, Shakespeare—the currents of scholarship and judgment follow the same pattern.

In the late nineteenth century, dismemberment was all the rage. In a single chapter of Luke, textual analysis revealed five distinct levels of authorship and interpolation. The plays attributed to that illiterate actor Shakespeare appeared to have been compiled by a committee which included Bacon, the Earl of Oxford, Marlowe, recusant Catholics, and printers' devils of extraordinary ingenuity. This fine fury of decomposition lasted well into the 1930's. As late as 1934, Gilbert Murray could discover no reputable scholar ready to defend the view that a single poet had written either or both the *Iliad* and the *Odyssey*.

Today, the wheel has come full turn. In Homeric, Biblical, and Shakespearean scholarship, unitarianism carries the day. To Professor Whitman of Harvard, the central personal vision and "ineradicable unity" of the *Iliad* are beyond doubt.

There are material and psychological reasons for this reversal of judgment. We have grown increasingly respectful of the tenacity of the written word. The higher criticism assumed that if a text was very ancient or had been often reproduced, it would necessarily be corrupt. We are no longer so sure. Comparisons between the Dead Sea scrolls and the canonic version of the Bible suggest that ancient literature, where it was regarded in a sacred light, was handed down with great fidelity. In reverence later scribes or scholiasts even reproduced errors or archaic words which they no longer understood.

What is even more important, a post-Freudian age regards the act of literary composition as one of extreme complexity. Where the nineteenth century editor saw a lacuna or interpolation, we tend to see the indirections or special logic of the poetic imagination. Our entire image of the mind has altered. The higher critics, Wilamowitz or Wellhausen, were anatomists; to get at the heart of a thing they took it to pieces. We, like the men of the sixteenth century, incline to regard mental processes as organic and integral. A modern art historian has written of *la vie des formes,* the implication being that in the life of art, as in that of organic matter, there are complications of design and autonomous energies which cannot be dissected. Wherever possible, we prefer to leave a thing whole.

Moreover, we no longer expect from genius a constant performance. We know that great painters on occasion produce bad pictures. The fact that *Titus Andronicus* is full of shoddy violence is no proof whatever that Shakespeare did not write it; or, more precisely, it is no proof that he wrote only the good lines. This change in perspective is vital with reference to the *Iliad* and *Odyssey*. A hundred years ago, a passage which struck an editor as inferior was confidently bracketed as an interpolation or textual corruption. Today, we simply invoke the fact that poets are not always at their best. Homer can nod.

Finally, there has occurred a deep change in our understanding of myth. We have come to realize that myths are among the subtlest and most direct languages of experience. They re-enact moments of signal truth or crisis in the human condition. But mythology is more than history made memorable; the mythographer—the poet—is the historian of the unconscious. This gives to the great myths their haunting universality. Not since the chiliastic panics of the late tenth century, when men believed that the Second Coming was at hand, moreover, has there been an age more nightmare-ridden by mythical imaginings than our own. Men who have placed the figure of Oedipus at the heart of their psychology, or who have fought for political survival against the myth of the superman and the thousand-year *Reich,* know that fables are deadly serious. More than our predecessors, therefore, we approach Homer on his own terms.

At the core of the Homeric poems lies the remembrance of one of the greatest disasters that can befall man: the destruction of a city. A city is the outward sum of man's nobility; in it, his condition is most thoroughly humanized. When a city is destroyed, man is compelled to wander the earth or dwell in the open fields in partial return to the manner of a beast. That is the central realization of the *Iliad.* Resounding through the epic, now in stifled allusion, now in strident lament, is the dread fact that an ancient and splendid city has perished by the edge of the sea.

Homer does not narrate the fiery death of Troy. Perhaps there is in this reticence an element of poetic tact (Dante's blindness at the climax of vision); perhaps a shrewd hunch that if the *Iliad* had shown Troy burning, the feelings of the audience would have shifted wholly to the Trojan side. Cunningly, Homer suggests the final catastrophe by depicting it on a miniature scale; we are shown Hector assailing the ramparts of the Greek encampment and threatening to fire the ships.

Lacking the close of the story, we do not know over precisely which city the wooden horse cast its murderous shadow. The topography of the *Iliad* would fit what archaeologists designate as Troy VI. But signs of violent ruin are strongest in that level of the mound designated as Troy VII A. Some scholars have even argued that the setting of the poem should be transposed from Asia Minor to the Greek mainland, where a fierce, protracted siege appears to have taken place in the early Mycenaean age.

Most probably, the *Iliad* reflects not only a single episode but a great catalogue of ruin. The fabled Knossos fell in circa 1400 B.C. The cause of its overthrow is not known, but legendary recollections of the event reappear in the Greek imagination for centuries thereafter. The next two hundred years are a period of extreme obscurity. Part of the problem lies in the identification of the mysterious Peoples of the Sea, whose attacks seem to have carried as far as Egypt. One thing is certain: on both sides of the Aegean, the Mycenaean world, with its great palaces and complex dynastic and commercial relations, met with violent disaster. The citadels of Pylos and Iolkos were burnt around 1200, and golden Mycenae itself was destroyed within the century. It is during this dark, confused period, in circa 1180, that Troy VII A was sacked.

The remembrance of these ancient terrors, of city gates broken and towers burned, beats loud in the *Iliad*. The *Odyssey* speaks of the aftermath. It is the epic of the displaced person. The cities are down, and survivors wander the face of the earth as pirates or beggars. This, in fact, is what seems to have taken place during the period from 1100 to 900. The Dorian invasions drove before them groups of Helladic refugees. These fugitives carried with them shattered yet rich fragments of their own culture. The main stream of migration seems to have passed through Attica between the early eleventh and late ninth centuries. Shortly after the year 1000 B.C., the uprooted peoples began colonizing Asia Minor and the islands. Some appear to have settled in and around Athens.

This could be an important point with respect to Homer. A number of contemporary scholars believe that Athens escaped the worst ravages of the Dark Ages. After the fall of the Achaean states, the city acted as a rallying point for Greek life. Within its walls the inheritance of the Mycenaean past was kept intact. Other archaeologists deny this: "Athens faded away exactly like more obviously destroyed sites; neither architecture nor art continued, only people." We simply do not know.

But even if we assume a continuity of civilization on the Greek mainland, a most difficult question arises. In the form in which we know them, the *Iliad* and the *Odyssey* were set down between circa 750 and 700 B.C. The siege of Troy, however, falls in the early part of the twelfth century, in the closing phase of the Mycenaean age. The manner of life dramatized in the *Iliad* is strongly Mycenaean; nearly all of the fighting embodies the weapons and tactics of the Bronze Age. The world of Agamemnon, as Sir John L. Myres said, is one of which later Greeks "knew little and understood less." How, then, were memories and traditions out of the archaic past transmitted over a gap of at least four hundred years?

A brilliant discovery made in 1952 by a young British architect, Michael Ventris, gives a lead toward a possible answer. He showed that the inscriptions on tablets found at various Mycenaean sites are written in a very ancient but recognizable form of Greek. A bridge of language spans the Dark Ages. But, despite the enthusiasm of certain scholars, such as Professor Webster of London, it is a tenuous bridge. The Greek in Linear B is half a millennium older than anything to compare it with. The tablets yielded inventories of goods and weapons, lists of names, some of which reappear in Homer, and fragmentary invocations to the gods. There is no evidence, so far, of Mycenaean literature in any real sense. The script is ill-suited to the writing of poetry, and the next written Greek, which belongs to the second half of the eighth century, is, of course, in our own kind of alphabet (as derived from the Phoenicians). What came between is still a mystery. A "Mycenaean *Iliad*" may have existed in some linear script, and the art of writing did survive in Cyprus. But what little evidence we have suggests that the Mycenaean inheritance of the *Iliad* came down to the eighth century by word of mouth. What we now know is that the word was Greek.

Does this mean that the *Iliad* and *Odyssey*—as distinct from the archaic material in them—were composed orally? Since Milman Parry, it is an established fact that much of Homeric verse is formulaic. It consists of set phrases which fill the natural metrical units of the lines. Thus, for example, there are forty-six noun epithets to describe Achilles. Each has a different metrical value, and the poet chooses the one most appropriate to the prosody of the line. He creates his epic as he chants it, using a vast stock of traditional motifs and formulas to sustain his invention or his variations on a given epic theme. Such heroic recitation still exists, notably in Yugoslavia and among the Berbers of North Africa. Narrations of the fall of Troy and the wanderings of Odysseus may have been recited on numerous occasions, each time in a different version. In this light, Homer emerges as one of many itinerant singers improvising on traditional motifs for an illiterate audience: "fortunately, some master of the new art of writing had the wit to set down on papyrus this outstanding singer's renderings of a couple of themes from the repertoire." This, in essence, is the thesis argued most recently by Albert B. Lord in *The Singer of Tales*.

This is a deceptive image. No doubt the Homeric epics contain much that is of an archaic and mnemonic character. And it is true that Yugoslav shepherds, squatting in front of tape recorders, have improvised lays of prodigious length. But what does this tell us of the composition of the *Iliad?* Not enough. The work of Homer, as we know it, is of dazzling intricacy. Its design is tight and deliberate. Set it beside the finest of recorded folk poetry, and the difference leaps to eye. We are dealing in the *Iliad* with a commanding vision of man, articulate in every detail, not with a tale of adventure automatically or randomly carried forward. The entrance into action via the oblique theme of Achilles' anger is art of high sophistication. The entire design, with its inner echoes and alternance of stress and repose, follows on the particular drama of the opening. Only Book X and, perhaps, the latter part of Book VII seem to stand apart as intrusions or late adjuncts.

It is the merit of Professor Whitman's *Homer and the Heroic Tradition* to have insisted on this essential truth. He contends that the *Iliad* is a counterpart, in language, of the famous geometric symmetry distinctive of Greek vases in the period 850 to 700. He argues that "the poem as a whole forms one large concentric pattern." Whitman's scheme is too neat, and it overlooks the fact that the division of the poem into twenty-four books is a later editorial convenience. But his main point is surely valid: the *Iliad* is a design of extreme complexity and formal control. That there should be embedded in it large sections of traditional, oral poetry is certain; but that the epic as a whole should have been composed and preserved without writing is most unlikely.

But in what writing? This, again, is an intricate problem on which scholars disagree. The Ionic script, in which the *Iliad* and *Odyssey* were handed down, came into official use only in the fifth century B.C. We know scarcely anything of its previous history. This leads Whitman to conclude that the Homeric epics were initially set down in what is known as the Old Attic alphabet and later transliterated (this could account for certain oddities in our present text). The first manuscript might date from the second half of the eighth century, "from the time, if not the hand, of Homer himself." Only thirty years ago, such a theory would have made scholars howl with derision!

We have no evidence to show that a written text of such length and elaboration could have been produced at so early a date. But the alphabet was available, and trade with Phoenicia could have provided the necessary papyrus. Moreover, if such a manuscript did not exist, how could we explain the startling fact that the *Iliad* and *Odyssey* have in them hardly any material, either linguistic or narrative, that can be dated as later than 700 B.C.? The theory that the two epics were memorized and transmitted perfectly by word of mouth until they could be written down in the fifth century simply won't hold.

Let me speculate here, not as a scholar but as a critic seeking to apprehend the genius of the poem. I venture to guess that Homer was the first great poet in Western literature because he was the first to have understood the infinite resources of the written word. In the zest of the Homeric narrative, in its superb architecture, flashes the delight of a mind which has discovered that it need not deliver its creation into the fragile trust of memory. The harsh gaiety of the *Iliad* and its constant equivocation between shortness of life and eternity of fame mirror the poet's new and proud sense of his own survival. In the beginning of poetry is the word, but very near the beginning of poetry on the scale of the *Iliad* is writing.

It is entirely possible that the original "Homer manuscript" was something unique and that it was kept in the jealous possession of a bardic guild (the *Homeridae*). The newly established Panhellenic festivals of the eighth century created an audience for the "sons of Homer." These singers may well have preserved the *Iliad* and *Odyssey* in a small number of canonic texts until their wider publications in sixth century Athens (what scholars call the Pisistratean Recension).

Nor need we assume that Homer himself was literate. He may have dictated to a scribe. Indeed, I would guess that the ancient and persistent tradition of his blindness is connected to this very point. Wishing to conceal from a later, more critical age the fact of the master's technical illiteracy, the Homeridae described him as blind. Above all else, the *Iliad* and *Odyssey* proclaim that men's lives go to forgotten dust unless they are given immortality by the song of a poet. Is not that the faith of a supreme artist who, for the first time in Western literature, had at his command, if not within his own resource, the full glory of the written word?

By far the greater part of recent Homeric scholarship deals with the *Iliad*. Excavation and decipherment seem to lead to Troy rather than to Ithaca. The *Odyssey* accords neither with the search for a Mycenaean tradition nor with the theory of a geometric style. This is revealing. It points to a conviction which many readers have held from the start. The two epics are profoundly different; different in tone, in formal structure and, most important, in their vision of life. The Homeric Question, therefore, goes beyond problems of authorship and text. It must deal with the literary and psychological relations between the *Iliad* and the *Odyssey*. What happens when we read the *Iliad* through the eyes of Odysseus?

Archaeologists differ on the way in which the world image of the *Iliad* was put together. Some assert that the narratives of battle are realistic and that efforts have been made to bring archaic details up to date (the classic instance being Homer's awkward treatment of Ajax's body shield, a piece of equipment which went out of use in the tenth century). Others regard the world of Homeric Troy as a "visionary structure" in which elements ranging from the Bronze Age to the eighth century are woven together by the set formulas and conventions of the heroic style. But one thing is clear: the *Iliad* expresses a specific view of the human condition.

In no other work of world literature, with the possible exception of *War and Peace,* do we find the same image of man. And certainly not in the *Odyssey.*

The poet of the *Iliad* looks on life with those blank, unswerving eyes which stare out of the helmet slits on early Greek vases. His vision is terrifying in its sobriety, cold as the winter sun:

> "So, friend, you die also. Why all this clamour about it?
> Patroklus also is dead, who was better by far than you are.
> Do you not see what a man I am, how huge, how splendid
> and born of a great father, and the mother who bore me immortal?
> Yet even I have also my death and my strong destiny,
> and there shall be a dawn or an afternoon or a noontime
> when some man in the fighting will take the life from me also
> either with a spearcast or an arrow flown from the bowstring."
> So he spoke, and in the other the knees and the inward
> heart went slack. He let go of the spear and sat back, spreading
> wide both hands; but Achilles drawing his sharp sword struck him
> beside the neck at the collar-bone, and the double-edged sword
> plunged full length inside. He dropped to the ground face downward,
> and lay at length, and the black blood flowed, and the ground was
> soaked with it.
>
> —*Iliad,* XXI; Richmond Lattimore's translation.

The narration proceeds with inhuman calm. The sharp directness of the poet's vision is never sacrificed to the demands of pathos. In the *Iliad* the truth of life, however harsh or ironic, prevails over the occasions of feeling. This is strikingly illustrated in the crowning moment of the epic: the night encounter of Priam and Achilles. There is a stillness in the midst of hell. Looking upon each other, the bereft king and the slayer of men, shadowed by his own near doom, give voice to their great griefs. Their sorrows are immeasurable. Yet, when they have spoken they feel hungry and sit down to an ample meal. For as Achilles says of Niobe, "She remembered to eat when she was worn out with weeping." No other poet, not even Shakespeare, would have run the risk of so humble a truth at such an instant of tragic solemnity.

But this magnificent clearheadedness derives not from bitter resignation. The *Iliad* is no lament over man's estate. There is joy in it, the joy that burns in the "ancient glittering eyes" of the sages in Yeats's "Lapis Lazuli." The poet revels in the gusto of physical action and in the stylish ferocity of personal combat. He sees life lit by the fires of some central, ineradicable energy. The air seems to vibrate around the heroic personages, and the force of their being electrifies nature. Achilles' horses weep at his impending fall. Even insensate objects are kindled by this excess of life. Nestor's drinking bowl is so palpably real that archeologists claim to have dug it up three thousand years after the event.

Pure energy of being pervades the *Iliad* like the surge of the wine-dark sea, and Homer rejoices at it. This is where Simone Weil's well-known essay on the poem goes so wrong. There *is* cruelty in the saga of Troy and a sheer redness of slaughter. But even in the midst of carnage, life is in full tide and beats forward with a wild gaiety. Homer knows and proclaims that there is that in men which loves war, which is less afraid of the terrors of combat than of the long boredom of the hearth.

In the sphere of Agamemnon, Hector, and Achilles, war is the measure of man. It is the only pursuit he has been trained for (in the shadow of death, Hector worries who will teach his son how to throw a spear). Beyond the shadow, moreover, gleams the light of returning dawn. Around the ashes of Patroclus, the Greek chieftains wrestle, race, and throw the javelin in celebration of their strength and aliveness. Achilles knows he is foredoomed, but "bright-cheeked" Briseis lies with him each night. War and mortality cry havoc, yet the center holds. That center is the affirmation that actions of body and heroic spirit are in themselves a thing of beauty, that renown shall outweigh the passing terrors of death, and that no catastrophe, not even the fall of Troy, is final. For beyond the charred towers and brute chaos of battle rolls the tranquil sea. Elsewhere dolphins leap and shepherds drowse in the peace of the mountains. Homer's famous similes, in which he compares some moment of battle to an episode from pastoral or domestic life, act as an assurance of ultimate stability. They tell us that the waves will race to the shore when the location of Troy is a disputed memory.

It is a specific and unique portrayal of man. Truer, says John Cowper Powys, than that given by any other poet: "it is more like what has happened, is happening, and will happen to us all, from the very beginning, in our history in this world until the end of human life upon this earth." This may well be; but the truth of the *Iliad* is not that of the *Odyssey*.

To the "ancient glittering eyes" of the *Iliad,* Odysseus opposes a roving and ironic glance. The war epic is hewn of great solid blocks; the story of the long voyage home is a cunning weave. Like the sea water which laps its every page, the vision of the poem is swift, changing, exploratory, prone to odd shallows and sudden depths. "This novel," said T. E. Lawrence. A marvel of design and variousness, but difficult to get into focus. The old fires of the heroic are banked, and the muscular simplicity of life around Troy has yielded to all manner of irony and complication. The work was revered by its ancient readers, but papyrus fragments of the *Iliad* far outnumber those of the *Odyssey*.

The geography of the tale is a riddle. It appears to include Greece and Ionia, Crete, Lycia, Western Sicily, Egypt, and even a hint of Mesopotamia. At times, it is clearly a geography of the imagination, bristling like medieval maps with fabled beasts and wind-daemons blowing out of every quarter. Certain elements in the *Odyssey* correspond to the period of the decline of Mycenaean feudalism (the fact that the societies shown are illiterate, the vague status of kingship in Ithaca, the queer economics of Penelope's marriage settlement). But other aspects of the poem seem to reflect the values of the new city-states as they began to emerge in the very late eighth century. What there is in the *Odyssey* of Mycenaean culture, moreover, appears to derive from those outposts and colonies of Mycenae which long survived in Asia Minor. For what is inescapable in the *Odyssey* is a sense of the Oriental.

That the poet knew the Babylonian *Gilgamesh* epic is probable. That very ancient Asiatic and African myths are echoed in the Wanderer's saga is almost certain. Consider one of the most haunting touches in the entire *Odyssey*. Speaking out of death, Tiresias prophesies to Odysseus that another voyage awaits him beyond Ithaca:

> go forth under your shapely oar till you come to a people who know not the sea and eat their victuals unsavoured with its salt: a people ignorant of purple-prowed ships and of the smoothed and shaven oars which are the wings of a ship's flying. I give you this token of them, a sign so plain that you cannot miss it: you have arrived when another wayfarer shall cross you and say that on your doughty shoulder you bear the scatterer of haulms, a winnowing-fan.
>
> —*Odyssey,* XI; T. E. Lawrence's translation.

Where is that saltless land, and what does the confusion between oar and winnowing-fan signify? We do not know. But in his remarkable study *Genèse de l'Odyssée,* the French anthropologist Gabriel Germain has shown that the tenor of the myth is profoundly un-Greek. To find the motif of a landlocked kingdom in which men know neither salt nor ships, we must look to the legend world of pre-Islamic North Africa.

Dante learnt of Tiresias' prophecy through Seneca (he had no direct knowledge of the Homeric *Odyssey*). He gave it a grim Christian reading. Making of Odysseus a Faustian man, too grasping of life and hidden science, he launched him on a last fatal voyage past Gibraltar (*Inferno,* XXVI). The mariner's ghost, however, would not stay put. It rose from damnation to assume countless shapes in Western art and literature. Most of these shapes—even those given it in our time by Joyce and Kazantzakis—are already implicit in the first Odysseus. The characters of the *Iliad* are of a rich simplicity and move in a clear light. The hero of the *Odyssey* is elusive as fire. He has enjoyed an afterlife even more various and fascinating than that accorded to an Achilles or a Hector precisely because his initial adventures comprise areas of thought and experience undreamt of by the bronze warriors before Troy.

Twice, at least, the winds that drive Odysseus blow out of Araby. He seems to come to Nausicaa straight from *A Thousand and One Nights.* The entire episode is an oriental fairy tale. The afflicted beggar is washed up by the sea. Invisible powers guide him to the royal palace, and there he reveals his true splendor. He departs laden with riches and falls into a magic sleep. Woven into this romance of beggar and caliph is the theme of a young girl's nascent love for a much older man. Again, there is in the tale a flavor which has little in common with the classic Greek sensibility. It foreshadows the romances of Alexandrine Hellenism.

Or take the only fully explored relationship in the *Odyssey,* the friendship of Athene and Odysseus. The goddess and the Wanderer delight in virtuosities of deception. They lie to each other in a gay rivalry of falsehood. They bargain like street merchants of Damascus, seeking to outwit one another with affectionate larceny. More than two thousand years before Shakespeare's Beatrice and Benedick, Homer knew that there can be between men and women affairs of the brain as well as of the heart. At one point, the goddess nearly admits herself beaten. Her loving mockery could come straight out of Shaw:

> Any man, or even any God, who could keep pace with your all-round craftiness must needs be a canny dealer and sharp-practised. O plausible, various, cozening wretch, can you not even in your native place let be these crooked and shifty words which so delight the recesses of your mind? Enough of such speaking in character between us two past-masters of these tricks of trade—you, the cunningest mortal to wheedle or blandish, and me, famed above other Gods for knavish wiles.
>
> —*Odyssey,* XIII

Once more, we are at a great distance from the tone and vision of the *Iliad.* The quarrels and lusts of the Olympians are, at times, satirized in the *Iliad.* But more often, the deities are seen as arrogant and daemonic forces destroying or favoring men at their caprice. Nowhere do we find the crafty, amused, deeply feminine amity which binds Athene to Odysseus. The flavor is Oriental.

The thought that the *Odyssey* is somehow anchored in the world of the Eastern Mediterranean is not new. In 1658 an Oxford scholar, Zachary Bogan, published a book entitled *Homerus Hebraizon,* and later another Greek scholar declared that both epics were written by King Solomon. Modern erudition is more cautious; but Victor Bérard has argued for a Phoenician *Odyssey,* and Joyce, with a characteristic leap of insight, made of his Ulysses a Jew.

But if the *Iliad* and *Odyssey* differ so notably in tone and in their view of human conduct, what is the relation between them? Many and contradictory answers have been given.

Whitman contends that the "vast and obvious" change occurring between the composition of the two epics corresponds to a change in the style of Greek ceramics. In contrast to the geometric, the proto-Attic style is "breezy, open and slightly orientalizing." The proto-Attic vase painter handles his subjects in a series of fluid episodes, as does the

Odyssey. We are no longer in the rigid, concentric world of the *Iliad.* Many scholars have rejected Whitman's entire thesis, arguing that poetry and ceramics cannot be compared. But Whitman has made one telling observation. The physical appearance of personages in the *Iliad* is stylized. The descriptive epithet is a stock formula; thus, women are almost invariably "white-armed." In the *Odyssey,* flesh tones appear; Odysseus is darkly tanned and Penelope's skin is like cut ivory. The same change occurs in vase painting. On proto-Attic ware, flesh tones make their first appearance. In both art and literature a comparable impulse toward naturalism and particularity of delineation can be discerned. The geometric style flourished about 750 B.C.; the proto-Attic emerges around the turn of the century. Whitman's theory would, therefore, match with the limit dates generally ascribed to the two epics and would corroborate the overwhelming impression that the *Odyssey* is somewhat later than the *Iliad.*

The two works may not only have been written at different times but in different places. Professor Denys Page insists that their vocabularies are so different that one cannot assign them to the same locality. The *Iliad* might have been composed in Attica; the *Odyssey* in Ionia, or even Sicily (as Robert Graves argues). This thesis has come under fire. Critics point out that an epic which deals with land warfare must necessarily use a different vocabulary from one mainly concerned with navigation. Nevertheless, it is hard to believe that the same ground was native to both. The Homer of the *Odyssey* seems to have verified with his own eyes certain settings and activities which the poet of the *Iliad* had only imagined.

Readers of Homer who are themselves writers or men of war nearly always reject the idea of a single authorship. Samuel Butler and Robert Graves discern in the *Odyssey* a woman's hand unraveling the ancient web of heroic action. John Cowper Powys states that the two poems "had different authors or originals and that there is an historic gap of three or four hundred years between them." T. E. Lawrence characterized the poet of the *Odyssey* as a "great if uncritical reader of the *Iliad*" and guessed that he was not much of a practical soldier. We seem to be dealing with contrasting qualities of mind.

Consider the image we get of the *Iliad* when looking at it through the *Odyssey.* It is exceedingly complex. We get nearest to it in Book VIII, when Demodocus, the minstrel, sings of the fall of Priam's towers in the hidden presence of Odysseus. This is one of the great moments of divided focus in all literature (it reminds one of the performance of an air from *The Marriage of Figaro* in the last scene of *Don Giovanni*). To the audience of the blind singer, the quarrels of Agamemnon and Achilles are remote. They have the muted radiance of legend. To Odysseus they are unbearably close. He draws his purple cloak around him and weeps. His position is ambiguous, for he is both within and outside the saga of Troy.

Hearing himself sung about, he knows that he has entered the realm of the legendary dead. But he is also a living man seeking return to Ithaca. Thus, he looks upon the Trojan War both in tragic remembrance and refutation. This is the crucial point. There is in the *Odyssey* a critique of the archaic values of the *Iliad* in the light of new energies and perceptions.

His critique is made dramatically explicit in the brief dialogue between Odysseus and the shade of Achilles:

> "How I envy your lot, Achilles, happiest of men who have been or will be! In your day all we Argives adored you with a God's honours: and now here I find you a Prince among the dead. To you, Achilles, death can be no grief at all." He took me up and said, "Do not make light of Death before me, O shining Odysseus. Would that I were on earth a menial, bound to some insubstantial man who must pinch and scrape to keep alive! Life so were better than King of Kings among these dead who have had their day and died."
>
> —*Odyssey*, XI

The glory-maddened Achilles of the *Iliad* would not have said this, even in death. He has his moods of harsh gloom, and carps at the predestined imminence of his fall. But he never rejects the excellence or necessity of the heroic ideal. Had he done so, there would have been peace before Troy. That Achilles should prefer to be alive as a poor man's slave rather than king of the immortal dead is to query the very meaning of the *Iliad*.

Though it is conceivable, it seems unlikely that the same poet should have articulated both conceptions of life. I find no other example in literature of a writer producing two masterpieces that look to each other with that mixture of awe and ironic doubt which the *Odyssey* displays toward the *Iliad*. And yet, time and again, a single voice seems to resound through the contrarieties of narrative technique and world view. Certain glories of the *Iliad* are fully visible only in the mirror of the *Odyssey*. When Achilles laments over Patroclus, he is compared to a father mourning the death of his newly married son. The exact converse of this simile expresses Odysseus' joy at seeing land after the destruction of his raft. Both similes, in turn, are hinted at in Penelope's recognition of the Wanderer. Subtle but tenacious strands relate the two poems.

How can we reconcile the sense of contrast to that of unity? The scholars give no convincing answer. Let me hazard one, unguarded by their authority.

I believe that the Homer whom we know, the poet who continues to shape many of the principal forms of the Western imagination, was the compiler of the *Iliad* and the inventor of the *Odyssey*. He assembled and ordered the fragmentary battle sagas of the Mycenaean tradition. He had the insight to group them around the dramatic and unifying motif of the rage of Achilles. He treated the ancient material and folk legends with profound respect. At times, he misunderstood the language and technical circumstances of the remote action. But he chose to retain what was obscure rather than improve upon it. He grasped the austere symmetries inherent in the archaic mode of narrative and saw life through the harsh, glittering eyes of battle. To the brief intensities of oral poetry, he made available the new amplitude and elaboration of the written form. The compiler of the *Iliad,* like the men who wove together the sagas of the Pentateuch, was an editor of genius; but the gold and the bronze lay ready in the crucible.

I imagine that he completed his task in the first powers of maturity. The *Iliad* has the ruthlessness of the young. But as he richened in experience and sensibility, the vision of the *Iliad* may have struck Homer as incomplete. One can readily conceive of him as a constant and observant voyager. "He had sailed upon and watched the seas," says T. E. Lawrence. In particular, I would suppose that he grew familiar with the complex, Orientalized civilizations of the Eastern Mediterranean. The part of the Orient in the *Iliad* has the stiffness of ancient legend. It is traditional material dating back to the commerce of the Bronze Age. The Orient of the *Odyssey* is more modern, more immediately observed.

In the afternoon of his life, this much-travelled man may have turned back to the world of the *Iliad* in order to compare its vision of human conduct with that of his own experience. From that comparison, with its delicate poise of reverence and criticism, grew the *Odyssey.* With marvelous acumen, Homer chose for his protagonist the one figure out of the Trojan saga nearest to the "modern" spirit. Already in the *Iliad,* Odysseus marks a transition from the simplicities of the heroic to a life of the mind more skeptical, more nervous, more wary of conviction. Like Odysseus, Homer himself abandoned the stark, rudimentary values inherent in the world of Achilles. When composing the *Odyssey,* he looked back to the *Iliad* across a wide distance of the soul—with nostalgia and smiling doubt.

This view of Homer does, at least, match the few facts available to us. The *Odyssey* is younger than the *Iliad,* but not, I think, by very much. The one poem is intensely alive in the other. The two epics express judgments of man's condition which differ considerably. But a related craftsmanship is at work in both. Behind each lie remote, partially misunderstood legacies from the Mycenaean past; in the *Iliad* they are more obtrusive. In the *Odyssey,* on the other hand, gleam the first dawn lights of the Socratic future. The bridge between Troy and Ithaca could be the personal life of an incomparable editor and poet.

We shall never really know. But the *Iliad* and the *Odyssey* remain as the unassailable fact. And although there are many books by which men have ordered their lives, I wonder whether any can do more than the Homeric poems to make us endure the exactions of mortality.

Homer and Shakespeare

by Leo Tolstoy

Whatever people may say, however they may be enraptured by Shakespeare's works, whatever merits they may attribute to them, it is certain that he was not an artist and that his works are not artistic productions. Without a sense of proportion there never was and could not be an artist, just as without a sense of rhythm there cannot be a musician. And Shakespeare may be anything you like—only not an artist.

"But one must not forget the times in which Shakespeare wrote," say his laudators. "It was a time of cruel and coarse manners, a time of the then fashionable euphuism, that is, an artificial manner of speech—a time of forms of life strange to us, and therefore to judge Shakespeare one must keep in view the times when he wrote. In Homer, as in Shakespeare, there is much that is strange to us, but this does not prevent our valuing the beauties of Homer," say the laudators. But when one compares Shakespeare with Homer, as Gervinus does, the infinite distance separating true poetry from its imitation emerges with special vividness. However distant Homer is from us we can without the slightest effort transport ourselves into the life he describes. And we are thus transported chiefly because, however alien to us may be the events Homer describes, he believes in what he says and speaks seriously of what he is describing, and therefore he never exaggerates and the sense of measure never deserts him. And therefore it happens that, not to speak of the wonderfully distinct, lifelike, and excellent characters of Achilles, Hector, Priam, Odysseus, and the eternally touching scenes of Hector's farewell, of Priam's embassy, of the return of Odysseus, and so forth, the whole of the *Iliad* and still more the *Odyssey,* is as naturally close to us all as if we had lived and were now living among the gods and heroes. But it is not so with Shakespeare. From his first words exaggeration is seen: exaggeration of events, exaggeration of feeling, and exaggeration of expression. It is at once evident that he does not believe in what he is saying, that he has no need to say it, that he is inventing the occurrences he describes, is indifferent to his characters and has devised them merely for the stage, and therefore makes them do and say what may strike his public; and so we do not believe either in the events or in the actions, or in the sufferings of his characters. Nothing so clearly shows the complete absence of aesthetic feeling in Shakespeare as a comparison between him and Homer. The works which we call the works of Homer are artistic, poetic, original works, lived through by their author or authors.

But Shakespeare's works are compositions devised for a particular purpose, and having absolutely nothing in common with art or poetry.

Homer or Virgil?

by Ezra Pound

Years ago a musician said to me: "But isn't there a place where you can get it all [meaning all of poetry] as in Bach?"

There isn't. I believe if a man will really learn Greek he can get nearly "all of it" in Homer.

I have never read half a page of *Homer* without finding melodic invention, I mean melodic invention that I didn't already know. I have, on the other hand, found also in Homer the imaginary spectator, which in 1918 I still thought was Henry James's particular property.

Homer says, "an experienced soldier would have noticed." The sheer literary qualities in Homer are such that a physician has written a book to prove that Homer must have been an army doctor. (When he describes certain blows and their effect, the wounds are said to be accurate, and the description fit for coroner's inquest.)

Another French scholar has more or less shown that the geography of the *Odyssey* is correct geography; not as you would find it if you had a geography book and a map, but as it would be in a "periplum," that is, as a coasting sailor would find it.

The news in the *Odyssey* is still news. Odysseus is still "very human," by no means a stuffed shirt, or a pretty figure taken down from a tapestry. It is very hard to describe some of the Homeric conversation, the irony, etc., without neologisms, which my publishers have suggested I eschew. The only readable translation of this part of Homer known to me was made by Amadis Jamyn, *secrétaire et lecteur ordinaire du Roy* (Henry III of France). He refers to Odysseus as *"ce rusé personnage."*

You can't tuck Odysseus away with Virgil's Aeneas. Odysseus is emphatically "the wise guy," the downy, the hard-boiled Odysseus. His companions have most of them something that must have been the Greek equivalent of shell shock.

And the language of the conversations is just as alive as when one of Edgar Wallace's characters says, "We have lost a client."

W. B. Yeats is sufficiently venerated to be cited now in a school book.

The gulf between Homer and Virgil can be illustrated profanely by one of Yeats's favorite anecdotes.

A plain sailor man took a notion to study Latin, and his teacher tried him with Virgil; after many lessons he asked him something about the hero.

Said the sailor: "What hero?"

Said the teacher: "What hero, why, Aeneas, the hero."

Said the sailor: "Ach, a hero, him a hero? Bigob, I t'ought he waz a priest."

Odysseus' Scar

by Erich Auerbach

Readers of the *Odyssey* will remember the well-prepared and touching scene in Book XIX, when Odysseus has at last come home, the scene in which the old housekeeper Eurycleia, who had been his nurse, recognizes him by a scar on his thigh. The stranger has won Penelope's good will; at his request she tells the housekeeper to wash his feet, which, in all old stories, is the first duty of hospitality toward a tired traveler. Eurycleia busies herself fetching water and mixing cold with hot, meanwhile speaking sadly of her absent master, who is probably of the same age as the guest, and who perhaps, like the guest, is even now wandering somewhere, a stranger; and she remarks how astonishingly like him the guest looks. Meanwhile Odysseus, remembering his scar, moves back out of the light; he knows that, despite his efforts to hide his identity, Eurycleia will now recognize him, but he wants at least to keep Penelope in ignorance. No sooner has the old woman touched the scar than, in her joyous surprise, she lets Odysseus' foot drop into the basin; the water spills over, she is about to cry out her joy; Odysseus restrains her with whispered threats and endearments; she recovers herself and conceals her emotion. Penelope, whose attention Athena's foresight had diverted from the incident, has observed nothing.

All this is scrupulously externalized and narrated in leisurely fashion. The two women express their feelings in copious direct discourse. Feelings though they are, with only a slight admixture of the most general considerations upon human destiny, the syntactical connection between part and part is perfectly clear, no contour is blurred. There is also room and time for orderly, perfectly well-articulated, uniformly illuminated descriptions of implements, ministrations, and gestures; even in the dramatic moment of recognition, Homer does not omit to tell the reader that it is with his right hand that Odysseus takes the old woman by the throat to keep her from speaking, at the same time that he draws her closer to him with his left. Clearly outlined, brightly and uniformly illuminated, men and things stand out in a realm where everything is visible; and not less clear—wholly expressed, orderly even in their ardor—are the feelings and thoughts of the persons involved.

In my account of the incident I have so far passed over a whole series of verses which interrupt it in the middle. There are more than seventy of these verses—while to the incident itself some forty are devoted before the interruption and some forty after it. The interruption, which comes just at the point when the housekeeper recognizes the scar—that is, at the moment of crisis—describes the origin of the scar, a hunting accident which occurred in Odysseus' boyhood, at a boar hunt, during the time of his visit to his grandfather Autolycus. This first affords an opportunity to inform the reader about Autolycus, his house, the precise degree of the kinship, his character, and, no less exhaustively than touchingly, his behavior after the birth of his grandson; then follows the visit of Odysseus, now grown to be a youth; the exchange of greetings, the banquet with which he is welcomed, sleep and waking, the early start for the hunt, the tracking of the beast, the struggle, Odysseus' being wounded by the boar's tusk, his recovery, his return to Ithaca, his parents' anxious questions—all is narrated, again with such a complete externalization of all the elements of the story and of their interconnections as to leave nothing in obscurity. Not until then does the narrator return to Penelope's chamber, not until then, the digression having run its course, does Eurycleia, who had recognized the scar before the digression began, let Odysseus' foot fall back into the basin.

The first thought of a modern reader—that this is a device to increase suspense—is, if not wholly wrong, at least not the essential explanation of this Homeric procedure. For the element of suspense is very slight in the Homeric poems; nothing in their entire style is calculated to keep the reader or hearer breathless. The digressions are not meant to keep the reader in suspense, but rather to relax the tension. And this frequently occurs, as in the passage before us. The broadly narrated, charming, and subtly fashioned story of the hunt, with all its elegance and self-sufficiency, its wealth of idyllic pictures, seeks to win the reader over wholly to itself as long as he is hearing it, to make him forget what had just taken place during the foot-washing. But an episode that will increase suspense by retarding the action must be so constructed that it will not fill the present entirely, will not put the crisis, whose resolution is being awaited, entirely out of the reader's mind, and thereby destroy the mood of suspense; the crisis and the suspense must continue, must remain vibrant in the background. But Homer—and to this we shall have to return later—knows no background. What he narrates is for the time being the only present, and fills both the stage and the reader's mind completely. So it is with the passage before us. When the young Eurycleia (vv. 401ff.) sets the infant Odysseus on his grandfather Autolycus' lap after the banquet, the aged Eurycleia, who a few lines earlier had touched the wanderer's foot, has entirely vanished from the stage and from the reader's mind.

Goethe and Schiller, who, though not referring to this particular episode, exchanged letters in April 1797 on the subject of "the retarding element" in the Homeric poems in general, put it in direct opposition to the element of suspense—the latter word is not used, but is clearly implied when the "retarding" procedure is opposed, as something proper to epic, to tragic procedure (letters of April 19, 21, and 22). The "retarding element," the "going back and forth" by means of episodes, seems to me, too, in the Homeric poems, to be opposed to any tensional and suspensive striving toward a goal, and doubtless Schiller is right in regard to Homer when he says that what he gives us is "simply the quiet existence and operation of things in accordance with their natures"; Homer's goal is "already present in every point of his progress." But both Schiller and Goethe raise Homer's procedure to the level of a law for epic poetry in general, and Schiller's words quoted above are meant to be universally binding upon the epic poet, in contradistinction from the tragic. Yet in both modern and ancient times, there are important epic works which are composed throughout with no "retarding element" in this sense but, on the contrary, with suspense throughout, and which perpetually "rob us of our emotional freedom"—which power Schiller will grant only to the tragic poet. And besides it seems to me undemonstrable and improbable that this procedure of Homeric poetry was directed by aesthetic considerations or even by an aesthetic feeling of the sort postulated by Goethe and Schiller. The effect, to be sure, is precisely that which they describe, and is, furthermore, the actual source of the conception of epic which they themselves hold, and with them all writers decisively influenced by classical antiquity. But the true cause of the impression of "retardation" appears to me to lie elsewhere—namely, in the need of the Homeric style to leave nothing which it mentions half in darkness and unexternalized.

The excursus upon the origin of Odysseus' scar is not basically different from the many passages in which a newly introduced character, or even a newly appearing object or implement, though it be in the thick of a battle, is described as to its nature and origin; or in which, upon the appearance of a god, we are told where he last was, what he was doing there, and by what road he reached the scene; indeed, even the Homeric epithets seem to me in the final analysis to be traceable to the same need for an externalization of phenomena in terms perceptible to the senses. Here is the scar, which comes up in the course of the narrative; and Homer's feeling simply will not permit him to see it appear out of the darkness of an unilluminated past; it must be set in full light, and with it a portion of the hero's boyhood—just as, in the *Iliad*, when the first ship is already burning and the Myrmidons finally arm that they may hasten to help, there is still time not only for the wonderful simile of the wolf, not only for the order of the Myrmidon host, but also for a detailed account of the ancestry of several subordinate leaders (XVI, vv. 155ff.). To be sure, the aesthetic effect thus produced was soon noticed and thereafter consciously sought; but the more original cause must have lain in the basic impulse of the Homeric style: to represent phenomena in a fully externalized form, visible and palpable in all their parts, and completely fixed in their spatial and temporal relations. Nor do psychological processes receive any other treatment: here too nothing must remain hidden and unexpressed. With the utmost fullness, with an orderliness which even passion does not disturb, Homer's personages vent their inmost hearts in speech; what they do not say to others, they speak in their own minds, so that the reader is informed of it. Much that is terrible takes place in the Homeric poems, but it seldom takes place wordlessly: Polyphemus talks to Odysseus; Odysseus talks to the suitors when he begins to kill them; Hector and Achilles talk at length, before battle and after; and no speech is so filled with anger or scorn that the particles which express logical and grammatical connections are lacking or out of place. This last observation is true, of course, not only of speeches but of the presentation in general. The separate elements of a phenomenon are most clearly placed in relation to one another; a large number of conjunctions, adverbs, particles, and other syntactical tools, all clearly circumscribed and delicately differentiated in meaning, delimit persons, things, and portions of incidents in respect to one another, and at the same time bring them together in a continuous and ever flexible connection; like the separate phenomena themselves, their relationships—their temporal, local, causal, final, consecutive, comparative, concessive, antithetical, and conditional limitations—are brought to light in perfect fullness; so that a continuous rhythmic procession of phenomena passes by, and never is there a form left fragmentary or half-illuminated, never a lacuna, never a gap, never a glimpse of unplumbed depths.

And this procession of phenomena takes place in the foreground—that is, in a local and temporal present which is absolute. One might think that the many interpolations, the frequent moving back and forth, would create a sort of perspective in time and place; but the Homeric style never gives any such impression. The way in which any impression of perspective is avoided can be clearly observed in the procedure for introducing episodes, a syntactical construction with which every reader of Homer is familiar; it is used in the passage we are considering, but can also be found in cases when the episodes are much shorter. To the word scar (v. 393) there is first attached a relative clause ("which once long ago a boar . . ."), which enlarges into a voluminous syntactical parenthesis; into this an independent sentence unexpectedly intrudes (v. 396: "A god himself gave him . . ."), which quietly disentangles itself from syntactical subordination, until, with verse 399, an equally free syntactical treatment of the new content begins a new present which continues unchallenged until, with verse 467 ("The old woman now touched it . . ."), the scene which had been broken off is resumed. To be sure, in the case of such long episodes as the one we are considering, a purely syntactical connection with the principal theme would hardly have been possible; but a connection with it through perspective would have been all the easier had the content been arranged with that end in view; if, that is, the entire story of the scar had been presented as a recollection which awakens in Odysseus' mind at this particular moment. It would have been perfectly easy to do; the story of the scar had only to be inserted two verses earlier, at the first mention of the word scar, where the motifs "Odysseus" and "recollection" were already at hand. But any such subjectivistic-perspectivistic procedure, creating a foreground and background, resulting in the present lying open to the depths of the past, is entirely foreign to the Homeric style; the Homeric style knows only a foreground, only a uniformly illuminated, uniformly objective present. And so the excursus does not begin until two lines later, when Eurycleia has discovered the scar—the possibility for a perspectivistic connection no longer exists, and the story of the wound becomes an independent and exclusive present.

The genius of the Homeric style becomes even more apparent when it is compared with an equally ancient and equally epic style from a different world of forms. I shall attempt this comparison with the account of the sacrifice of Isaac, a homogeneous narrative produced by the so-called Elohist. The King James version translates the opening as follows (Genesis 22:1): "And it came to pass after these things, that God did tempt Abraham and said to him, Abraham! and he said, Behold, here I am." Even this opening startles us when we come to it from Homer. Where are the two speakers? We are not told. The reader, however, knows that they are not normally to be found together in one place on earth, that one of them, God, in order to speak to Abraham, must come from somewhere, must enter the earthly realm from some unknown heights or depths. Whence does he come, whence does he call to Abraham? We are not told. He does not come, like Zeus or Poseidon, from the Ethiopians, where he has been enjoying a sacrificial feast. Nor are we told anything of his reasons for tempting Abraham so terribly. He has not, like Zeus, discussed them in set speeches with other gods gathered in council; nor have the deliberations in his own heart been presented to us; unexpected and mysterious, he enters the scene from some unknown height or depth and calls: Abraham! It will at once be said that this is to be explained by the particular concept of God which the Jews held and which was wholly different from that of the Greeks. True enough—but this constitutes no objection. For how is the Jewish concept of God to be explained? Even their earlier God of the desert was not fixed in form and content, and was alone; his lack of form, his lack of local habitation, his singleness, was in the end not only maintained but developed even further in competition with the comparatively far more manifest gods of the surrounding Near Eastern world. The concept of God held by the Jews is less a cause than a symptom of their manner of comprehending and representing things.

This becomes still clearer if we now turn to the other person in the dialogue, to Abraham. Where is he? We do not know. He says, indeed: Here I am—but the Hebrew word means only something like "behold me," and in any case is not meant to indicate the actual place where Abraham is, but a moral position in respect to God, who has called to him—Here am I awaiting thy command. Where he is actually, whether in Beersheba or elsewhere, whether indoors or in the open air, is not stated; it does not interest the narrator, the reader is not informed; and what Abraham was doing when God called to him is left in the same obscurity. To realize the difference, consider Hermes' visit to Calypso, for example, where command, journey, arrival and reception of the visitor, situation and occupation of the person visited, are set forth in many verses; and even on occasions when gods appear suddenly and briefly, whether to help one of their favorites or to deceive or destroy some mortal whom they hate, their bodily forms, and usually the manner of their coming and going, are given in detail. Here, however, God appears without bodily form (yet he "appears"), coming from some unspecified place—we only hear his voice, and that utters nothing but a name, a name without an adjective, without a descriptive epithet for the person spoken to, such as is the rule in every Homeric address; and of Abraham too nothing is made perceptible except the words in which he answers God: *Hinne-ni,* Behold me here—with which, to be sure, a most touching gesture expressive of obedience and readiness is suggested, but it is left to the reader to visualize it. Moreover the two speakers are not on the same level: if we conceive of Abraham in the foreground, where it might be possible to picture him as prostrate or kneeling or bowing with outspread arms or gazing upward, God is not there too: Abraham's words and gestures are directed toward the depths of the picture or upward, but in any case the undetermined, dark place from which the voice comes to him is not in the foreground.

After this opening, God gives his command, and the story itself begins: everyone knows it; it unrolls with no episodes in a few independent sentences whose syntactical connection is of the most rudimentary sort. In this atmosphere it is unthinkable that an implement, a landscape through which the travelers passed, the serving-men, or the ass, should be described, that their origin or descent or material or appearance or usefulness should be set forth in terms of praise; they do not even admit an adjective: they are serving-men, ass, wood, and knife, and nothing else, without an epithet; they are there to serve the end which God has commanded; what in other respects they were, are, or will be, remains in darkness. A journey is made, because God has designated the place where the sacrifice is to be performed; but we are told nothing about the journey except that it took three days, and even that we are told in a mysterious way: Abraham and his followers rose "early in the morning" and "went unto" the place of which God had told him; on the third day he lifted up his eyes and saw the place from afar. That gesture is the only gesture, is indeed the only occurrence during the whole journey, of which we are told; and though its motivation lies in the fact that the place is elevated, its uniqueness still heightens the impression that the journey took place through a vacuum; it is as if, while he traveled on, Abraham had looked neither to the right nor to the left, had suppressed any sign of life in his followers and himself save only their footfalls.

Thus the journey is like a silent progress through the indeterminate and the contingent, a holding of the breath, a process which has no present, which is inserted, like a blank duration, between what has passed and what lies ahead, and which yet is measured: three days! Three such days positively demand the symbolic interpretation which they later received. They began "early in the morning." But at what time on the third day did Abraham lift up his eyes and see his goal? The text says nothing on the subject. Obviously not "late in the evening," for it seems that there was still time enough to climb the mountain and make the sacrifice. So "early in the morning" is given, not as an indication of time, but for the sake of its ethical significance; it is intended to express the resolution, the promptness, the punctual obedience of the sorely tried Abraham. Bitter to him is the early morning in which he saddles his ass, calls his serving-men and his son, Isaac, and sets out; but he obeys, he walks on until the third day, then lifts up his eyes and sees the place. Whence he comes, we do not know, but the goal is clearly stated: Jeruel in the land of Moriah. What place this is meant to indicate is not clear—"Moriah" especially may be a later correction of some other word. But in any case the goal was given, and in any case it is a matter of some sacred spot which was to receive a particular consecration by being connected with Abraham's sacrifice. Just as little as "early in the morning" serves as a temporal indication does "Jeruel in the land of Moriah" serve as a geographical indication; and in both cases alike, the complementary indication is not given, for we know as little of the hour at which Abraham lifted up his eyes as we do of the place from which he set forth—Jeruel is significant not so much as the goal of an earthly journey, in its geographical relation to other places, as through its special election, through its relation to God, who designated it as the scene of the act, and therefore it must be named.

In the narrative itself, a third chief character appears: Isaac. While God and Abraham, the serving-men, the ass, and the implements are simply named, without mention of any qualities or any other sort of definition. Isaac once receives an appositive; God says, "Take Isaac, thine only son, whom thou lovest." But this is not a characterization of Isaac as a person, apart from his relation to his father and apart from the story;

he may be handsome or ugly, intelligent or stupid, tall or short, pleasant or unpleasant—we are not told. Only what we need to know about him as a personage in the action, here and now, is illuminated, so that it may become apparent how terrible Abraham's temptation is, and that God is fully aware of it. By this example of the contrary, we see the significance of the descriptive adjectives and digressions of the Homeric poems; with their indications of the earlier and as it were absolute existence of the persons described, they prevent the reader from concentrating exclusively on a present crisis; even when the most terrible things are occurring, they prevent the establishment of an overwhelming suspense. But here, in the story of Abraham's sacrifice, the overwhelming suspense is present; what Schiller makes the goal of the tragic poet—to rob us of our emotional freedom, to turn our intellectual and spiritual powers (Schiller says "our activity") in one direction, to concentrate them there—is effected in this Biblical narrative, which certainly deserves the epithet epic.

We find the same contrast if we compare the two uses of direct discourse. The personages speak in the Bible story too; but their speech does not serve, as does speech in Homer, to manifest, to externalize thoughts—on the contrary, it serves to indicate thoughts which remain unexpressed. God gives his command in direct discourse, but he leaves his motives and his purpose unexpressed; Abraham, receiving the command, says nothing and does what he has been told to do. The conversation between Abraham and Isaac on the way to the place of sacrifice is only an interruption of the heavy silence and makes it all the more burdensome. The two of them, Isaac carrying the wood and Abraham with fire and a knife, "went together." Hesitantly, Isaac ventures to ask about the ram, and Abraham gives the well-known answer. Then the text repeats: "So they went both of them together." Everything remains unexpressed.

It would be difficult, then, to imagine styles more contrasted than those of these two equally ancient and equally epic texts. On the one hand, externalized, uniformly illuminated phenomena, at a definite time and in a definite place, connected together without lacunae in a perpetual foreground; thoughts and feeling completely expressed; events taking place in leisurely fashion and with very little of suspense. On the other hand, the externalization of only so much of the phenomena as is necessary for the purpose of the narrative, all else left in obscurity; the decisive points of the narrative alone are emphasized, what lies between is nonexistent; time and place are undefined and call for interpretation; thoughts and feeling remain unexpressed, are only suggested by the silence and the fragmentary speeches; the whole, permeated with the most unrelieved suspense and directed toward a single goal (and to that extent far more of a unity), remains mysterious and "fraught with background."

I will discuss this term in some detail, lest it be misunderstood. I said above that the Homeric style was "of the foreground" because, despite much going back and forth, it yet causes what is momentarily being narrated to give the impression that it is the only present, pure and without perspective. A consideration of the Elohistic text teaches us that our term is capable of a broader and deeper application. It shows that even the separate personages can be represented as possessing "background"; God is always so represented in the Bible, for he is not comprehensible in his presence, as is Zeus; it is always only "something" of him that appears, he always extends into depths. But even the human beings in the Biblical stories have greater depths of time, fate, and consciousness than do the human beings in Homer; although they are nearly always caught up in an event engaging all their faculties, they are not so entirely immersed in its present that they do not remain continually conscious of what has happened to them earlier and elsewhere; their thoughts and feelings have more layers, are more entangled. Abraham's actions are explained not only by what is happening to him at the moment, nor yet only by his character (as Achilles' actions by his courage and his pride, and Odysseus' by his versatility and foresightedness), but by his previous history; he remembers, he is constantly conscious of, what God has promised him and what God has already accomplished for him—his soul is torn between desperate rebellion and hopeful expectation; his silent obedience is multilayered, has background. Such a problematic psychological situation as this is impossible for any of the Homeric heroes, whose destiny is clearly defined and who wake every morning as if it were the first day of their lives: their emotions, though strong, are simple and find expression instantly.

How fraught with background, in comparison, are characters like Saul and David! How entangled and stratified are such human relations as those between David and Absalom, between David and Joab! Any such "background" quality of the psychological situation as that which the story of Absalom's death and its sequel (II Samuel 18 and 19, by the so-called Jahvist) rather suggests than expresses, is unthinkable in Homer. Here we are confronted not merely with the psychological processes of characters whose depth of background is veritably abysmal, but with a purely geographical background too. For David is absent from the battlefield; but the influence of his will and his feelings continues to operate, they affect even Joab in his rebellion and disregard for the consequences of his actions; in the magnificent scene with the two messengers, both the physical and psychological background is fully manifest, though the latter is never expressed. With this, compare, for example, how Achilles, who sends Patroclus first to scout and then into battle, loses almost all "presentness" so long as he is not physically present. But the most important thing is the "multilayeredness" of the individual character; this is hardly to be met with in Homer, or at most in the form of a conscious hesitation between two possible courses of action; otherwise, in Homer, the complexity of the psychological life is shown only in the succession and alternation of emotions; whereas the Jewish writers are able to express the simultaneous existence of various layers of consciousness and the conflict between them.

The Homeric poems, then, though their intellectual, linguistic, and above all syntactical culture appears to be so much more highly developed, are yet comparatively simple in their picture of human beings; and no less so in their relation to the real life which they describe in general. Delight in physical existence is everything to them, and their highest aim is to make that delight perceptible to us. Between battles and passions, adventures and perils, they show us hunts, banquets, palaces and shepherds' cots, athletic contests and washing days—in order that we may see the heroes in their ordinary life, and seeing them so, may take pleasure in their manner of enjoying their savory present, a present which sends strong roots down into social usages, landscape, and daily life. And thus they bewitch us and ingratiate themselves to us until we live with them in the reality of their lives; so long as we are reading or hearing the poems, it does not matter whether we know that all this is only legend, "make-believe." The oft-repeated reproach that Homer is a liar takes nothing from his effectiveness, he does not need to base his story on historical reality, his reality is powerful enough in itself; it ensnares us, weaving its web around us, and that suffices him. And this "real" world into which we are lured, exists for itself, contains nothing but itself; the Homeric poems conceal nothing, they contain no teaching and no secret second meaning. Homer can be analyzed, as we have essayed to do here, but he cannot be interpreted. Later allegorizing trends have tried their arts of interpretation upon him, but to no avail. He resists any such treatment; the interpretations are forced and foreign, they do not crystallize into a unified doctrine. The general considerations which occasionally occur (in our episode, for example, v. 360: that in misfortune men age quickly) reveal a calm acceptance of the basic facts of human existence, but with no compulsion to brood over them, still less any passionate impulse either to rebel against them or to embrace them in an ecstasy of submission.

It is all very different in the Biblical stories. Their aim is not to bewitch the senses, and if nevertheless they produce likely sensory effects, it is only because the moral, religious, and psychological phenomena which are their sole concern are made concrete in the sensible matter of life. But their religious intent involves an absolute claim to historical truth. The story of Abraham and Isaac is not better established than the story of Odysseus, Penelope, and Eurycleia; both are legendary. But the Biblical narrator, the Elohist, had to believe in the objective truth of the story of Abraham's sacrifice—the existence of the sacred ordinances of life rested upon the truth of this and similar stories. He had to believe in it passionately; or else (as many rationalistic interpreters believed and perhaps still believe) he had to be a conscious liar—no harmless liar like Homer, who lied to give pleasure, but a political liar with a definite end in view, lying in the interest of a claim to absolute authority.

To me, the rationalistic interpretation seems psychologically absurd; but even if we take it into consideration, the relation of the Elohist to the truth of his story still remains a far more passionate and definite one than is Homer's relation. The Biblical narrator was obliged to write exactly what his belief in the truth of the tradition (or, from the rationalistic standpoint, his interest in the truth of it) demanded of him—in either case, his freedom in creative or representative imagination was severely limited; his activity was perforce reduced to composing an effective version of the pious tradition. What he produced, then, was not primarily oriented toward "realism" (if he succeeded in being realistic, it was merely a means, not an end); it was oriented toward truth. Woe to the man who did not believe it! One can perfectly well entertain historical doubts on the subject of the Trojan War or of Odysseus' wanderings, and still, when reading Homer, feel precisely the effects he sought to produce; but without believing in Abraham's sacrifice, it is impossible to put the narrative of it to the use for which it was written. Indeed, we must go even further. The Bible's claim to truth is not only far more urgent than Homer's, it is tyrannical—it excludes all other claims. The world of the Scripture stories is not satisfied with claiming to be a historically true reality—it insists that it is the only real world, is destined for autocracy. All other scenes, issues, and ordinances have no right to appear independently of it, and it is promised that all of them, the history of all mankind, will be given their due place within its frame, will be subordinated to it. The Scripture stories do not, like Homer's, court our favor, they do not flatter us that they may please us and enchant us—they seek to subject us, and if we refuse to be subjected we are rebels.

Let no one object that this goes too far, that not the stories, but the religious doctrine, raises the claim to absolute authority; because the stories are not, like Homer's, simply narrated "reality." Doctrine and promise are incarnate in them and inseparable from them; for that very reason they are fraught with "background" and mysterious, containing a second, concealed meaning. In the story of Isaac, it is not only God's intervention at the beginning and the end, but even the factual and psychological elements which come between, that are mysterious, merely touched upon, fraught with background; and therefore they require subtle investigation and interpretation, they demand them. Since so much in the story is dark and incomplete, and since the reader knows that God is a hidden God, his effort to interpret it constantly finds something new to feed upon. Doctrine and the search for enlightenment are inextricably connected with the physical side of the narrative—the latter being more than simple "reality"; indeed they are in constant danger of losing their own reality, as very soon happened when interpretation reached such proportions that the real vanished.

If the text of the Biblical narrative, then, is so greatly in need of interpretation on the basis of its own content, its claim to absolute authority forces it still further in the same direction. Far from seeking, like Homer, merely to make us forget our own reality for a few hours, it seeks to overcome our reality: we are to fit our own life into its world, feel ourselves to be elements in its structure of universal history. This becomes increasingly difficult the further our historical environment is removed from that of the Biblical books; and if these nevertheless maintain their claim to absolute authority, it is inevitable that they themselves be adapted through interpretative transformation. This was for a long time comparatively easy; as late as the European Middle Ages it was possible to represent Biblical events as ordinary phenomena of contemporary life, the methods of interpretation themselves forming the basis for such a treatment. But when, through too great a change in environment and through the awakening of a critical consciousness, this becomes impossible, the Biblical claim to absolute authority is jeopardized; the method of interpretation is scorned and rejected, the Biblical stories become ancient legends, and the doctrine they had contained, now dissevered from them, becomes a disembodied image.

As a result of this claim to absolute authority, the method of interpretation spread to traditions other than the Jewish. The Homeric poems present a definite complex of events whose boundaries in space and time are clearly delimited; before it, beside it, and after it, other complexes of events, which do not depend upon it, can be conceived without conflict and without difficulty. The Old Testament, on the other hand, presents universal history: it begins with the beginning of time, with the creation of the world, and will end with the Last Days, the fulfilling of the Covenant, with which the world will come to an end. Everything else that happens in the world can only be conceived as an element in this sequence; into it everything that is known about the world, or at least everything that touches upon the history of the Jews, must be fitted as an ingredient of the divine plan; and as this too became possible only by interpreting the new material as it poured in, the need for interpretation reaches out beyond the original Jewish-Israelitish realm of reality—for example to Assyrian, Babylonian, Persian, and Roman history; interpretation in a determined direction becomes a general method of comprehending reality; the new and strange world which now comes into view and which, in the form in which it presents itself, proves to be wholly unutilizable within the Jewish religious frame, must be so interpreted that it can find a place there. But this process nearly always also reacts upon the frame, which requires enlarging and modifying. The most striking piece of interpretation of this sort occurred in the first century of the Christian era, in consequence of Paul's mission to the Gentiles: Paul and the Church Fathers reinterpreted the entire Jewish tradition as a succession of figures prognosticating the appearance of Christ, and assigned the Roman Empire its proper place in the divine plan of salvation. Thus while, on the one hand, the reality of the Old Testament presents itself as complete truth with a claim to sole authority, on the other hand that very claim forces it to a constant interpretative change in its own content; for millennia it undergoes an incessant and active development with the life of man in Europe.

The claim of the Old Testament stories to represent universal history, their insistent relation—a relation constantly redefined by conflicts—to a single and hidden God, who yet shows himself and who guides universal history by promise and exaction, gives these stories an entirely different perspective from any the Homeric poems can possess. As a composition, the Old Testament is incomparably less unified than the Homeric poems, it is more obviously pieced together—but the various components all belong to one concept of universal history and its interpretation. If certain elements survived which did not immediately fit in, interpretation took care of them; and so the reader is at every moment aware of the universal religio-historical perspective which gives the individual stories their general meaning and purpose. The greater the separateness and horizontal disconnection of the stories and groups of stories in relation to one another, compared with the *Iliad* and the *Odyssey*, the stronger is their general vertical connection, which holds them all together and which is entirely lacking in Homer. Each of the great figures of the Old Testament, from Adam to the prophets, embodies a moment of this vertical connection. God chose and formed these men to the end of embodying his essence and will—yet choice and formation do not coincide, for the latter proceeds gradually, historically, during the earthly life of him upon whom the choice has fallen. How the process is accomplished, what terrible trials such a formation inflicts, can be seen from our story of Abraham's sacrifice. Herein lies the reason why the great figures of the Old Testament are so much more fully developed, so much more fraught with their own biographical past, so much more distinct as individuals, than are the Homeric heroes. Achilles and Odysseus are splendidly described in many well-ordered words, epithets cling to them, their emotions are constantly displayed in their words and deeds—but they have no development, and their life-histories are clearly set forth once and for all. So little are the Homeric heroes presented as developing or having developed, that most of them—Nestor, Agamemnon, Achilles—appear to be of an age fixed from the very first. Even Odysseus, in whose case the long lapse of time and the many events which occurred offer so much opportunity for biographical development, shows almost nothing of it. Odysseus on his return is exactly the same as he was when he left Ithaca two decades earlier. But what a road, what a fate, lie between the Jacob who cheated his father out of his blessing and the old man whose favorite son has been torn to pieces by a wild beast!—between David the harp player, persecuted by his lord's jealousy, and the old king, surrounded by violent intrigues, whom Abishag the Shunnamite warmed in his bed, and he knew her not! The old man, of whom we know how he has become what he is, is more of an individual than the young man; for it is only during the course of an eventful life that men are differentiated into full individuality; and it is this history of a personality which the Old Testament presents to us as the formation undergone by those whom God has chosen to be examples. Fraught with their development, sometimes even aged to the verge of dissolution, they show a distinct stamp of individuality entirely foreign to the Homeric heroes. Time can touch the latter only outwardly, and even that change is brought to our observation as little as possible; whereas the stern hand of God is ever upon the Old Testament figures; he has not only made them once and for all and chosen them, but he continues to work upon them, bends them and kneads them, and, without destroying them in essence, produces from them forms which their youth gave no grounds for anticipating. The objection that the biographical element of the Old Testament often springs from the combination of several legendary personages does not apply; for this combination is a part of the development of the text. And how much wider is the pendulum swing of their lives than that of the Homeric heroes! For they are bearers of the divine will, and yet they are fallible, subject to misfortune and humiliation—and in the midst of misfortune and in their humiliation their acts and words reveal the transcendent majesty of God. There is hardly one of them who does not, like Adam, undergo the deepest humiliation—and hardly one who is not deemed worthy of God's personal intervention and personal inspiration. Humiliation and elevation go far deeper and far higher than in Homer, and they belong basically together. The poor beggar Odysseus is only masquerading, but Adam is really cast down, Jacob really a refugee, Joseph really in the pit and then a slave to be bought and sold. But their greatness, rising out of humiliation, is almost superhuman and an image of God's greatness. The reader clearly feels how the extent of the pendulum's swing is connected with the intensity of the personal history—precisely the most extreme circumstances, in which we are immeasurably forsaken and in despair, or immeasurably joyous and exalted, give us, if we survive them, a personal stamp which is recognized as the product of a rich existence, a rich development. And very often, indeed generally, this element of development gives the Old Testament stories a historical character, even when the subject is purely legendary and traditional.

Homer remains within the legendary with all his material, whereas the material of the Old Testament comes closer and closer to history as the narrative proceeds; in the stories of David the historical report predominates. Here too, much that is legendary still remains, as for example the story of David and Goliath; but much—and the most essential—consists in things which the narrators knew from their own experience or from firsthand testimony. Now the difference between legend and history is in most cases easily perceived by a reasonably experienced reader. It is a difficult matter, requiring careful historical and philological training, to distinguish the true from the synthetic or the biased in a historical presentation; but it is easy to separate the historical from the legendary in general. Their structure is different. Even where the legendary does not immediately betray itself by elements of the miraculous, by the repetition of well-known standard motives, typical patterns and themes, through neglect of clear details of time and place, and the like, it is generally quickly recognizable by its composition. It runs far too smoothly. All crosscurrents, all friction, all that is casual, secondary to the main events and themes, everything unresolved, truncated, and uncertain, which confuses the clear progress of the action and the simple orientation of the actors, has disappeared. The historical event which we witness, or learn from the testimony of those who witnessed it, runs much more variously, contradictorily, and confusedly; not until it has produced results in a definite domain are we able, with their help, to classify it to a certain extent; and how often the order to which we think we have attained becomes doubtful again, how often we ask ourselves if the data before us have not led us to a far too simple classification of the original events! Legend arranges its material in a simple and straightforward way; it detaches it from its contemporary historical context, so that the latter will not confuse it; it knows only clearly outlined men who act from few and simple motives and the continuity of whose feelings and actions remains uninterrupted. In the legends of martyrs, for example, a stiff-necked and fanatical persecutor stands over against an equally stiff-necked and fanatical victim; and a situation so complicated—that is to say, so real and historical—as that in which the "persecutor" Pliny finds himself in his celebrated letter to Trajan on the subject of the Christians, is unfit for legend. And that is still a comparatively simple case. Let the reader think of the history which we are ourselves witnessing; anyone who, for example, evaluates the behavior of individual men and groups of men at the time of the rise of National Socialism in Germany, or the behavior of individual peoples and states before and during the last war, will feel how difficult it is to represent historical themes in general, and how unfit they are for legend; the historical comprises a great number of contradictory motives in each individual, a hesitation and ambiguous groping on the part of groups; only seldom (as in the last war) does a more or less plain situation, comparatively simple to describe, arise, and even such a situation is subject to division below the surface, is indeed almost constantly in danger of losing its simplicity; and the motives of all the interested parties are so complex that the slogans of propaganda can be composed only through the crudest simplification—with the result that friend and foe alike can often employ the same ones. To write history is so difficult that most historians are forced to make concessions to the technique of legend.

It is clear that a large part of the life of David as given in the Bible contains history and not legend. In Absalom's rebellion, for example, or in the scenes from David's last days, the contradictions and crossing of motives both in individuals and in the general action have become so concrete that it is impossible to doubt the historicity of the information conveyed. Now the men who composed the historical parts are often the same who edited the older legends too; their peculiar religious concept of man in history, which we have attempted to describe above, in no way led them to a legendary simplification of events; and so it is only natural that, in the legendary passages of the Old Testament, historical structure is frequently discernible—of course, not in the sense that the traditions are examined as to their credibility according to the methods of scientific criticism; but simply to the extent that the tendency to a smoothing down and harmonizing of events, to a simplification of motives, to a static definition of characters which avoids conflict, vacillation, and development, such as are natural to legendary structure, does not predominate in the Old Testament world of legend. Abraham, Jacob, or even Moses produces a more concrete, direct, and historical impression than the figures of the Homeric world—not because they are better described in terms of sense (the contrary is the case) but because the confused, contradictory multiplicity of events, the psychological and factual cross-purposes, which true history reveals, have not disappeared in the representation but still remain clearly perceptible. In the stories of David, the legendary, which only later scientific criticism makes recognizable as such, imperceptibly passes into the historical; and even in the legendary, the problem of the classification and interpretation of human history is already passionately apprehended—a problem which later shatters the framework of historical composition and completely overruns it with prophecy; thus the Old Testament, in so far as it is concerned with human events, ranges through all three domains: legend, historical reporting, and interpretative historical theology.

Connected with the matters just discussed is the fact that the Greek text seems more limited and more static in respect to the circle of personages involved in the action and to their political activity. In the recognition scene with which we began, there appears, aside from Odysseus and Penelope, the housekeeper Eurycleia, a slave whom Odysseus' father Laertes had bought long before. She, like the swineherd Eumaeus, has spent her life in the service of Laertes' family; like Eumaeus, she is closely connected with their fate, she loves them and shares their interests and feelings. But she has no life of her own, no feelings of her own; she has only the life and feelings of her master. Eumaeus too, though he still remembers that he was born a freeman and indeed of a noble house (he was stolen as a boy), has, not only in fact but also in his own feeling, no longer a life of his own, he is entirely involved in the life of his masters. Yet these two characters are the only ones whom Homer brings to life who do not belong to the ruling class. Thus we become conscious of the fact that in the Homeric poems life is enacted only among the ruling class—others appear only in the role of servants to that class. The ruling class is still so strongly patriarchal, and still itself so involved in the daily activities of domestic life, that one is sometimes likely to forget their rank. But they are unmistakably a sort of feudal aristocracy, whose men divide their lives between war, hunting, marketplace councils, and feasting, while the women supervise the maids in the house. As a social picture, this world is completely stable; wars take place only between different groups of the ruling class; nothing ever pushes up from below. In the early stories of the Old Testament the patriarchal condition is dominant too, but since the people involved are individual nomadic or half-nomadic tribal leaders, the social picture gives a much less stable impression; class distinctions are not felt. As soon as the people completely emerges—that is, after the exodus from Egypt—its activity is always discernible, it is often in ferment, it frequently intervenes in events not only as a whole but also in separate groups and through the medium of separate individuals who come forward; the origins of prophecy seem to lie in the irrepressible politico-religious spontaneity of the people. We receive the impression that the movements emerging from the depths of the people of Israel-Judah must have been of a wholly different nature from those even of the later ancient democracies—of a different nature and far more elemental.

With the more profound historicity and the more profound social activity of the Old Testament text, there is connected yet another important distinction from Homer: namely, that a different conception of the elevated style and of the sublime is to be found here. Homer, of course, is not afraid to let the realism of daily life enter into the sublime and tragic; our episode of the scar is an example, we see how the quietly depicted, domestic scene of the foot-washing is incorporated into the pathetic and sublime action of Odysseus' home-coming. From the rule of the separation of styles which was later almost universally accepted and which specified that the realistic depiction of daily life was incompatible with the sublime and had a place only in comedy or, carefully stylized, in idyl—from any such rule Homer is still far removed. And yet he is closer to it than is the Old Testament. For the great and sublime events in the Homeric poems take place far more exclusively and unmistakably among the members of a ruling class; and these are far more untouched in their heroic elevation than are the Old Testament figures, who can fall much lower in dignity (consider, for example, Adam, Noah, David, Job); and finally, domestic realism, the representation of daily life, remains in Homer in the peaceful realm of the idyllic, whereas, from the very first, in the Old Testament stories, the sublime, tragic, and problematic take shape precisely in the domestic and commonplace: scenes such as those between Cain and Abel, between Noah and his sons, between Abraham, Sarah, and Hagar, between Rebekah, Jacob, and Esau, and so on, are inconceivable in the Homeric style. The entirely different ways of developing conflicts are enough to account for this. In the Old Testament stories the peace of daily life in the house, in the fields, and among the flocks, is undermined by jealousy over election and the promise of a blessing, and complications arise which would be utterly incomprehensible to the Homeric heroes. The latter must have palpable and clearly expressible reasons for their conflicts and enmities, and these work themselves out in free battles; whereas, with the former, the perpetually smouldering jealousy and the connection between the domestic and the spiritual, between the paternal blessing and the divine blessing, lead to daily life being permeated with the stuff of conflict, often with poison. The sublime influence of God here reaches so deeply into the everyday that the two realms of the sublime and the everyday are not only actually unseparated but basically inseparable.

We have compared these two texts, and, with them, the two kinds of style they embody, in order to reach a starting point for an investigation into the literary representation of reality in European culture. The two styles, in their opposition, represent basic types: on the one hand fully externalized description, uniform illumination, uninterrupted connection, free expression, all events in the foreground, displaying unmistakable meanings, few elements of historical development and of psychological perspective; on the other hand, certain parts brought into high relief, others left obscure, abruptness, suggestive influence of the unexpressed, "background" quality, multiplicity of meanings and the need for interpretation, universal-historical claims, development of the concept of the historically becoming, and preoccupation with the problematic.

Homer's realism is, of course, not to be equated with classical-antique realism in general; for the separation of styles, which did not develop until later, permitted no such leisurely and externalized description of everyday happenings; in tragedy especially there was no room for it; furthermore, Greek culture very soon encountered the phenomena of historical becoming and of the "multilayeredness" of the human problem, and dealt with them in its fashion; in Roman realism, finally, new and native concepts are added. We shall go into these later changes in the antique representation of reality when the occasion arises; on the whole, despite them, the basic tendencies of the Homeric style, which we have attempted to work out, remained effective and determinant down into late antiquity.

Since we are using the two styles, the Homeric and the Old Testament, as starting points, we have taken them as finished products, as they appear in the texts; we have disregarded everything that pertains to their origins, and thus have left untouched the question whether their peculiarities were theirs from the beginning or are to be referred wholly or in part to foreign influences. Within the limits of our purpose, a consideration of this question is not necessary; for it is in their full development, which they reached in early times, that the two styles exercised their determining influence upon the representation of reality in European literature.

Telemachos Remembers

by Edwin Muir

Twenty years, every day,
The figures in the web she wove
Came and stood and went away.
Her fingers in their pitiless play
Beat downward as the shuttle drove.

Slowly, slowly did they come,
With horse and chariot, spear and bow,
Half-finished heroes sad and mum,
Came slowly to the shuttle's hum.
Time itself was not so slow.

And what at last was there to see?
A horse's head, a trunkless man,
Mere odds and ends about to be,
And the thin line of augury
Where through the web the shuttle ran.

How could she bear the mounting load,
Dare once again her ghosts to rouse?
Far away Odysseus trod
The treadmill of the turning road
That did not bring him to his house.

The weary loom, the weary loom,
The task grown sick from morn to night,
From year to year. The treadle's boom
Made a low thunder in the room.
The woven phantoms mazed her sight.

If she had pushed it to the end,
Followed the shuttle's cunning song
So far she had no thought to rend

In time the web from end to end,
She would have worked a matchless wrong.

Instead, that jumble of heads and spears,
Forlorn scraps of her treasure trove.
I wet them with my childish tears
Not knowing she wove into her fears
Pride and fidelity and love.

Fire and Other Elements

by Cedric H. Whitman

It has been said that the oral poet feels no urge to coin new and striking phrases, as does the poet who writes.[1] The oral poet conceives his art, as indeed he must, as a continuous recombination of formulae. These formulae have already, as we have seen, partially solved the problem of making language presentational, leaving the poet more free to center his attention upon the arrangement and consistency of his poem. Since the whole is carried in the mind, and each unit is imagistic, in the sense defined in the last chapter, it is almost inevitable that certain images should group themselves systematically around leading ideas or characters; the creative process can be described in part as a movement from image to image, a movement controlled on one side by the demands of narrative, and on the other by the particular associations of the individual poet. Yet these images do not form a schematic set of deliberate correspondences; they change and shift constantly, according to the demands of the larger scene-image in which they stand, and the consistency which they show is the consistency of the whole design. By association with action and character, they grow into symbols, but like all symbols, they reflect in their unity a Gestalt, or organism of mental pictures and processes which do not correspond to any single concept. Their wording may change, but this basic set of associations, developing slowly throughout the narrated action, reveals the main threads of the poet's concern. If the formulaic method explains how an oral poet managed to compose at all, the image-patterns of the epic give the clue to his artistic plan. All poets plan their images, of course; but an oral poet's leading motifs must, to be manageable and communicable, remain austerely simple and strict in their economy. Herein the practical need of the performer and the meaning of his art serve each other, and well-nigh merge.

The total imagery of the *Iliad* exhibits the most extraordinary range of observation, especially in the formal similes, and the most startling of

[1] M. Parry, *Les Formules et la métrique d'Homère* (Paris, 1928), p. 61.

these, such as the comparison of the Achaean battleline to an honest woman measuring wool, or of Hector to a stone rolling down a cliff, occur once only. But there are also numerous kinds of image which, as part of the more expectable vocabulary of a warlike tradition, recur many times: comparisons of advancing hosts to the waves of the sea, of heroes to fierce animals, tall trees, whirlwinds, cliffs, and eagles. These are stock in trade on the one hand; yet it is precisely in this type of imagery that Homer's poetic economy makes itself evident. These motifs are not used indiscriminately, but with great subtlety, always emphasizing and sometimes symbolizing the larger movements of the poem. For the most part, these images occur in groups, in limited parts of the poem, changing to reflect changes of action. Only one stretches from beginning to end of the *Iliad,* reflecting the progress of the main action. This is the image of fire.

In one form or another, fire occurs about two hundred times in the *Iliad,* and of these only ten can really be said to be casual uses, unconnected with the main scheme. For the rest, fire itself, or comparisons of things to fire, forms a remarkable pattern of associations, all centering around the theme of heroic passion and death. Nothing could provide a more clinical case history of the working of a poet's mind upon a traditional theme than Homer's use of fire. For clearly, in the epic tradition, the motif existed chiefly in the form of men in armor flashing, or dashing, like fire. This is by far the most frequent form in which the image occurs, and there are numerous formulae for it, and sundry variations. Fire, or "heat" thus becomes a simple metonym for war, so that a battle with stones can even be referred to as "a divine-kindled fire of stones." In Homer's hands, however, not only do the heroes behave like fire; fire itself behaves like the heroes. With the exception of the few passages noted, every spark of flame, no matter how naturally and inevitably it is lit, is drawn eventually into the tragic symbolism.

It begins naturally enough with sacrifices and funeral pyres. The first fire we hear of is in the prayer of Chryses, who reminds Apollo of the sacrifices he has burned. Shortly thereafter the pyres of the dead blaze in the Greek camp; Chryses' sacrifices were doubtless of a festive nature; but the fire of sacrifices to the gods takes on darker coloring as the poem proceeds. The next one is the propitiatory and repentant sacrifice of Odysseus at Chrysa, and after that the sacrifices of the Achaeans on the brink of a disastrous battle, and of Agamemnon himself, whose prayers Zeus has refused. While he entertains the Embassy, Achilles roasts meat for a meal; but later in Phoenix' account of his wrath against his father, the image of meat roasting in the fire merges mysteriously with the watchfire of the guard set upon Phoenix, whose rage would not cool, so that the fire could not be quenched for nine nights. By this point in the poem, as we shall see, anger and fire are inseparably associated, so that a special meaning surrounds the later narrative of Nestor's earliest memory of

Achilles in the light of a sacrificial fire. Finally the idea of sacrifice becomes really doom-laden. Its last three occurrences are in contexts far removed from the festive. As he watches Hector fleeing from Achilles, Zeus says,

> My heart mourns for Hector who burned many thighs of bulls
> On the peaks of Ida of the many glens, and sometimes in the acropolis.
> Now divine Achilles pursues him with swift feet round Priam's city.

The sight of the pious man whom he cannot save, driven to death on the site of his many sacrifices, may well move Zeus. The sacrificer becomes the sacrificed, and Andromache's burning of Hector's clothes is like the last of his profitless sacrifices. It is in lieu of a funeral; in fact sacrifice and funeral have blended, in part, and they become actually identical when the twelve Trojan youths are immolated at the funeral of Patroclus. Surely there is a consciousness here of an inverted order of things: Andromache burns Hector's empty clothes, while his corpse remains unburnt; Achilles sacrifices twelve living men to swell the pyre of Patroclus. The limits of funeral and sacrifice have somehow become confused, and their functions perverted.

Pyres for the dead are, of course, numerous in the *Iliad*, but in general they follow the action closely, appearing at climactic moments. They appear first as the direct result of Agamemnon's insult to Chryses, the germ of the plot. In Andromache's narrative to Hector, the pyre of her father enters as a poignant commentary upon her own tragic isolation, and incidentally upon the character of Achilles also.[2] At the end of the first day's fighting in the poem, the passage known as the Gathering of the Dead, with its long description of the Greek and Trojan funerals, seems to serve a special purpose. As yet the Achaeans have suffered no special defeat, yet they decide, on Nestor's advice, to build a wall to defend themselves and their ships. The problem of Book VII is to bridge the gap between the victorious displays of Diomedes in V and VI, and the sudden worsting of the Greeks in VIII. A wall is needed to keep these reversals from becoming an immediate rout. And in order to motivate the wall adequately, the poet binds its construction closely to the taking up of the dead; Nestor proposes both the truce for burial and the wall-building in a single speech—a unique example of compendiousness on his part. But the reason for it is to create a specious motivation for this

[2] VI.417-420. Death, fire, and the magnanimity of Achilles are here first associated, in a most unique passage. Soon again, in the challenge of Hector, VII.79, the stipulation of honorable burial for the loser reflects the same association. Cf. the threat in XV.350, where the reverse is implied. To give bodies to dogs, rather than to fire, is a threat of utter annihilation. See Schrade, *Götter und Menschen Homers* (Stuttgart, 1952), pp. 216ff. Terrifying as fire is in the *Iliad*, the denial of it is worse, for then glory is lost. In tbe context of funerals, and in the context of the Διὸς βουλή (see below), fire has much to do with heroic glory.

sudden act of defensiveness, and the burning and burial of the fallen provides just the imagistic atmosphere needed. From the logical point of view, there is a weak link in the structure here; Homer has tried to hide it in the dazzle of funeral pyres.

The funeral motif has two climaxes, the pyre of Patroclus and the pyre of Hector, and both reflect upon the character of Achilles. The burial of his friend takes place in an atmosphere of horror and savage grief. He delays it until he can carry out to the full his threatened vengeance; he repeatedly drags Hector round the bier, until the ghost of Patroclus himself begs for some haste with the formalities. Something of Achilles' own feeling that he cannot do enough for his friend is reflected in the reluctance of the fire to burn; special winds must be summoned, and then at last the pyre flames. The contrast between such scenes of wrenching agony and the long perspective on sorrow in Book XXIV is profound. When he restores the body of Hector to Priam, Achilles repeats his honorable treatment of Andromache's father, and his own fulfilled dignity is echoed in the long but restrained triptych of lamentation, as Andromache, Hecuba, and Helen conduct Hector's funeral. When the embers of this pyre die down, the tragic fire-motif which spreads wildly throughout the poem, somehow returns to its limits at last.

As one looks back from this point, lurid flame seems to start from every portion of the poem. The eyes of Agamemnon in the quarrel glare darkly like fire. In the king's hope of victory, we foresee the flare of burning Troy.[3] As the marshalled host marches out, they are like wasting fire that burns in a wooded mountain glen, the first of a famous chain of similes. Rage, destruction, heroic valor, and heroic honor are all fire. Sometimes the hero simply moves like fire; sometimes it is his eyes that burn terribly under the nodding helmet. Achilles' own fierce choler sometimes blazes clear, and sometimes is compared to a growing cloud of smoke. Athena drops from Olympus to the battlefield like a meteor shooting sparks; sometimes she comes in a burning chariot. When Hector smashes the Achaean gates with a stone and leaps inside the wall, he seems all clothed in fire, with his arms and eyes flaring; but it is a dusky, threatening flame, for he is also like the night.[4] Later, as he threatens to burn the ships, he is like a blazing eagle, so that in his most victorious moment, his fire is joined by the bird of Zeus, who gives him the victory. Even proper names get caught significantly in the conflagration. As Hector begins his great attack, he addresses his four horses, two of which have fiery names, Aithon (Blazing) and Lampus (Torch), and the first man slain by Patroclus as he drives the Trojans back from the ships

[3] II.414. Though the *Iliad* never narrates the sack of Troy, the image of it constantly rises.

[4] XII.462-466. Cf. the bright Apollo, who also in a threatening moment comes "like the night," I.47. The night of Apollo's anger and that of Hector's victory are from the same source.

is Pyraichmes, "Fiery Spearhead." While images of tree-felling as a rule prevail in the pitched battle, forest fire is the regular image for a rout.

But it is in connection with the wrath of Achilles and the plan of Zeus itself that the fire motif undergoes its principal development. In this connection it becomes symbolic, from simply imagistic, and thus gives to every passage involving it the tragic context of the hero himself. There could scarcely be a more apt symbol of Greek heroism, which turns upon the poles of divinity and death. The fire of the funeral pyres betokens one side of the heroic nature; the other reaches toward the gods through the lightning flashes, which presently become the explicit sign of Zeus' acceptance of the hero's cause.[5]

The plan of Zeus to defeat the Achaeans in Achilles' absence does not actually begin to take effect until Book VIII, but at the end of the preceding book, the sign of Zeus' participation in the war begins. The Achaeans and Trojans are at their evening meal:

> All night long then the long-haired Achaeans feasted,
> And the Trojans also in the city, and their allies;
> And all night long Zeus the Councillor was planning evil against them,
> Terribly thundering; and pale fear seized them.

It is not yet made clear to either side who is to be the object of Zeus' evil plan, but it soon becomes specific enough when the battle is joined next morning:

> While it was dawn and the sacred day was rising, steadily
> Missiles of both hosts flew to the mark, and the men were falling;
> But when the sun bestrode the midst of the sky,
> Verily then the father spread out the golden scales,
> Casting therein two fates of long and grievous death,
> Fates of the Trojans, masters of horses, and bronze-vested Achaeans;
> Taking the center he poised them; the Achaeans' day drooped fatal;
> Down to the full-nourishing earth the fates of the Achaeans
> Settled, and the Trojans' rose up toward the broad heaven.
> Mightily he himself thundered from Ida, and hurled a flaming
> Lightning-bolt at the host of Achaeans, and they perceiving
> Wondered aghast, and pale fear secretly stole over all.

The use of the scales here symbolizes, as usual in Homer, fatality, meaning what must happen because of the nature of things. The scales never

[5] Apropos of the association of the Διὸς βουλή with the μῆνις, cf. V.34, where the phrase Διὸς μῆνιν occurs, referring to the ban on the gods' participation in the war, which has not yet taken place. Note too that Zeus and Achilles, during the Wrath, are both νόσφι λιασθείς, I.349; XI.80, a formula used nowhere else.

indicate a miraculous, unnatural, or supernatural event; their readings are, in Homer's phrase, "according to fate." Here they point to the inevitable weakness of the Achaeans without Achilles, and by their token the plan of Zeus is shown as grounded in fact and made organic with the human situation. The lightning flash which dismays the Achaeans is the direct reflex of Achilles' retirement. The action of the god and the inaction of the hero are essentially one.

On the other hand, the lightning flash itself presently takes on the appearances of a special, personal rebuke. Diomedes, flushed with recent triumphs, rescues Nestor from the tangle of his wounded horses, and turns against the Trojans with such fury that "they would have been pent up in Ilium like sheep," had not Zeus again hurled the lightning. There follows a little tussle between Diomedes and Zeus, and the god has to hurl three more bolts before Diomedes will swallow Hector's taunts and retreat. Here lightning, the symbol of the necessity of Greek defeat, has become an actor on the scene, the agent of things as they are, according to the decree of the scales of Zeus. On the surface of it, this is direct interference, yet it is also in character for Diomedes. It would be impossible to allow Diomedes, whose brilliant exploits in Books V and VI have included the wounding of two gods and a bold resistance to Apollo himself, to yield too easily to a divine sign and turn his back on the enemy. His heroism has reached a high and inspired level, though not that of Achilles. Moreover, he is the least dismayed of all the princes by the retirement of Achilles, and on three occasions he recommends his own valor to Agamemnon, who would give up in discouragement. It is in character, therefore, that he should give in least easily. His resistance to Zeus is coupled with that of the two goddesses who inspired him in V. Exactly as they came to Diomedes in V, Hera and Athena start on their way now, in a chariot to the battlefield, and they too have to be threatened individually with lightning. The scene which follows on Olympus then dramatizes in terms of the gods' own personalities the passionate and wayward courses of the warriors below. Diomedes in a rage of frustration, had prayed for the earth to swallow him. Hera, in a rage of frustration, trembles on her throne and shakes Olympus. But Zeus, unmoved, says that she may plunge into the depths of the earth, but he would not care. The image of being swallowed up by the earth spreads from Diomedes to Hera.

But now the lightning flashes are understood by Hector as a sign of victory. Hector calls to his fiery horses and drives the Achaeans steadily back toward the wall. As Agamemnon in terror appeals to Zeus for the army's safety, Homer brings in a new symbol. Zeus sends an eagle to reassure the king; the eagle has a fawn in its claws, probably a sign of the taking of Troy.[6] It is as if Zeus here indicated the limits of his plan; later on again, the ultimate victory of the Greeks is foreshadowed by an

[6] VIII.246-250; cf. eagles and hare in Aeschylus, *Agamemnon*, 115ff.

eagle, which goes unnoticed by the Trojans.[7] For the moment the lightning carries the day; fire is on the Trojan side, and burns threateningly in the form of the watchfires which at the end of Book VIII dot the plain, and burn throughout the succeeding night.[8]

Presently the threat takes a more definite form: Hector will burn the ships. This is his first thought when he recognizes the meaning of the lightning flashes; throughout the Embassy, the essence of the Greeks' fear is the image of burning ships, and during the whole central battle it remains the principal deed which Hector envisions in his victory, growing ever more imminent until at last he is at the ships and calls to his companions to bring the fire. It is of course literal, physical fire which Ajax keeps warding away as he strides from deck to deck, battling desperately with a boathook for a spear; but the fire has not lost its connection with Zeus' intention and with Achilles: Idomeneus, at one point, feels sure that the Achaeans can hold off the fire, *unless Zeus himself* hurls it onto the ships. Moreover, the frequent stock comparisons of Hector and the Trojans to fire now have the effect of identifying Hector and his threat as the agents of the Plan of Zeus. War itself is fire, yet here the real fire which threatens is the blaze of the tragic wrath. Nor has the related thunder signal been forgotten;[9] one of the finest uses of it comes when Zeus thunders in answer to a prayer of Nestor's. The god meant to encourage Nestor, and Nestor understands the omen. But the Trojans, to whom now the omen of thunder and lightning is a token of their own victory, are equally encouraged; they set on the Greeks more fiercely, and drive them back even more.

Such ambiguity is increased during the counterattack which the Greeks make, led by Poseidon. Fire still appears in connection with Hector and the threat to the ships, but only while Poseidon's help must be in secret; when Zeus is deceived by Hera into napping, Poseidon assists the Greeks openly. But from the moment of the god's arrival, the fire shows signs of changing sides, and begins to play around Idomeneus, whom Poseidon directly inspires. Idomeneus comes to the battlefield like a lightning flash; a little later he is again compared to fire, and further on to a wild boar with fiery eyes. This is while Zeus is still awake; after he falls asleep, Poseidon takes the field openly, leading the Greeks with a sword which is like lightning. Then comes the climax; the lightning which had been his sign of victory turns against Hector, and he falls beneath the stone of Ajax, like a lightning-blasted oak. Thereafter, Zeus awakes and

[7] XII.200ff.; XIII.821. Three omens seem to bear out the poet's explanation of the limits of Zeus' intentions, XIII.345-360, especially 348ff. But the whole passage indicates his meaning in allowing Poseidon to enter the battle.

[8] VIII.509, 554; IX.77, 88 (where the Greek watchfires are also set on Nestor's advice), 234; X.12, 418. As Agamemnon looks at these campfires, his groans are like the thunder of Zeus, X.5ff.

[9] XI.4, 184. In the first of these passages, the Scholiast suggests that lightning is what is meant by the τέρας πολέμοιο.

restores the order of the day; but this part of the action illustrates both the suppleness and careful economy of the fire image. Ambiguous and varied as it is, it goes by plan.

When the first fire actually falls on the ships, the motif passes from the momentary image into the action itself. This moment is most carefully prepared, and the poet gives it a separate, brief invocation of the Muses. The breaking of Ajax' spear, which the hero recognizes as the direct work of the gods, is only the last of a series of such happenings, which include the lightning flashes of Book VIII, the wounding of the chiefs, and the breaking of Teucer's bowstring.[10] With Ajax momentarily helpless, the Trojans finally set fire to the first ship, and Achilles sees it. The identification of the wills of Achilles and Zeus is hinted at in this moment, since not long before, Zeus was waiting to see the flame arise. Both were waiting to see it, and both of course saw it, but Homer notes only that Zeus waited for it, and Achilles saw it. He smites his thigh and calls to Patroclus to hurry, for now for the first time he feels that the latter's urgency is justified. He repeats, in fact, Patroclus' own gesture when he hurried away from Eurypylus to rouse Achilles. Thus in the single moment of the first firing of the ship, the two sides of Achilles' nature are brought into sharp confrontation—the intransigent will, which has become the plan of Zeus, and the humane concern which yields to Patroclus and the emergency. Now Patroclus goes, and quenches the fire.

But from here on, the fire of the Plan of Zeus becomes ever less evident. Significantly enough, lightning does not appear in connection with Patroclus, brilliant as his deeds are, for Patroclus, who represents the human side of Achilles, could hardly be attended by the symbol of his wrath; nor would the lightning which betokens victory for the Trojans be appropriate to Patroclus, who momentarily repels them. Real lightning, in fact, returns only once. This is when the body of Patroclus is being dragged off by Menelaus, and the Trojans press forward, encouraged by one last thunderbolt, to drive the Greeks in rout. Hector, still victorious, continues to be compared to fire, and so does the battle itself. But the heavenly sign has disappeared. Actually, there is no longer any propriety in it, for when Patroclus set out, the wrath of Achilles, as he himself says, was already waning, and was now simply grief. Achilles' own indecisive period of waiting for Patroclus to return is reflected, perhaps, in a certain indecisiveness in Zeus' position. Since he does not yet know that Patroclus is dead, Achilles cannot foresee his own next move. Meanwhile, the wrath being partly abated, the plan of Zeus hangs in abeyance, though it is not formally declared at an end until after Achilles formally renounces the wrath. But already before that, fire has begun to take new, and more miraculous forms, centering around Achilles himself. His breastplate, which he lends to Patroclus, is like a star, and the flash of

[10] XV .464ff. Teucer also recognizes herein the operation of the Plan of Zeus.

it is seen several times, both on Patroclus and Hector.[11] But when Achilles goes to the trench and shouts, the fire of the hero himself appears. Athena crowns his head with a golden cloud from which flame shoots heavenward like the beacon of a besieged city. The Trojans see it and quail. The image of the besieged city foreshadows the end of the war, and the burning of Troy. This is the true fire, where the thunder and lightning signals had been deceptive.

The fire that shoots from Achilles' head denotes the *peripeteia* of the *Iliad.* The great battle which began in Book XI with the shout of Eris, holding in her hands the *teras* or "symbol" of war (which the Scholiast says was lightning), is ended by the shout and fire of Achilles. From here on, all deception breaks, the truth is out. Achilles is indispensable, but Patroclus is dead. Agamemnon was deceived, Hector was deceived; Pulydamas alone had read the omens right, and no one listened to him. Even Achilles, who foresaw so much about himself, did not foresee the death of his friend. Now he has paid the price of human loss for his godlike intransigence. Once the issue is clear, with the return of Achilles to the field, the far-flung action of the *Iliad* begins to narrow to a single course, led on by the fire ignited by Athena around Achilles over the trench. All the associations of the image—death, rage, heroic greatness, the fall of Troy, and divinity itself—now play against each other constantly. From the vision at the trench, we pass instantly to the corpse of Patroclus, and shortly thereafter Achilles declares his plans for the pyre, with its human sacrifice. Presently a fire is lit to heat water for bathing the corpse. But the principal kind of fire in Book XVIII is divine fire, and when Thetis goes to Olympus, we meet the god of fire himself, Hephaestus. The forging scene opens with twenty bellows blowing up the coals for the work to begin. The *thorax* is brighter than the gleam of fire. The great shield is too transcendent an image to be wholly dominated by fire images, but it includes them; sun, moon, and stars, the fiery bodies of heaven (to all of which Achilles, dressed in these arms, is later compared), occupy a prominent position together with the other three elements, earth, sky, and sea. There are also the fires of wedding torches and of flashing men in arms. But all things are in their places on the shield; the gift of the god is entirely true to the way things are. If Achilles, when he wears these arms, becomes all but identified with fire, it is because the gods' gifts are precisely those which lift a man perilously from his place and destroy him. In an agonized moment, Achilles wishes his father had taken a mortal wife; as it is, he will pay the price of his half-divinity; he will put on armor wrought in Olympian fire, slay Hector and, therewith, himself.

The terror of the divine gift is apparent at once. Thetis puts the arms down in front of Achilles, and even the Myrmidons are unable to look at

[11] XVI.134; cf. the helmet, 70f., and also the appearance of Hector "flaming" in Achilles' arms, XVII.213f.

them. Fear seizes them. But rage seizes Achilles; his eyes gleam like fire, and he takes delight in handling the god's gifts. It is not the supernal vision of the shield, the Olympian view of things as they are, which enters into him, but fire and fire alone; for this is the only one of the elements which applies to Achilles here—the most swift, short-lived, and dangerous. As he puts on the panoply, the motif of fire is closely conjoined with images of agony, lonely despair, and the heavenly bodies: in his eyes is the flash of fire, but in his heart his unendurable grief sets him in contrast to the other Myrmidons, under whose gleaming bronze the whole earth laughs. The shield is like the glance of the moon, or like a distant forest fire seen by lonely sailors driven far from their friends by adverse winds. The helmet glimmers like a star. Moreover, the arms seem to weigh nothing, but lift their wearer like wings, an image provoked perhaps by the swiftness and upward course of flames. The total vision of the hero armed is like the shining Hyperion himself. Throughout the arming scene, the single symbol of fire connotes directly all the anguish, semidivine glory, and utter isolation of Achilles. Less directly, it still flickers with intimations of rage, loss, and imminent death.

During the great *aristeia* which follows, fire, though concentrated primarily on Achilles, follows to some extent the general action. The plain is filled with the flash of bronze. Aeneas' arms gleam, and Hector, in a moment of retaliatory passion for the death of his brother Polydorus, faces Achilles "like fire." There are remote references to the flame which will consume Troy, and this foreshadowing of the city's doom is subtly associated with Achilles, who is compared to fire in a city.[12] But the really striking thing about Books XX and XXI is the contest between fire and water. The narrative in this section skillfully intertwines two actions, the *Theomachia,* or Battle of the Gods, and the River Fight. Released from the ban of Zeus, the gods take the field, pairing off according to their Greek or Trojan sympathies. Among the eminent Olympians appears the somewhat obscure figure of Xanthus, genius of the stream by Troy, who confronts Hephaestus. Nothing is made of this at once, for the gods, always dependent on human action, interrupt their fight while Achilles pursues the Trojans who flee like locusts from a fire. But when Achilles reaches the river, his *aristeia* is no longer merely that. It becomes a battle of the elements, in which the protective river of Troy rises up against the hero and attempts to drown him. Natural as it is for a stream choked with corpses to overflow, Homer is not interested in leaving the scene on the naturalistic level. The river appeals to Achilles to desist, and he, as always, yields to a divine injunction; he tries to get up the bank, but the river pursues him. His footing is washed away, and in spite of appeals to Zeus and the help of Poseidon and Athena, Achilles is helpless

[12]XXI.522ff. cf. Zeus' fear that Achilles will take Troy (XX.29f.), or Poseidon's that he will slay Aeneas (*ibid.,* 336), ὑπὲρ μόρον. According to the *Aethiopis,* Achilles did make a furious assault on Troy, after slaying Memnon, cf. Schadewaldt and Pestalozzi.

to extricate himself from the flooding stream. The latter, no longer concerned merely for his own state, calls to his brother Simois to help defend Troy, lest Achilles sack it. And now the meaning of the earlier confrontation of Xanthus and Hephaestus becomes clear, and with it the meaning of the whole *Theomachia;* Hera calls to Hephaestus:

> Up, lame-foot, my son, we deem that eddying Xanthus
> Rises in strife against you.

Two things here deserve notice: first that the *Theomachia* had been suspended in the previous book, on the advice of Poseidon, because he felt certain of victory, and was content to let the mortals fight; he said, however, that if Apollo or Ares began a fight, or if any one held back Achilles from fighting, then the pro-Greek Olympians would show their strength. Xanthus, by holding back Achilles, precipitates the battle of the gods, and Hera, the quick-to-wrath, calls upon Hephaestus. The second point is that Hera regards Xanthus' action *as river* against Achilles as identical with an attack *as personal god* on Hephaestus, his official opponent. Homer is seldom as directly symbolic with his divine figures as this, but he has a special reason. Xanthus threatens to quench the fire of Achilles, and fire itself must answer the challenge. Hephaestus "aims the divine fire" like a spear, burning first the plain with the bodies on it, and begins to restrain the water. Trees and shrubs are consumed. The fish are tormented, and at last the water itself burns, or boils, and cries out in surrender. Achilles himself, in the middle of it, is untouched. All naturalism is here left far behind, and the basic imagery of the *aristeia* of Achilles has completely run away with the action. It is, in fact, an inversion of nature for fire to lick up water. But this is the fire of Achilles himself, which most recently has taken the form of arms made by Hephaestus, and the whole passage, like the *Theomachia* proper which follows it, becomes a dumb show of the taking of Troy. This fact is proven by the terms of Xanthus' surrender: he swears no longer to protect Troy, not even when the Achaeans burn it.[13] So the fire here is also prophetic.

The comic duels which follow this scene are a mere epilogue, for the real battle is won. Only Apollo is really serious in this scene. He represents the tragic valor of the Trojans, and, after refusing, out of respect, to struggle with his father's brother, he departs with intact dignity to defend Troy to the last. The threat of fire is upon it, and looking back, one can see how carefully Homer prepared for the duel between this inevitable fire and the waters of the Troad. Action and imagery are in accord throughout. As he hurls the body of Lycaon into the stream, Achilles utters a challenge:

[13] XXI.373ff. See Schadewaldt, *Iliasstudien* (Leipzig, 1938), p. 156, n. 4, for a collection of references to the taking of Troy in the latter half of the *Iliad*.

Perish, till we come to the citadel of holy Troy,
You fleeing, and I behind you slaying.
No help will the fair-flowing, silver-eddying stream
Bring you.

And again, after he has slain Asteropaeus, the son of the River Axius, his challenge to all the waters of the world is based on the lightning of his ancestor Zeus:

Lie thus! it is hard for you, though son of a river
To strive with the sons of Zeus.
You say you are the offspring of a broad-flowing river,
But I boast of the race of great Zeus. . . .

Thus Zeus is greater than rivers coiling seaward,
And greater is Zeus' offspring than any river. . . .

With him (Zeus) not even lordly Achelous is equal,
Nor the might of deep-channeled Ocean,
From whom all rivers, all the sea,
All springs and trailing rivulets flow.
But even he fears the lightning bolt of mighty Zeus,
And the dread thunder, when it crashes from heaven.

Here the meaningful confrontation of deadly fire and its gentler opposite, water, is clear, as is the connection between the helplessness of the stream and the taking of Troy in the previous passage on Lycaon. These two particular passages can have been elaborated as they are for no other reason than to emphasize the imagistic structure. Neither does the threat to take Troy enter in any merely casual way. When Apollo goes to Troy at the end of the *Theomachia,* his concern is that the city should not be taken "beyond fate." This "fate," *moros,* like all Homer's words for fate, indicates the process by which things are as they are; and part of the worldly process is time. Led by Achilles, the Achaeans now, as earlier in the *Patrocleia,* threaten to take Troy "beyond fate," or "before its time," and Zeus had originally allowed the gods to rejoin the war in order that Troy might not be so taken. This can only mean that the gods, especially Zeus, are in a way the keepers of the world process, custodians of time, though they themselves see things not as they happen, but entire, finished. In their own persons, they are absolute, and their gifts to man, such as the arms of Achilles, are tokens of man's own grasp of the absolute. Achilles' fire also is an absolute, hence it threatens to upset fate, or the temporal world process, even as it licks up the waters of Troy. Hence presumably, one may explain the fear of Aidoneus, the god of death, at the very beginning of Achilles' great attack. He feared the earth would be rent and the houses of death itself appear naked to all. This is not merely grandiose rhetoric. It is on the one hand part of the cosmic imagery characteristic of these two books,[14] and on the other hand it reflects the pervasive fear of things happening beyond fate. To reveal death all at once would be to see it absolute, and not as the veiled end of the temporal process; yet such is Achilles' deathly earnest, so absolute is his fire, that this is precisely what he threatens to do. It may well be asked why, if that is so, did Achilles not take Troy; why did not this absolute fire, which consumes water, rush on unhindered? The answer of course is that nothing ever actually happens beyond fate; Achilles' absolute, like every heroic absolute, finds its *telos,* or fulfillment, not in dislocating the world as it is, but in self-destruction. Achilles' *aristeia,* since it destroyed Hector, did in a way destroy the city. Hence the appropriateness of the symbolic shadow-show by which Homer implies what he does not narrate. But Achilles' own limit is also fixed. The all-destructive rage with which he assails the Trojans is directed in the last analysis against himself. Like Patroclus, he will have his meeting with Apollo. Homer does not narrate the death of Achilles, but in the scene where Apollo deflects him while the Trojans save themselves inside the gates, he symbolizes the limits of what Achilles can do. Here Apollo has done exactly what he went to Troy to do. In delaying Achilles, he defends the *moros,* here "portion," or "lot," of Troy. Achilles angrily retorts that he would slay Apollo if he could. But this admission that there is anyone he cannot slay shows exactly where the limit of his great slaughter lies—in Apollo himself. And from this point on, the fire image begins to contract again, and to grow more confined to the action of the moment.

As Achilles turns from Apollo and races back toward Troy, Priam watching from the walls sees him in the likeness of a star:

> Rushing over the plain, gleaming bright as a star,
> The star that comes in autumn, and eminently its fires
> Shine in the darkness of night, among the many stars;
> That one they call by the name, Dog of Orion;
> Brightest it is, and fashioned for a token of evil,
> And brings much fever on suffering mortals. . . .

The comparison of a hero to a star does not occur only here. Diomedes, at the opening of his *aristeia,* is compared to a star—indeed the same autumn star—but how differently:

> Fire exhaustless flamed from his helm and shield,
> Starlike, the star of autumn, that gleams brightest
> Washed in the ocean. . . .

[14] Besides fire and water, earth and air are also constantly involved.

In the latter case the traditional theme is compressed; the star is shorn of its threatening feverish association, and only its brightness is emphasized. In the former passage, the star partakes of the deadly significance of the moment. Hector also is compared to a star once, near the beginning of the great battle:

> As a baleful star appears from the clouds,
> Shining, and then dips back into dusky cloud,
> So Hector sometimes in the forefront shone,
> Sometimes marshaling the rear; and all in bronze
> He shone like the lightning of the aegis-bearer, father Zeus.

Though for the moment the lightning of the Plan of Zeus attends him, Hector's glory is intermittent; it comes and goes, which is in character for the man whose hopes are raised so high, and who lies so low at the end. It is in such instances that we can really see the poet's own work. Though the epithet may be a fixed, inherited lens through which to behold not individuals but heroic norms, themes of this sort—stock comparisons, as well as even episodes—are subject to great variation, and regularly in the work of Homer they take their shape from the individual concern of the action where they occur. Achilles' fiery star is of the same fire which we have seen springing from him and all but consuming the Trojan plain itself. It foretells the fire which will destroy the city. Now it is concentrated like a star, while Achilles is in the distance: as he draws nearer, the bronze looks "like fire or the rising sun." The poet keeps to heavenly bodies, for the nonce, and a later comparison narrows the focus again, and even further, from Achilles himself to the spear point which he poises, looking for a chink in his opponent's armor:

> . . . And he lowered his head under the shining
> Four-plumed helm; and the fine manes tossed
> Golden, which Hephaestus set in abundant crests;
> And as a star goes among stars in the dark of night,
> The evening star, which stands in heaven the fairest star,
> So started the flash from the edged spear—

Deserted by the gods, Hector faces Achilles alone. His noblest and fairest moment comes at the end of his long day of battle, with its glory and defeat; and the spear which transfixes him a few lines later is like the evening star. The fire of Achilles is distilled to a purposive and fatal point, and at the very last, as the star of the dying day, responds to the passion and beauty of both heroes.

The last two books of the poem are full of the sacrifice and funeral fires described earlier. Like a double frame, these natural but subtly intertwined forms of fire enclose the vast symbolic permutations which the theme undergoes in the main action. The first sacrifices and the first funerals of the *Iliad* were in general terms, the last are specific, tragic; and in this passage from the normative, formulaic motif to a particularized enlargement, without loss of the universal shape, we have only another form of that same artistic spirit which characterizes all classic art—the interdependence of the individual and the generic.

The foregoing analysis of the *Iliad*'s use of fire may seem somewhat to overbid the material. Torn from its context, this fire may seem even a little monotonous. Such treatment, however, may be excused as an attempt to give the case history of a single traditional motif in the hands of a supremely gifted oral poet. This image of fire stood in Homer's eyes, impelling and controlling his work; he could not read or write, but he could remember. Though interpretations might differ as to its significance in particular passages, the fact certainly cannot be denied that fire is the one clearly imagistic motif which continues throughout the poem, that it goes through more kinds of change and more varied association than any other. Yet—and this is most important—its symbolism is limited, in that there are things to which it might have been but never is applied, such as love. Like the metaphysical terms in philosophy, it transcends categories; it is also metaphysical in that it specifically connects the wrath of Achilles with the Plan of Zeus, and Achilles himself with the gods. Wherever it occurs in connection with heroes, it emphasizes their inspired energy and stress, and in Achilles' case it typifies his extraordinary self-identification with the absolute. These and all the other associations of fire—death, sacrifice, the fall of Troy—coexist in each occurrence of it, or very nearly, but only in the *Iliad*. One would look in vain for any such associations in the *Odyssey*, where fire plays no very great role, and is in part supplanted by the continuing motif of the sea. These associations are the joint creation of the formulaic method and the poet's total vision. It is not to be thought that any pre-established connection existed in Homer's mind among all the things which are connected in his poem with fire. It is simply that fire, or fiery objects such as sun and stars, was traditionally and in certain phrases compared to all these things, while of course it existed in its own shape as the natural destroyer of dead bodies, invaders' ships, and beleaguered cities. Its meaning grew with the song, but it could do so only if controlled by a master singer. And Homer's fire is never out of hand. Few themes in any art have been developed with such fullness and restraint.

One such symbolic pattern must be looked upon as the token of a concentrated ingenuity, haunted by an especially appropriate and supple image. If all the imagery of the *Iliad* were so developed, it would—supposing it were possible—point to a fantastically schematized and mannered conception of poetry. Most of the great similes come once and once only, and even the scenes and objects which appear in them are not, with the exception of fire, drawn into any strict pervasive rhythm.

Yet a few images, especially the fundamental ones of earth, air, and sea, undergo partial, momentary elaboration. Although the treatment of them is far less extended, it does not differ essentially from the treatment of fire—where simple formulaic similes of warfare, such as "fighting like fire," or "flashing like fire," were carefully budgeted within certain associations until fire, having a symbolic life of its own, could act for itself and achieve its own climax. In a similar though lesser way, the formulae of earth, air, and sea behave not merely as units of speech but also of thought and structure, moving in and out of the factual bones of the story, and confusing themselves with them.

Although it seldom enters decisively into the emotional or dramatic scheme of the *Iliad* as it does in the *Odyssey,* the sea is always there as the vast backdrop of the poem. When Thetis on occasion comes from it wrapped in mist, her presence is primarily felt as that of goddess and mother; yet she is also the sea goddess, and there is even some hint of the *Urmutterschaft* of the ocean in Patroclus' accusation to Achilles: "Not Thetis, but the grey sea bore you," as also in the quasi-funeral of Book XVIII, when the Nereids form a lamenting chorus. Yet on one occasion the sea distinctly enters the action, first in the guise of Poseidon himself. At the beginning of Book XIII, Zeus momentarily turns his eyes from the war, and Poseidon, "keeping no sightless watch," swoops in three paces from Samothrace to Aigae, and thence drives his dolphin chariot to the coasts of Tenedos and the Troad. For the space of the next two books he is, as we have seen, first in secret, then openly, the helper of the Greeks, who are battling desperately for their ships; during his presence on the field, the heroic fire changes from the Trojan to the Greek side, and the lightning flash of Zeus disappears in favor of a "sword-like lightning" in the hand of Poseidon. But at the moment when Zeus finally dozes and Poseidon overtly leads on the Greeks in renewed strength, Homer suddenly injects this line:

> And the sea crashed among the tents and ships of the Argives.

This is the decisive moment. Not only in his personal form, but also in his elemental form, Poseidon assists the Achaeans, and the confusion between god and element is the same as in the case of Xanthus and Hephaestus in the *Theomachia*. For the moment, fire and water are on the same side, and Homer seems perfectly conscious of the fact, for in the splendid simile immediately following he links them closely: the din of the battle is compared first to breakers on the shore, then to forest fire in mountain glens, and finally (for good measure, and also because wind is a highly developed image in the Great Battle), to the wind in lofty oak trees. These crashing breakers in a way complete an earlier sea image: Nestor, watching the battle, was indecisive as a billow that does not break till Zeus decides its course. Now the wave breaks—a different wave, certainly, and not according to Zeus' decision, but the sea wave is currently in the poet's mind, and may take on the likeness of decision or of indecision. It remains in his mind, moreover, even after Poseidon has left the Greeks and the tide turns against them: two images of shipwreck, when the wave passes over the swamped vessel, described the Trojans swarming over the wall. And thereafter, the sea ceases to participate in the battle, either as god, element, or image.

The resistance of the sea god to the Trojan effort to burn the ships is a little like the *Theomachia* in reverse: there, fire and water were represented by Hephaestus and Xanthus, here by Hector and Poseidon. There the triumph of fire foreshadowed the fall of Troy; here nothing so far-reaching is intended, but it is by no means a fantasy to see in Poseidon's help something more than the mere use of a god. The wave that crashes at his heels among the ships and tents, and the prevalence of sea imagery, reveals the tenor of the poet's thinking. To the polytheistic mind, the safety of ships is the work of a benevolent Poseidon, a favoring sea. If that favor is removed, shipwreck ensues. The difference between the personal god and his element is merely a matter of aspect, as usual in Homer. At other moments in the poem, other gods are active in helping the Greeks, but when it is a question of the defense of ships, even if the ships are drawn up on the shore, Poseidon is the figure who naturally comes to mind, and with him a whole train of images inevitable to the consciousness of a sea-faring people. The poet scarcely needed to plan this; he merely had to keep the scene before him. In the case of the *Theomachia* and River Fight, a greater degree of conscious planning must be recognized.

Interwoven with the other nature imagery, especially in the Great Battle, is the image of wind. It is joined often by clouds, dust, rain, snow, or sea, and in general blows harder and harder as Hector's attack nears its climax. Before this attack begins, the Achaeans withstand the Trojans like clouds on a windless day:

> Firmly they stood like clouds, such as the son of Cronos
> Stations in windless weather, over high-ranging mountains,
> Motionless, while the might of Boreas sleeps and all other
> Violent winds, that ever with shrilling gusts
> Blow and scatter apart the shadowy clouds: even so
> Steadfast the Danaoi withstood the Trojans, nor turned in flight. . . .

But when Hector and Paris rejoin the fight after their sojourn in Troy, they seem to their tired comrades like a favoring wind that Zeus gives to sailors. A little later the seated armies, with their multitudinous spears bristling along the plain, are compared to the prickling dark patches of the sea under a freshening zephyr. After the Interrupted Battle of Book VIII the wind is blowing in earnest: the consternation of the

Greeks is like a sea storm aroused by Boreas and Zephyr; they foresee the rout which the next day becomes a fact, when Hector, after the wounding of Agamemnon,

> Fell upon the battle like a hard-blowing squall,
> Which leaps down on the violet-faced sea and stirs it.[15]

He slaps nine chieftains in rapid succession, then assaults the host in general:

> . . . as when Zephyr drives the clouds
> Of the clear south wind, smiting with a deep whirlwind;
> Many a swollen wave rolls, and aloft the spume
> Scatters in the howl of the far-wandering wind.
> So thick at Hector's hands fell the heads of the host.

In the next phase of the struggle, the wind takes on more forms, from the brief formula comparing Hector to a blast to the more developed description of the two Lapith brothers, sons of Pirithous, who make a stand against the Trojans, like mountain oaks resisting wind and rain. Tree images are frequent for men who stand firm in battle, as tree-felling comparisons regularly characterize those who are cut down fighting. Here the generic tree faces a wind which has become in particular this special Trojan thrust. Later, when the Lycians support the Trojans, they too are like a black whirlwind. Two similes of stones falling like snowflakes illustrate the different emphasis obtainable through combination of traditional motifs:

> . . . And they [the stones] fell to the ground like snowflakes
> Such as hard-breathing wind, driving the shadowy clouds,
> Pours down swarming on the full nourishing earth;
> So from their hands the missiles streamed, from Achaeans and
> Trojans alike; and the helmets rang out dully
> Smitten with the round stones, and the great-bossed shields also. . . .

Here the wind is blowing hard, and the emphasis falls on the swift, violent flight of the stones, the smitten helmets and shields. In the other simile, there is no wind:

> . . . As flakes of the snow fall
> Thick on a winter day, when councillor Zeus is minded
> Sending down snow to manifest forth his shafts to men;

[15] XI.297f. This and the following image, which also involves the sea, may already prepare the way for the identification of the Greek cause with the sea and Poseidon.

Laying the winds asleep, he steadily pours, till it buries
Towering mountains' heads, and the lofty headlands,
Flowering fields and the rich ploughed lands of men;
Even on the whitening sea it falls, on harbors and beaches,
Curbing the billow that beats against it; all things else lie
Wrapped from above, when the storm of Zeus falls heavy;
So the stones flew thick, one side to the other.

Here the silence of the windless snowstorm burying mountain and meadow, though compared to a fight when a great din arose, underlines the grimness and steady determination on both sides. Descriptions of two battle lines holding firmly against each other, neither having the advantage, usually prompt in Homer images of some very peaceful nature, and the effect is always a rather startling one.[16]

But now the wind begins to undergo variations. It combines with still other images which subsequently supplant it. Already it has appeared with sea, snow, and clouds—inevitably, of course, since wind is detected by what it blows. But from the middle of Book XII on, it becomes less casual and more associated with the activity of Zeus, and the confusions arising from the plan to honor Achilles. A line of Aeschylus nicely sums up the way human action, and with it its characteristic imagery, in Homer is taken up by the gods:

God as well, whenever man himself takes action, joins with him.[17]

Homer's divinities depend on human promptings for their deeds; their knowledge is independent and transcendent, but their action as a rule is immanent in human action, or character. Hence all divine participation has something of the effect of apotheosis, and this is true no less of Homer's system of the continuing images than it is of action itself. As Zeus' plan to honor Achilles is a kind of apotheosis of Achilles, so too is the supernatural development of fire in the later books, though the image had begun as a mere comparison. Now the vain, misled gallantry of Hector, which has repeatedly called forth wind images, draws toward a climax. Hector again refuses to listen to the temperate advice of Pulydamas, who has perceived the eagle of Zeus, and read therein the fruitlessness of the Trojan effort. Hector trusts in the lightning flashes, and leads his men forward. At this point Zeus rouses a blast of wind,

Which bore dust toward the ships, and of the Achaeans
He beguiled the mind, and gave glory to Hector and the Trojans.

[16] Cf. the honest woman measuring wool, XII.432f.; the shipwright with a chalk-marker, XV.410; the woodcutter at noon, XI.84ff.

[17] Aeschylus, *Persae*, 742.

Lo, trusting in his signs and in their strength,
They tried to break the great wall of the Achaeans.[18]

Actually, Hector is more beguiled here than the Achaeans, who are simply suffering the consequences of the quarrel. The storm of dust emphasizes the confusion on both sides, the weakening of Achaean nerve, and the mistaken hopes of the Trojans. But the wind still blows against the Greeks, and now it is divinely sent. The wild wind of Hector's attack has become a daemonic moil, and the cloud thus engendered becomes a motif which characterizes, with sundry variations, the *mise en scène* of the next books. "Blinding storm" might be the best description for the variety of phenomena which occur. The two images of snowstorms and the assault of the Lycians "like a black whirlwind" have already been mentioned. At the beginning of Book XIII, wind and fire enter in brief comparisons, the two images of Trojan supremacy. But presently the dust storm returns, this time around Idomeneus, whose inspired counterattack repulses the onset of the enemy:

As whenever the squalls of the shrill winds hurry
On a day when the dust is plenty along the roads,
Winds all together lift up a vast cloud of the dust,
So to one place their battle came. . . .

Wind has not changed sides as clearly as the fire did, but it now centers around a Greek hero, rather than around Hector. It has also been joined by "mist"—a "mist of dust"—which will be the next major modulation of the idea of "blinding storm." The Trojan rally at the end of Book XIII is marked by a simile of wind, lightning, and sea storm;[19] during the direct assistance of Poseidon, the comparable simile of the four elements which describes the noise of the battle has already been noted.[20] Such broad combinations of elemental imagery seem to occur when the battle is still undecided and raging on both sides.

Meanwhile, the idea of cloud or mist becomes dominant.[21] Balancing the dust-cloud on earth, with its motif of "beguilement" is the golden cloud which enwraps Zeus, now the beguiled, and Hera the beguiler on Mount Ida.[22] It is now Patroclus, whose coming is like a clear sky after clouds:

[18] XII.254-257. Motif of *θέλξις* also at XV.317-322, and 594. Should Hector's wind be connected by paronomasia with *ἀνεμώλια βάξαι*?

[19] XIII.795ff. Note that for the third time, the stormy images of Trojan victory (fire, lightning, wind, sea-storm) are here answered by the single symbol of ultimate salvation for the Achaeans, the eagle.

[20] Wind also plays a part in the shipwreck images denoting the departure of Poseidon.

[21] Dust is compared to mist, "better for a thief than night," in III.10ff.

[22] XVI.66. Is this cloud to be thought of as a contrast with *φάος*, safety, victory? See Ajax' prayer.

As, when from the towering head of a great mountain
Zeus the lightning-gatherer moves the close-packed cloud,
Hilltops all are revealed, and lofty headlands,
Valleys too, and the boundless air of heaven breaks clear,
So having thrust from the ships the deadly fire, the Danaoi
Breathed a little. . . .[23]

and later, he is like a whirlwind blowing away clouds:

As when the cloud passes from Olympus melting into sky
Out of the divine ether, when Zeus stretches out the whirlwind.

The Trojan wind raised dust and enveloped the Achaeans; Patroclus is a clearing wind, for the time being. A little later, not in a comparison at all, but in the description of the Trojans fleeing and crowding the roads,

The horses strained, and on high the wind
Spread down from the clouds.

Again the imagery is so far in the front of the poet's mind, he does not even make it a comparison. The cloud of dust, the cloud of Trojans, the clouds to which the Lycians were compared are all equally metaphoric clouds. Homer was not sure whether Patroclus was simply like a wind, or whether a real wind came with him.

The imagery of mist and wind continues consistent. Little need be made of the use of the formula for death, "mist wrapped his eyes," but when the flight of the Trojans is compared to a rainstorm driven by a whirlwind, Homer seems to add what is in his heart; the clouds of threatening but misled Trojans, and the veiled deceits of the Plan of Zeus, are about to be blown away. Perhaps for this reason, the storm of this simile is one which Zeus sends because he is angry with mortals for their injustice. It is a purgatorial storm, driven by a *laelaps,* a whirlwind. It clears the air morally.

But the clouds are by no means gone altogether. As the death of Sarpedon approaches, Zeus sheds a bloody dew in grief, and a little later draws a "baleful night" around the battle over his body. Horror has taken a supernatural form consistent with the ever-darkening atmosphere which precedes the return of Achilles. This same darkness continues, or is renewed throughout Books XVI and XVII, and stands in acute contrast with the bright blaze of the *aristeia* of Achilles. When Patroclus is to fall, Apollo approaches him wrapped in thick fog,[24] and when he is

[23] XVI.297ff. Achilles' horses which Patroclus drives run like wind, XVI.149.

[24] XVI.790. Contrast Athena who comes to the aid of the Greeks wrapped in a rainbow, XVII.547.

dead, his body in its turn becomes the center of a battle in a blinding fog. Mist, clouds, and darkness are again in the air; Patroclus could clear it only for a little. Twice the none-too-frequent formula "in his glowering heart," occurs; Hector all by himself is called a "cloud of war," and when his brother-in-law is slain, a "black cloud of pain enfolds him." It is at this moment that Zeus for the last time signalizes a success by the lightning flash, as Hector leads one last drive at the Greeks; but simultaneously he wraps Mount Ida in clouds. Thus literal and figurative clouds are mingled into one broad image of the confusion and agony of war. As the terror of the fight over Patroclus increases, the Achaeans are compared to a frightened cloud of starlings. But this is merely an added touch, arising casually from the general cloud-imagery. The active climax comes a little before, when Ajax, peering into the mist, cannot find anyone to send to Achilles with the news of Patroclus' death; suddenly he prays to Zeus in words which Longinus took as a special example of sublimity:

> Father Zeus, save the sons of Achaeans from the mist,
> Make a clear sky, and let our eyes see;
> And slay us in the light, since that is your pleasure.

And then finally the mist clears, the sun shines, and the whole battlefield becomes visible. By the sudden return of the light, Antilochus is sent to Achilles with the terrible news.

Image-making is basically a subrational process, and creates its own characteristic tenor differently in different poetic minds. In Greek epic, the process is predetermined to a degree by the formulaic material, which is the germinal of its imagery; but the selective principle, operating at high speed in oral composition, is the individual singer's own responsibility and opportunity. Beneath that selective principle, and directing it, must lie half-conscious or unconscious patterns of association and symbolific consistency which constitute at least one root of the poetic urge itself. Therefore, where the resultant images form a design consistent with and illustrating the action of a long narrative, and sometimes even supplanting it, it is difficult to see how more than one mind could have worked upon such a structure. However many bards may have sung its constituent episodes before, the *Iliad* which we possess is structurally and imagistically a single reconception of all that is in it, a unity in traditional terms, both in intention and in execution.

Homer

by Albert B. Lord

The practice of oral narrative poetry makes a certain form necessary; the way in which oral epic songs are composed and transmitted leaves its unmistakable mark on the songs. That mark is apparent in the formulas and in the themes. It is visible in the structure of the songs themselves. In the living laboratory of Yugoslav epic the elements have emerged and they have been segregated. We have watched singers in the process of learning songs, we have seen them change songs, and we have seen them build long songs from short ones. A panorama of individual singers, some of them true artists, has passed before us, and the details of their art no longer mystify us. With this new understanding, which further research will eventually deepen, we must turn again to the songs that we have inherited from the past in precious manuscripts. Do they also show the marks of oral composition as we have come to know them?

* * *

What is called oral tradition is as intricate and meaningful an art form as its derivative, "literary tradition." In the extended sense of the word, oral tradition is as "literary" as literary tradition. It is not simply a less polished, more haphazard, or cruder second cousin twice removed, to literature. By the time the written techniques come onto the stage, the art forms have been long set and are already highly developed and ancient.

There is now no doubt that the composer of the Homeric poems was an oral poet. The proof is to be found in the poems themselves; and it is proper, logical, and necessary that this should be so. The necessity of oral form and style has been discussed; their characteristic marks have been noted. What marks of formulaic technique and of thematic structure does examination of the Homeric poems reveal?

Parry's analyses have, I believe, answered the first part of this question.[1] His discovery of the intricate schematization of formulas in the Homeric poems has never been challenged; though there have been critics who have not been willing to accept his interpretation of the meaning and implication of the phenomenon of formula structure. It is highly important to emphasize the fact that the formulas are not limited to the familiar epithets and oft-repeated lines, but that the formulas are all-pervasive. . . . Considering the limited amount of material available for analysis—only two poems, approximately 27,000 lines—the percentage of demonstrably formulaic lines or part lines is truly amazing. It is even more to be wondered at because of the subtlety and intricacy of the Greek hexameter. The task before the ancient Greek bards was not easy, and one should have the most profound respect for their accomplishment in creating a formulaic technique so perfect and rich in expressive possibilities. It is a complex and delicately balanced artistic instrument.

The Greek hexameter is probably the best known meter in all literature, and for this study of formulas it needs no further elucidation than has already been given it. But something must be said about formula length. . . . In the Yugoslav poems there are formulas of four, six, and ten syllables in length. The structure of the Yugoslav line, with its strict break after the fourth syllable, is comparatively simple. The Greek hexameter allows for greater variety, because the line may be broken at more than one place by a caesura. It is probably correct to say that this flexibility is closely allied to the musical pattern in which the poetry was sung or chanted, but since we know nothing of this music, any such statement is speculative. The caesura can occur in any one of the following points in the line: (a) after the first syllable of the third foot, (b) after the second syllable of the third foot if it is a dactyl, and (c) after the first syllable of the fourth foot. To these should be added (d) the bucolic diaeresis (after the fourth foot) and (e) the pause after a run-over word at the beginning of the line, which occurs most frequently after the first syllable of the second foot. One can, therefore, expect to find formulas of one foot and a half, two feet and a half, two feet and three quarters, three feet and a half, four feet, and six feet in length measured from the beginning of the line, and complementary lengths measured from the pause to the end of the line.

* * *

The formula technique in the Homeric poems is, indeed, so perfect, the system of formulas, as Parry showed, is so "thrifty," so lacking in identical alternative expressions, that one marvels that this perfection could be reached without the aid of writing.[2] We have already shown

[1] For Parry's analyses see "Studies in the Epic Technique of Oral Verse-Making. I: Homer and Homeric Style," *Harvard Studies in Classical Philology*, 41:118ff. (1930).

[2] See C. M. Bowra, *Heroic Poetry* (London, 1952), pp. 233ff.

that the thrift of the Yugoslav poetry is greater than was previously believed. To determine the thrift of a poetry, one should confine oneself to the work of a single singer, . . . and one should take into consideration all the poetic elements in a formula, including its acoustic pattern. The misunderstanding of Yugoslav thrift has come about by reading hastily through collections from many different singers from different regions and from different times. This method is not precise enough to yield reliable results. Moreover, even were one to limit oneself to a single singer and make use of only sung texts, one would still not arrive at a just picture of the situation for comparison with the Homeric poems. One must always make allowances and adjustments for sung texts and their deviations which arise from the pressure of rapid composition. Dictated texts of a carefully controlled type must be used for the comparison. When this was done, we saw that we had statistics comparable to those for the Homeric poems, which must of necessity be dictated and not sung texts. By making one's methods more exact, by considering the nature of the texts chosen in the Yugoslav experiment, and by understanding the type of text represented in the Homeric poems, one sees that the discrepancies between the statistics for the two traditions disappear.

The formulaic techniques, therefore, in the Greek and South Slavic poetries are generically identical and operate on the same principles. This is the surest proof now known of oral composition, and on the basis of it alone we should be justified in the conclusion that the Homeric poems are oral compositions. But there are other characteristics which can corroborate this conclusion.

In his study of enjambment in the Homeric poems Parry indicated that necessary enjambment is much less common in the epics of Homer than in Virgil or Apollonius.[3] The line is a metrical unit in itself. In Yugoslav

[3] "The Distinctive Character of Enjambement in Homeric Verse," *Transactions and Proceedings of the American Philological Association*, 60:200-220 (1929). For the term "necessary enjambment" see A. B. Lord, "Homer and Huso III: Enjambment in Greek and South-slavic Heroic Song," *TAPhA*, 79:113-124 (1948). I follow the definition of enjambment given by Parry, pp. 203-204: "Broadly there are three ways in which the sense at the end of one verse can stand to that at the beginning of another. First, the verse end can fall at the end of a sentence and the new verse begin a new sentence. In this case there is no enjambment. Second, the verse can end with a word group in such a way that the sentence, at the verse end, already gives a complete thought, although it goes on in the next verse, adding free ideas by new word groups. To this type of enjambment we may apply Denis' term *unperiodic*. Third, the verse end can fall at the end of a word group where there is not yet a whole thought, or it can fall in the middle of a word group; in both of these cases enjambment is *necessary*. . . . To know where there is no enjambment we must gauge the sentence. The varying punctuation of our texts, usually troublesome, will not do. I define the sentence as any independent clause or group of clauses introduced by a coordinate conjunction or by asyndeton; and by way of showing that this definition is fitting I would point out that the rhetoricians paid little heed to the sentence as we understand it: for them the

song necessary enjambment is practically nonexistent. The length of the hexameter is one of the important causes of the discrepancy between the two poetries. It is long enough to allow for the expression of a complete idea within its limits, and on occasion it is too long. Then a new idea is started before the end of the line. But since there is not enough space before the end to complete the idea it must be continued in the next line. This accounts for systems of formulas that have been evolved to fill the space from the bucolic diaeresis to the end of the line, with complementary systems to take care of the run-over words in the following line.

Parry pointed out the situation in the Homeric poems, and I have already compared this with statistics from the Yugoslav poetry in a separate article.[4] Here, too, it was necessary, as always, to be aware of the differences of language, length of line, and possible influence of a different type of musical accompaniment in order to understand the discrepancy between the Greek and Yugoslav poetries in the higher instance and end-stop lines in the latter than in the former. Again, by paying particular attention to matters of method, one was able to arrive at an understanding of this basic stylistic feature. The test of enjambment analysis is, as a matter of fact, an easily applied rule of thumb that can be used on first approaching a new text to determine the possibility of oral composition. It should be done, however, with a knowledge of the musical background, if such information is available, and with an awareness of differences that may be brought about by length of line and peculiarities of the languages involved.

Another corroborating test for oral composition is less easily applied—though just as decisive—because it requires a greater amount of material for analysis than is usually available from the poetries of the past. This is the investigation of thematic structure.[5]

The Homeric poems have probably been analyzed more often and more variously than any other poems in world literature. It would be a brave man who would undertake another analysis of them, unless he were convinced that there are really new and significant grounds for so doing, and that the analysis would bring decisive results.

The first step in thematic analysis must be to prove the existence of themes in the poem under consideration. In other words we must find, either in the poem under scrutiny or in other poems by the same singer

---

unit of style was the clause, and the only group of clauses of which Aristotle speaks is the period." The statement of Jakobson, following perhaps a more widely known definition of enjambment, that there is no enjambment in Serbocroatian epic, is correct, although rare exceptions can be found.

[4] "Homer and Huso III: Enjambement in Greek and Southslavic Heroic Song," *TAPhA*, 79:113-124 (1948).

[5] See my "Composition by Theme in Homer and Southslavic Epos," *TAPhA*, 82:71-80 (1951).

or otherwise belonging to the same tradition, the same situations repeated at least once. The method is the same used for formula analysis; but the units are larger and exact word-for-word correspondence is not necessary. In fact, exact word-for-word correspondence, as we have seen, is not to be expected.

One of the more readily isolated themes in the Homeric poems, indeed in all epic literature, is that of the assembly. It is easily isolated because it has an obvious beginning and an obvious end. Let us observe this theme in Books I and II of the *Iliad.* The first assembly in the *Iliad* is an informal and unofficial one, and it is brief. Chryses comes to the Achaean fleet, and makes his petition to the people in general and to the Atridae in particular. The people applaud, but Agamemnon sends the priest away with harsh words. This form of the theme of the assembly is a hybrid. It is halfway between the general theme of interchange of words between two characters and the general theme of the formal assembly, because it takes place in the presence of the people, yet it lacks the calling and dismissing of an assembly.

The next assembly in the poem is a full-dress affair, called by Achilles at the instigation of Hera, complete with the risings and sittings of the speakers and with the dismissal of the assembly. This assembly can serve as a model for the full use of the theme.

The third assembly in Book I, and the final scene in the book, is that of the gods, where Hera and Zeus bandy words and Hephaestus takes his mother's part. Here again is a special form of the general theme, because this group of gods is usually always together except for individuals away on a mission. It needs to be called into formal council only when there is special and important business. It is like a family scene, or like the aghas of the Border in the Yugoslav Moslem songs, who are always gathered together in the green bower in Udbina. There is no need usually to call an assembly, hence no need to dismiss one. It is not unlike the first assembly described above, except that in that case the conversation was started by a newly arrived stranger, and in this instance it is confined to the family group.

The relationship between these three examples of the assembly theme in Book I could be expressed as A (the assembly called by Achilles), B_1 (the assembly of the gods), and B_2 (the quarrel between Chryses and Agamemnon).

Book II furnishes a number of instructive cases of this theme. First comes the council of elders called by Agamemnon as a result of the deceptive dream. It is a formal affair and belongs in the A category. If we designate the full assembly of the people as A_1, we may call the council of elders A_2, although structurally there is no difference between them. In the example under consideration in Book II, however, the council of elders is introduced within the framework of the full assembly. Heralds are sent out to summon an assembly of the people, and while the men are gathering together a council of elders is held. A_2 is here included in A_1. This popular assembly is not formally dismissed for some time; it is broken up by the men themselves, who have to be brought back by the efforts of Odysseus. We might term this interrupted and reconvened assembly of the people A_{1a}.

There are two more examples of our theme in Book II. The first may be considered as a special variety of A_2, the council of elders. Agamemnon calls together the elders and chief men; there is a sacrifice and dinner (both of which are themselves themes, of course), followed by a brief speech of instruction and command by Nestor. We might call this A_{2a}. Although I am including this theme with the assembly themes, it might perhaps more properly belong with feasting and sacrifice themes. This ambiguity emphasizes the overlapping of themes, or, more precisely, the way in which minor themes are useful in more than one major theme. The summoning of the elders is a minor theme in point, as is also the speech of Nestor. This can be seen again in the lines that immediately follow the speech and tell of the sounding of the call to battle and the assembling of the army. The lesser theme of summoning is itself useful in numerous situations: in this case in the larger theme of summoning an army, which is the prelude to the theme of the catalogue. The architectonics of thematic structure are wondrous to observe.

The final assembly in Book II is one already in progress on the Trojan side. It is a popular assembly, and hence a form of A_1. It has been addressed by Iris and will be dismissed by Hector. We see only the end of the assembly.

Thus, in the first two books of the *Iliad* we find some seven examples of the theme of the assembly. The second example in Book I provides a good model. The rest seem to be variations in different tonalities on this theme. We have already become aware in this analysis of the interweaving and overlapping of major themes; we have begun to glimpse the complexity of thematic structure in the *Iliad*.

We have now applied the three sets of tests that we recognize as valid in determining whether any given poem is oral or not. The Homeric poems have met each of these tests. We now realize fully that Homer is an oral poet. Some of the implications of that fact have already been apparent from our thematic analysis. But we cannot leave it at that.

First, this knowledge places Homer inside an oral tradition of epic song. He is not an outsider approaching the tradition with only a superficial grasp of it, using a bit here and a bit there, or trying to present a "flavor" of the traditional, yet ever thinking in terms essentially different from it. He is not a split personality with half of his understanding and technique in the tradition and the other half in a parnassus of literate methods. No, he is not even "immersed" in the tradition. He *is* the tradition; he is one of the integral parts of that complex; for us, as undoubtedly for his own audiences, he is the most gifted and fascinating part of that tradition. His vividness and immediacy arise from the fact that he is a practicing oral poet. Those who would make of Homer a "literary" poet, do not understand his "literariness"; he has none of the artificiality of those who use traditional themes or traditional devices for nontraditional purposes. From ancient times until the present we have been misled about the true nature of Homer's art and greatness. And the reason has been that we have tried to read him in our own terms, which we have labelled "universal terms of art."

We have exercised our imaginations and ingenuity in finding a kind of unity, individuality, and originality in the Homeric poems that are irrelevant. Had Homer been interested in Aristotelian ideas of unity, he would not have been Homer, nor would he have had composed the *Iliad* or *Odyssey*. An oral poet spins out a tale; he likes to ornament, if he has the ability to do so, as Homer, of course, did. It is on the story itself, and even more on the grand scale of ornamentation, that we must concentrate, not on any alien concept of close-knit unity. The story is there and Homer tells it to the end. He tells it fully and with a leisurely tempo, ever willing to linger and to tell another story that comes to his mind. And if the stories are apt, it is not because of a preconceived idea of structural unity which the singer is self-consciously and laboriously working out, but because at the moment when they occur to the poet in the telling of his tale he is so filled with his subject that the natural processes of association have brought to his mind a relevant tale. If the incidental tale or ornament be, by any chance, irrelevant to the main story or to the poem as a whole, this is no great matter; for the ornament has a value of its own, and this value is understood and appreciated by the poet's audience.

Each theme, small or large—one might even say, each formula—has around it an aura of meaning which has been put there by all the contexts in which it has occurred in the past. It is the meaning that has been given it by the tradition in its creativeness. To any given poet at any given time, this meaning involves all the occasions on which he has used the theme, especially those contexts in which he uses it most frequently; it involves also all the occasions on which he has heard it used by others, particularly by those singers whom he first heard in his youth, or by great singers later by whom he was impressed. To the audience the meaning of the theme involves its own experience of it as well. The communication of this supra-meaning is possible because of the community of experience of poet and audience. At our distance of time and space we can approach an understanding of the supra-meaning only by steeping ourselves in as much material in traditional poetry or in a given tradition as is available.

But we are getting ahead of our story. Having determined that the method of composition of the Homeric poems is that of oral poetry, we must next decide what degree of oral composition they represent. What degrees can we distinguish? First, there is the *actual performance.*

Let us make one thing clear at this point. An interested audience, with time and desire to listen for a long period and from one day to another, coupled with a singer of talent in a rich tradition might produce songs as long as the Homeric poems. But our texts as we have shown in a previous chapter could not have been written down during performance. Actual performance is too rapid for a scribe. One might possibly suggest that the scribe might write as much as he could at one performance, correct it at the next, and so on until he had taken down the text of the whole from several singings. I mention this because Parry had an assistant in the field at the beginning who thought that he could do this, but the variations from one singing to another were so great that he very soon gave up trying to note them down. It should be clear by now that such a suggestion makes sense only when there is a fixed text being repeated. In oral epic performance this is not the case. Without recording apparatus, it is impossible to obtain an exact text of actual performance, and hence we cannot say that our texts of the Homeric songs represent oral poetry in the first degree.

The second degree is close to the first in matter of composition. This degree is the dictated text. This is the nearest one can get to an actual performance without the use of a recording machine, but there are important differences. In the hands of a good singer and competent scribe this method produces a longer and technically better text than actual performance, for reasons that we have already analyzed. It seems to me that this is where we should most logically place the Homeric poems. They are *oral dictated texts.* Within this class of texts, we can differentiate between those skillfully and those ineptly done. The first will have regular lines and fullness of telling. The second will have many irregularities in lines and the general structure will be apocopated. Even allowing for later editing, we must see in the Homeric texts models of the dictating and scribal technique.

The third degree of oral composition is when the oral poet is literate and himself writes down a poem. At best the result may be the same as in the second degree described above, except that the pen is in the hand of the singer, and there is no scribe involved. This may be attractive to those who must have a literate Homer writing. Theoretically, it makes little difference, if any, in the results at this stage. Yet it is not a normal situation, and the experience which we have of such cases would indicate that texts thus produced (which we have termed *oral autograph texts*) are inferior in all respects to oral dictated texts. There seems to be little sense in grasping at this solution for purely sentimental reasons. In putting a pen into Homer's hand, one runs the danger of making a bad poet of him. The singer not only has a perfectly satisfactory method of composition already in the highly developed oral technique of composition, but is actually hampered and restricted by writing. The method he knows came into being for the very purpose of rapid composition before a live audience, as we have said. Writing is a slow process even at best, and the oral poet would find it annoying, indeed, not worth the bother.[6] I cannot accept Homer as semiliterate, whatever that may mean. His skill demands that he be either the best of oral poets or the best of literary poets, not a nondescript hybrid. Anyone actually acquainted with "semiliterate" texts would, I believe, strongly resist any pressure to place Homer in such a category.

Those who wish may seek to find comfort and corroboration in the discovery of pre-Homeric literacy as shown by Linear B. They will be prone to "discount" and ignore the wise caution of Professor Sterling Dow,[7] who has pointed out the limited use of Linear B and the disappearance of the script on the mainland perhaps around 1200 B.C. He writes (p. 128):

> Four or five hundred years the Greeks had lived in Greece before they learned to write. In other skills and arts, including those of power, they had advanced tremendously. In literacy—the very nerve of Classical civilization—the Mykenaian Greeks, after they once got it, made no advance at all. . . . Literacy arrived tightly associated with practical day-by-day bread and butter purposes. Created for these purposes, it was all too adequate for them. . . . The origin was in government and commerce, not in *belles lettres.* When, with the coming of the Dorians and the Dark Ages, the purposes which writing served—commerce and elaborate government—were choked off, writing ended; whereas literature—oral, that is—went on. . . .
>
> Europe's first taste of literacy was comparatively brief, meager, and unpromising. However severe the cataclysm that caused it, the loss of that literacy was not itself an unqualified disaster. The oral tradition which gave us the Homeric poems may well have been saved at an early stage (i.e. before the twelfth century) by the restricted nature of Mainland literacy, which doubtless excluded it from the field of heroic poetry; and heroic poetry remained oral, i.e., unthreatened, during its great period of growth, because in that period literacy, instead of expanding, perished.

[6] There is an excellent treatment of the slowness of reading and writing in medieval times in *From Script to Print* (1945), by H. J. Chaytor, Master of St. Catherine's College, Cambridge. He writes:

> The medieval reader, with few exceptions, did not read as we do; he was in the stage of our muttering childhood learner; each word was for him a separate entity and at times a problem, which he whispered to himself when he had found the solution [p. 10]. . . . The history of the progress from script to print is a history of the gradual substitution of visual for auditory methods of communicating and receiving ideas [p. 4].

The task, yes, the very physical task, of writing down the *Iliad* and the *Odyssey* is a tremendous one.

[7] "Minoan Writing," *American Journal of Archaeology,* 58:77-129 (1954).

And in the same article (p. 108) Professor Dow has indicated our tendency to naïveté concerning literacy:

> Literacy is usually spoken of, for instance, as a simple indivisible essence (so that we say "the Mykenaians were literate"), whereas in reality literacy is a complex skill applicable to a wide variety of purposes, in fact, to practically all the purposes of human communication. It would obviously be hazardous to assume that as soon as a person—child, barbarian, or Minoan—learns to write, he will use writing for the full range of purposes familiar to us.

But even were we to assume that writing flourished in the service of literature in Homer's day, it does not follow that we must also assume that Homer wrote. We have already seen that oral literature can and does exist side by side with written literature. The discovery of an entire literature, including written epics, in Linear B would not in any way alter the fact that the Homeric poems are oral.

And so we see Homer as the men of his own time saw him, a poet singer among poet singers. That there was a Greek tradition of oral epic we have abundant reason to believe. The *Odyssey* gives us a picture of the practice, and what we know of the Cyclic epics gives us some idea of what kind of stories were told in this tradition. Homer was one of many singers in his own day; he was preceded by generations of singers like him; and certainly, scanty though our evidence may be here, the tradition of oral epic in Greece scarcely stopped with Homer. It would be the height of naïveté to conceive of Homer as the inventor of epic poetry in Greece or in our Western culture. The tradition in which he belonged was a rich one. He heard many good singers, and he himself had great talent, so that he was well known wherever songs were sung.

The singer who performed the *Iliad* and the *Odyssey* was obviously no novice in the art. Both poems are too well done, show too great a mastery of technique (and by this I mean oral technique) to be by a young man in the stages of learning. To attain such mastery, Homer must have been a singer with a large repertory of songs. He must also have performed his songs, and especially the tale of Achilles and that of Odysseus, many times. He was not a two-song man; nor was he one who sang but once a year at a festival. He sang these two songs often. It is normal to assume that he learned them from other singers. The songs were current in the tradition; Homer did not make them up. We do not have to depend on the analogy with Yugoslav epic or with any single Yugoslav singer to come to this conclusion. The songs themselves betray the fact that they have been long in the tradition. If Separatist scholarship has taught us nothing more, if it has not proved the kind of multiple authorship which it had ever in its mind, it has brought to our attention the mingling of themes, which is an indication of a long period of existence in the traditional repertory. It should be understood, however, that we are speaking about the songs, the tales of Achilles and of Odysseus, and not about the *Iliad* and the *Odyssey,* which are fixed texts (at a given period) by a given singer whom we call Homer. We shall consider that moment and those texts shortly, but it is necessary first to see what can be said about the two songs before they became the *Iliad* and the *Odyssey*.

We shall never be able to determine who first sang these songs, nor when they were first sung, nor where, nor what form they had. We can only be sure that it was a long time before Homer's day; for, as I have said, the songs themselves show that they have had a long history. We can with some certainty assume that their original form, their first singing, was crude as compared with our texts and only in basic story similar.[8] And it is only fair to recognize that the generic tales and many of the themes were already formed and in Greek tradition long before they were applied to Achilles and to Odysseus. Our *Iliad* and *Odyssey* were many centuries in the making.

The poet who first sang these songs changed them in the second singing in the manner which we have already demonstrated in the Yugoslav tradition, and this change continued in each successive singing. He never thought of his song as being at any time fixed either as to content or as to wording. He was the author of each singing. And those singers who learned from him the song of Achilles or that of Odysseus continued the changes of oral tradition in their performances; and each of them was author of each of his own singings. The songs were ever in flux and were crystallized by each singer only when he sat before an audience and told them the tale. It was an old tale that he had heard from others but that telling was his own. He did not claim it, yet all could see that it was his; for he was there before them.

This is the way of oral tradition. To call it multiple authorship is to belittle the role not only of Homer but of all the singers in an oral tradition. It is based upon a false premise, namely, that at one time someone created a fixed original for each song in the tradition and that thereafter whatever happened to the tales was a change of something that had been formed from a marble monolith. As long as scholars felt that they were dealing with firm entities, they could speak of multiple authorship and of interpolation. A part of one monolith could be chiseled away and set upon another. But it should be clear from our investigation of oral tradition in the field in Yugoslavia that one is not dealing with monoliths but with a pliable protean substance. When the same or similar ideas are properly useful in many tales, they belong to none, or perhaps even better, they belong to all of them. Interpolation implies, I believe, that

[8] As an example of a song that has not been perfected by much singing and is close in frequency of performance, if not in time, to its first singing, see Salih Ugljanin's song of the Greek War (Parry and Lord, *Serbocroatian Heroic Songs*, I and II, No. 10).

an element belonging to only one song is moved consciously into another. In the flux of oral tradition where a theme is fitting in many tales, the term interpolation is misapplied. And the same may be said for multiple authorship. Once Homer's texts of a particular performance of our two songs were set in the *Iliad* and in the *Odyssey,* interpolations were possible; for here for the first time probably in Greek epic tradition were two definite monoliths. But that belongs to the story of what happened to the manuscripts of the Homeric poems after Homer had sired them.

He must have sung them many times before and many times after those momentous occasions that gave us the *Iliad* and the *Odyssey*. And then came one of the greatest events in the cultural history of the West, the writing down of the *Iliad* and the *Odyssey* of Homer. We know the results of that moment of history, but other than the poems themselves we know nothing about the actual moment. We are in the dark about why the poems were written down. We may be fairly certain, however, that it was not Homer's idea. He would have no need for a written text; he would not know what to do with it. Surely, as master of the oral technique, he needed no mnemonic device. That he might wish to see his songs preserved may seem a valid reason for us, but no oral poet thinks even for a moment that the songs he sings and which others have learned from him will be lost. Nor has he a concept of a single version which is so good that it must be written down to be kept. In suggesting such reasons we are putting into the mind of an oral poet something logical for us but foreign to him. I feel sure that the impetus to write down the *Iliad* and the *Odyssey* did not come from Homer himself but from some outside source.

One reads such statements as "Homer composed the *Iliad* and the *Odyssey* for performance at a festival." [9] Homer did not need a written text. He indeed may have and probably did sing the tales of Achilles and of Odysseus at festivals. At a much later period, once the poems were written down, there were singers who memorized the written text and performed them at festivals. But these were not oral poets. A festival might give an oral poet an opportunity to sing a song over several days and thus to sing a long song. Homer might have sung these songs long at such a festival. But I am afraid that even here we are straining to explain the length of the *Iliad* and the *Odyssey*. In some ways it seems to me that a festival would be the least likely circumstance to afford opportunity for a long song. There is too much going on at a festival. The audience is constantly distracted and is constantly moving about. A long song seriously delivered to an appreciative audience can be produced only in peace and quiet.

Our texts of Homer can have come only from an ideal condition of dictating, inasmuch as there were no recording apparatuses in ancient

[9] See especially H. T. Wade-Gery, *The Poet of the Iliad* (Cambridge, 1952).

Greece! Since there is only one way in which the *Iliad* and the *Odyssey* could have been taken down from our oral epic singer, Homer, the problem of the festival lasting several days to allow time for Homer to sing his songs becomes irrelevant. I have already suggested that such festivals or circumstances which would allow for the singing of moderately long songs are important only for the development of a rich tradition; hence they would have only an indirect influence on the actual texts of the poems we have. It is more likely that epics were sung in brief or in moderately long versions on such occasions. What we can be sure of is that in the course of Greek oral tradition there must have been opportunity for the singing of epics of several thousand lines. A tradition does not become as rich in ornamental themes as the ancient Greek tradition if singers have opportunity to perform songs of only a few hundred lines. Yet the length of the *Iliad* and of the *Odyssey* must have been exceptional.

The length of the songs in the Epic Cycle may provide a rough measurement of the length of the ordinary songs in the tradition in ancient Greece. They seem to belong to a collection that someone made from various singers, or possibly from a compilation of several manuscript collections of various dates.[10] We are told that the *Oidipodeia* had 6,600 verses, the *Thebaid* (ascribed to Homer), 7,000 verses, and the *Epigonoi* (also ascribed to him), 7,000 verses. Other indications of length are in terms of books. If we compare them with the Homeric poems, then the *Cypria,* with its eleven books, was a little less than half the length of those poems; and so proportionately with the five books of the *Aithiopis* and the *Nostoi,* the four books of the *Ilias Mikra,* and the two books of the *Sack of Ilium* and of the *Telegonia.* In other words the longest of the poems in the Epic Cycle were not more than half as long as the *Iliad* and *Odyssey.* To Homer belongs the distinction of having composed the longest and best of all oral narrative songs. Their unusual length predicates exceptional circumstances of performance. If I be not mistaken, dictation to a scribe provides this opportunity. Would not the fact that Homer was the man who dictated the "long songs" account for the reputation which both he and the songs came to enjoy? Would not the city-states have vied with one another for the credit of having nurtured this unusual man?

Yet we still have no answer to the question of why someone chose to ask Homer to dictate 27,000 Greek hexameters to him. The most recent conjecture is found in Cedric Whitman's *Homer and the Heroic Tradition.*[11] After recognizing the fact that "Homer's mode of composition seems to be, from beginning to end, strictly that of the oral poet" (p. 79), Whitman continues by excluding the possibility that Homer himself

[10] *Hesiod, the Homeric Hymns, and Homerica,* edited by H. G. Evelyn-White, Loeb Classical Library (Cambridge and London, 1943), pp. 480ff.

[11] *Homer and the Heroic Tradition* (Cambridge, Mass., 1958), pp. 79ff.

wrote down his songs. Whitman then points to an example noted by J. Notopoulos[12] previously, of a Greek revolutionary who from being an oral singer became a writer of his own memoirs, as an indication of

> a dissatisfaction with the improvised accounts in verse which he had formerly sung to his companions. In an age when the art of writing has gone far toward thrusting back the boundaries of illiteracy, it can hardly fail to strike a creative artist sooner or later that the medium of pen and paper has something new to offer. One might even say that, with writing, a new idea of permanence is born; oral communication is shown for what it is—inaccurate and shifting. Writing has a godlike stability, and to anyone with an eye for the future, its significance is scarcely to be mistaken. . . . If one seeks the motivation for the transference of oral verse to written form it must lie in the disseminated knowledge of writing itself, in its disintegration of the belief that unwritten songs never change, and in the promise of real fixity. One ought, therefore, to associate the great epic, in contrast to the short epic song, not only with festal audiences, but also with writing, not because writing is necessary for its creation, but because the monumental purpose of the large epic is profoundly served by anything which bestows fixity of form. In the century which saw the rise of the city-state, the festivals, and the first flowering of the great colonial movement, the Greek mind cannot have failed to recognize that written characters have a peculiar permanence, whatever had been commonly believed about the immutability of oral tradition.

I have quoted Whitman at some length for convenience in analyzing his thinking on this subject.

First, the example of the Greek revolutionary is not really apt for Homer, unless we assume much more writing in Greece in Homer's time, and that of a literary sort, than there is evidence of, at the moment at least. Revolutionary Greece had a rich tradition of written literature, and Makriyannis' progress from illiteracy to literacy was a progress from a more backward, peasant social group to a more advanced, and more privileged social stratum. It is to be doubted that his dissatisfaction with the older oral songs (which was probably very real) sprang at all from any recognition of the possibilities of a fixed text as against the lack of them in an oral text. It is far more likely that he was dissatisfied with them because they belonged to the peasant society and he had now graduated into the company of the elite. Are we to assume that there was such a literate and elite group of littérateurs in Homer's day? If so, where is the evidence for it? Makriyannis moved into a milieu with a long-established tradition not only of writing (we might even say from Homer's day), but of fine writing in the form of literature. "The boundaries of illiteracy" were of a different kind in modern Greece from what

[12] J. A. Notopoulos, "The Warrior as an Oral Poet: A Case History," *Classical Weekly*, 46:17-19 (1952).

they were in ancient, more specifically, late eighth century B.C. Greece, and the gulf between the oral singer and "the creative artist" was both broad and deep in Makriyannis' time. In Homer's day, on the contrary, the oral singer was a creative artist; in fact there was no distinction—I believe that the idea of the "creative artist," the "inspired poet," and so forth, is derived from the mantic and sacred function of the singer. In assessing the situation in Homer's day in Greece, we must reckon with the fact that we have no other literary texts from that time, no written literary tradition. Yet suddenly 27,000 Greek hexameters appear! Are we supposed to believe that Homer, or someone else, saw the lists of chattels and, realizing what this meant for epic, sat down to record the *Iliad* and *Odyssey*? Makriyannis had much more than jar labels to read when he learned his ABC's. A slow progress with small written beginnings in the field of literature, recording short pieces, over a long period of time is believable, and Whitman allows for some possibility of this later when he says, "For all we know, some of his [Homer's] predecessors may have committed their work to paper somehow." Without interference from outside of Greece, this is the only way one could have arrived at the point of writing down so many lines of verse.

The trouble with Whitman's "creative artist" is that, in spite of the fact that he is said to compose entirely as an oral poet, he is not in the tradition; he is not an oral *traditional* poet. *And oral poets who are not traditional do not exist.* With this in mind, if one should substitute "the best oral traditional singer" for "creative artist" in Whitman's statement, it would read, "it can hardly fail to strike the best oral traditional singer sooner or later that the medium of pen and paper has something new to offer." I cannot help, when the statement reads this way, but ask *why* the idea of "something new" is so inevitable for the oral poet, even the greatest and best of them. Why should permanence and fixity be so attractive to an oral poet? And how does he come to recognize and to distrust oral communication as "inaccurate and shifting?" Remember that the man with whom we are dealing is an oral poet in a society with writing, but not extensive writing in literature, if any at all. Whitman has tacitly and naturally assumed that the oral poet has the same sense of propriety for the "form" of his song, even for "his song" that the written poet has. He hears the "creative artist" saying, "This is *my* song, *my* masterpiece, every word of it"; but the oral poet does not say this because he is in the tradition. What he says is, "I learned this song from someone else, and I sing it as he sang it." Does this man with his sense of the tradition see permanency so readily, if at all, for the tradition's song? It is not in the psychology of the oral poet to concern himself with stability of form, since stability of meaning and story already exist for him. Oral communication is not "inaccurate and shifting" until you have the idea that a given *form, one* given performance, is worth fixing. And this idea may come readily to the "creative artist" who is self-consciously creating something which he is accustomed to think of as his very own, but it is a large order for the oral poet who is intent upon preserving a meaningful traditional song. We must not suddenly endow the oral poet with the mentality of the developed literary artist in a written tradition, with his sense of ownership.

Perhaps we shall never have a certain solution to the riddle of the writing down of the Homeric poems, but we can hypothesize on what is most likely. We have already seen that the idea would not have come from Homer, and it is logical that the group to which he belonged and which regularly listened to him would not have had any reason (other than what we might project backward from our own thinking) for wanting these two songs, or any songs, written down. We should do well, therefore, to look about in the world of ancient Greece, before, let us say, 700 B.C., if perchance we might discover people who were recording or had already recorded in writing their literature, people with whom the Greeks may well have come into contact.

In the ninth century in Palestine the oldest of the documents of the Old Testament seems to have been written, namely, the J Document, and in the following century the E Document came into being.[13] These writings or records told of the creation of the world and of the history of the founders of the Jewish people or of man in general. They contained the epics and myths of these people. In the eighth century Sargon II (722-705) established the library at Nineveh and under him the Assyrian Empire was at its greatest extent. His library contained tablets inscribed with epic, mythic, magic, and historical material in several languages, including Sumerian, and dating from as early as 2000 B.C. Here were to be found the Epic of Creation and the Epic of Gilgamesh, among other texts.[14] Two bodies of recorded lore, one already ancient in ancient times, the other new and exciting in its serious intensity, were thus available to any Greeks who might turn in their direction. And it seems that it would be normal for them to look to the East during these centuries; for it was in the East that the cultural center was then located.

Hence, I should like to suggest that the idea of recording the Homeric poems, and the Cyclic epics, and the works of Hesiod, came from observation of or from hearing about similar activity going on further to the East. The list of works on Sumerian tablets given by Kramer in his *Sumerian Mythology*[15] reminds one of the kind of literature recorded at the earliest period in both Palestine and Greece: "epics and myths, hymns and lamentations, proverbs and 'wisdom' compositions." And the wisdom compositions consist of "a large number of brief, pithy, and pointed proverbs

[13] See Robert H. Pfeiffer, *Introduction to the Old Testament* (New York, 1941; revised edition, 1948), pp. 282ff.

[14] For these texts see James B. Pritchard, ed., *Ancient Near Eastern Texts Relating to the Old Testament* (Princeton, 1950).

[15] S. N. Kramer, *Sumerian Mythology* (Philadelphia, 1944), pp. 13ff.

and aphorisms; of various fables, such as 'The Bird and the Fish,' 'The Tree and the Reed,' 'The Pickax and the Plow,' 'Silver and Bronze'; and finally of a group of didactic compositions, long and short, several of which are devoted to a description of the process of learning the scribal art and of the advantages which flow from it." The Greeks and the Hebrews were reliving in their own terms the cultural experiences of older civilizations. The scribe who wrote down the Homeric poems was doing for the Greeks what the scribes of Sumer had done for their people many centuries before.

The Shield of Achilles

by W. H. Auden

She looked over his shoulder
  For vines and olive trees,
Marble well-governed cities,
  And ships upon untamed seas,
But there on the shining metal
  His hands had put instead
An artificial wilderness
  And a sky like lead.

A plain without a feature, bare and brown,
  No blade of grass, no sign of neighborhood,
Nothing to eat and nowhere to sit down,
  Yet, congregated on its blankness, stood
  An unintelligible multitude.
A million eyes, a million boots in line,
Without expression, waiting for a sign.

Out of the air a voice without a face
  Proved by statistics that some cause was just
In tones as dry and level as the place:
  No one was cheered and nothing was discussed;
  Column by column in a cloud of dust
They marched away enduring a belief
Whose logic brought them, somewhere else, to grief.

She looked over his shoulder
  For ritual pieties,
White flower-garlanded heifers,
  Libation and sacrifice,
But there on the shining metal
  Where the altar should have been,
She saw by his flickering forge-light
  Quite another scene.

Barbed wire enclosed an arbitrary spot
Where bored officials lounged (one cracked a joke)
And sentries sweated, for the day was hot:
A crowd of ordinary decent folk
Watched from without and neither moved nor spoke
As three pale figures were led forth and bound
To three posts driven upright in the ground.

The mass and majesty of this world, all
That carries weight and always weighs the same,
Lay in the hands of others; they were small
And could not hope for help and no help came:
What their foes liked to do was done, their shame
Was all the worst could wish; they lost their pride
And died as men before their bodies died.

She looked over his shoulder
For athletes at their games,
Men and women in a dance
Moving their sweet limbs
Quick, quick, to music,
But there on the shining shield
His hands had set no dancing-floor
But a weed-choked field.

A ragged urchin, aimless and alone,
Loitered about that vacancy; a bird
Flew up to safety from his well-aimed stone:
That girls are raped, that two boys knife a third,
Were axioms to him, who'd never heard
Of any world where promises were kept
Or one could weep because another wept.

The thin-lipped armorer,
Hephaestos, hobbled away;
Thetis of the shining breasts
Cried out in dismay
At what the god had wrought
To please her son, the strong
Iron-hearted man-slaying Achilles
Who would not live long.

Odysseus Did Not Die in Ithaca

by Ernst Bloch

Reach further, Storm, and further yet,
Uprear upon your mighty crest
The highest star, the humblest gnat,
And bear us home to final rest!

LENAU, *Faust*

It is more than right that the hungry man should long for food. He who is frozen strives toward the hearth, the man gone astray seeks his dwelling, the traveller rejoices at the thought of wife and child. But when the much driven-about head of the family is called Odysseus or some such name, the matter of a homeward journey is no longer quite so evident, nor is it clear that one's own bed will close the voyage. Wind-tossed Odysseus was not only Odysseus the much-suffering man, he was also errant Odysseus, he had seen the cities and realms of many men, and Calypso and Nausicaa to boot.

Naïve, slovenly interpretations of Odysseus' saga would have it that it exemplifies how an honorable *paterfamilias* will labor incessantly and against all perils to reach home and family. This is the Odysseus whom Daumier caricatured, wearing a nightcap, sitting beside his sharp-nosed spouse, helmet and sword displayed like trophies on the wall—*et habet bonam pacem, qui sedet post fornacem*. No doubt, the homeward journey is a significant concept and condition; but this means that its dangers and seductions, like those of passive rest, are all the greater. If Ithaca was not a symbol, it would be a dilemma; and it is across this dilemma that Homer drew a curtain once the rites of hearth and marriage bed had been fulfilled.

But legend did not fall silent; it spun around a later, wild, unknown Odysseus the garb of a Flying Dutchman. In such guise it is not even certain that he returns to Ithaca. He journeys onward into the unfathomed places and makes of his past destiny the very bent and fabric of his own being. This startling turn can be seen in the *Divine Comedy* (*Inferno* XXVI, 79-142). Here the involuntary sufferer attains an altogether wilfull audacity; indeed, he becomes a Faustus of the seas. Through the flames that envelop him, Virgil inquires of Odysseus how his terrestrial life ended. Odysseus answers that after leaving Circe he could find no rest; neither tender affection for his son, nor reverence for his aged father, nor love of Penelope had power to hold him. None of these could

> conquer in me the ardour that I had to
> gain experience of the world, and of human
> vice and worth.

Thus Odysseus, together with a band of mariners, once more took to the high seas. Having trimmed the sails of their square-rigger, they went before the wind. A wondrous breeze bore them into open waters, and took them along the African coast to Spain and the Pillars of Hercules, the ancient boundary of the ancient world. But there, although his crew had grown old and winded, Odysseus summoned them to the boldest voyage of all—toward an Ithaca of ultimate truth and fulfilment:

> "O brothers!" I said, "who through a hundred
> thousand dangers have reached the West, do
> not deny to what little there remains
>
> in you of sensual awareness, the experience
> of that unpeopled world which lies
> behind the setting Sun.
>
> Consider your lineage: you were not formed
> to live like brutes, but to pursue
> virtue and knowledge."

The voyage proceeded into the Atlantic, bearing due west, then south, and after five months Odysseus sighted land, a lofty mountain in the distance, in the "unpeopled world" on the far side of creation. But a whirlwind sprang up from the mountain, for it was the Mount of Purgatory; no living man may set foot on it, and pagan Odysseus may not do so even after death. Man's crossing of boundaries comes to an end; Purgatory, which bears upon its summit the earthly Paradise, is glimpsed but remains untrodden. Thus far Dante's astounding version; from it emerges an altered, Gothic Odysseus.

The shape of a Sinbad, to whom the wonders and perils of the deep have become the very essence of life, is already present in Homer's Odysseus, but it was not acknowledged. The classic consciousness did not harbor defiance against Poseidon, Odysseus' sworn foe, and it lacked a sense of gigantic horizons. In the baroque tale, the Flying Dutchman sought to round Cape Horn despite the adverse winds unleashed by Heaven; as a result he was doomed to furrow the seas until the end of time. In Dante's version, Odysseus the Trespasser, the "Captain of *Hubris*," perishes; but Dante makes of him the first of the titans, a man descended not from the image of sufferance but from that of the chivalric quest. He is the first of the mightily obsessed; he embodies that spirit of "entirety," of uncompromising totality, which appears later in Don Juan and Faust, and of which Don Quixote is a comic counterpart.

He is a strange voyager, this later Odysseus; he is hewn from more than his own timber. In him are prefigured not only Faustus, but also an actual human being: Columbus. There is warrant for neither Faust nor Columbus in the Homeric Odysseus or in subsequent Hellenistic and Roman versions. It is true, however, that the Homeric wanderer was given wider scope. Marcus Terrentius Varro wrote a prolongation "by half" of the *Odyssey*; in it Odysseus is made to roam about another five years. Lucian based his satiric book of travels about fabled lands in the West—the *Vera Historia*—on the testimony of an inventive Odysseus. But all this was meant satirically and not in admiration. The literary legacy of long-suffering Odysseus was that of a Baron Münchausen, not of a man of overweening audacity.

In Homer also Odysseus sets out on a new voyage, but by no means of his own volition. He is to carry out the task assigned him by the prophet Tiresias in the Underworld (*Odyssey* XI, 119ff.). He must set forth once again, an oar upon his shoulder, and wander until someone inquires of him why he is carrying a winnowing fan; at this signal, Odysseus is to halt and offer a sacrifice to Poseidon. But though Odysseus' reminiscence of this prophecy, as he recounts it to Penelope, does portend a renewed separation and does signify a voyage into the remote unknown, it has no implication of a sea-journey, nor is anything said, as in Dante, of a desire to sail beyond the sun (*Odyssey* XXIII, 267ff.). In fact, the journey leads to a land so ignorant of the sea that there an oar is mistaken for a winnowing fan. And above all: there is no question of trespass, of *Hubris* at work. On the contrary: a mighty god is to be placated; perhaps his worship is to be extended to a new land. That is the principal motive for this obeissant voyage.

Thus there is no connection whatever between the landlocked motif in Homer and the purely maritime, audacious version in the *Divine Comedy*. It has been suggested that there is a formal link—that Dante may have darkly confounded Odysseus' journey to Hell with the voyage foretold by Tiresias. This so-called confusion brought forth the unprecedented figure of a Faustus of the seas who sets out to see the world and to experience and ascertain all things, going even unto that Mountain on which no living man may set foot. By contrast, the Homeric Odysseus returns from his pilgrimage to old Ithaca, where, according to Tiresias' prophecy, death finds him a prosperous ruler and patriarch in the midst of his people (*Odyssey* XXIII, 281ff.).

In Dante's time there was hardly any specific knowledge of the *Odyssey*. Dante combined the general notion of a seafarer with the new image of one attempting to cross the Atlantic. *Ne plus ultra*—no further!—was written on the Pillars of Hercules; Dante's Odysseus sails beyond them, and thus prefigures, in an amazing way, the voyage of Columbus. That this Odysseus discovered America, so to speak, may be inferred from the course he took—if not from his destination. The *mondo senza gente*, the "Unpeopled World" as Dante calls it, referred in medieval geography to the whole of the supposedly uninhabited hemisphere south of the Equator. This, of course, included sub-Saharan Africa: in 1291 an expedition had left Genoa under the command of Vivaldi, sailing beyond Ceuta in an endeavor to circumnavigate the African continent; it perished. Conceivably, Dante joined to his Odysseus this stroke of contemporary heroism. But hints of an African goal are incompatible with a westward course—*diretro al Sol*—with the emphatic foolhardiness of the visionary journey, with the notion of a five-months' solitude and with the absence of any landfall. Lastly, the thought of Africa is contradicted by the fact that Dante locates his Mount of Purgatory on an island. The giant continent of Africa, conceived even in its southern latitudes as a coherent land mass, could not emerge from the ocean in the shape of a mountain. The land of Purgatory does lie in the western hemisphere; such distance alone is commensurate with the audacity, with the o'erleaping boldness, with which Dante endowed his late Odysseus.

No news of the discovery of America by the Greenlander Leif Ericson, three hundred years earlier, could have reached Dante's Florence. Even in Greenland it was soon forgotten. From Roman antiquity, however, there has come down a notable conjecture, a leap of mind beyond the known confines of the ancient world. It is contained in a passage from Seneca to which Columbus often referred. Spoken by the Chorus in Seneca's *Medea*, the lines were definitely known in Dante's time. The Odysseus of the *Inferno* could be set in the context of those future centuries in which, according to Seneca—

> The ocean would loosen its bonds,
> And the wide world stand open,
> When Thetis would reveal new lands
> And Thule no longer be the last of earth.

Odysseus himself loosened the bonds which would have made of him a king in some provincial hole, a retired sea-captain living on his pension.

Not only is he impatient to see the world—he incarnates impatience. Impatience constitutes the specific and distinctive quality of his being. His life becomes synonymous with a constant breaking of bounds, with a quest for virtue and knowledge (*virtute e conoscenza*). In the midst of the medieval world, Dante gives the password of the nascent, forward-thrusting *bourgeoisie:* to leap the barrier (*trespassar del segno*).

Odysseus, moreover, came to be understood as a kind of knight errant from an unknown Round Table; or rather, as King Arthur himself with the Round Table on his ship. His quest is not undertaken in a Christian condition; he is, therefore, the more imperilled during his wondrous voyage beyond the confines of the known world. His courage is greater than that of Sir Gawain or Roland the Paladin. He casts no comic shadow, unlike so many of the stiffly sublime Arthurian heroes or the last of the high dreamers of the knightly quest—Don Quixote. For the goal of Dante's Odysseus—to know oneself in action, to be ever outward bound—cannot wane or grow stale as did the ideal of knighthood.

The goal lies ahead—in the *mondo senza gente,* in a world not yet humanized, among men who do not yet own a world adequate to the human condition. It lies ahead—in spite of, as well as because of, the perilous crossing.

To Narrate or Describe?

by Georg Lukács

What is it that gives objects in epic poetry a poetic quality? Can a description however skillfully done, however faithful in every technical and visual detail render the intrinsic, poetic quality of the theater, say, or the market-place, or the stock-exchange? We doubt that it can. Boxes and orchestra, stage, sets, and wardrobes are in themselves dead, uninteresting, completely unpoetic objects. And they remain unpoetic even when filled with human figures in so far as the human destinies of those represented are incapable of arousing us poetically. The theater or the stock-exchange is a crossroads of human endeavors, an arena of human interaction and conflict. And only in this connection—that is, only in so far as the theater or the stock-exchange becomes the immediate, concrete matrix of concrete human interrelation and interaction—does it take on literary significance and become poetic.

A "poetry of things" independent of man and of human destinies does not exist in literature. And it is more than questionable, whether the elaborate accuracy of description with its faithfulness to technical details which is so highly praised today, is able to convey a real idea of the object described. When a relevant action of a person who moves us poetically is properly narrated, then every object which plays a real part in this action becomes poetically significant by virtue of its very context. One need merely recall the deeply poetic effect of the tools which Robinson Crusoe recovers after the shipwreck.

In contrast, let us pick at random a description from Zola. Let us take for example a backstage scene from *Nana*:

> A painted canvas was lowered. It was the backdrop for the third act: the grotto of Aetna. The stage-hands planted poles into the trapdoors; others hauled scenery, screwed it together and fastened it with ropes to the poles. In the background a stage-hand set up a spot-light whose flames burned behind red glass panes: that was the wild glare of fire from Vulcan's smithy. The entire stage was frantic pell-mell, a seemingly inextricable rush and tangle, and yet each little move was necessary, every motion of a hand

To Narrate or Describe? From *Probleme des Realismus,* by Georg Lukács. (Berlin: Aufbau-Verlag, 1955). Translated by Hanna Loewy.

ordered and regulated. Amidst this hustle and bustle the prompter strolled up and down in leisurely fashion with small steps in order to stretch his legs.

To whom can such a description mean anything? He who does not know the theater already can derive no real conception of it from this passage. For one who has expert knowledge of the theater, on the other hand, such a description offers nothing new. Poetically it is completely superfluous. The striving for greater factual "authenticity," however, entails a serious danger to the novel. One need not know about horses to ride with Vronsky when he races. The descriptions of the naturalistic writer, however, aim continuously at an ever more specialized "authenticity" in their terminology; they increasingly use the professional jargon of the milieu or domain which they describe. Thus, just as Zola speaks of "movable scenery" in the technical terms of the theater, so, whenever possible, the painter's studio is described in the jargon of the painter and the workshop in the jargon of the metal worker. In this way there arises a body of literature directed at specialists and literati who happen to appreciate the painstaking efforts expended by the knowledgeable authors in absorbing technical jargon into literary language. The Goncourt brothers have expressed this tendency most clearly and paradoxically. They once wrote:

According to d'Alembert: "Those works of art whose beauty appeals only to artists are failures." This is one of the stupidest things that could ever have been asserted.

In attacking the profound truth expressed by d'Alembert, that great *philosophe* of the enlightenment, those co-founders of naturalism, the Goncourts, commit themselves unreservedly to the studio ideal of "art for art's sake."

Objects have poetic life only through their relationships to human destiny. Therefore the true epic poet does not describe them. He speaks of the task objects have in the nexus of human destinies, and he does so only when the objects have a share in those destinies, when they partake in the deeds and sufferings of men. Lessing understood this fundamental poetic truth: "I find that Homer paints nothing but actions in progress, and all bodies, all separate objects he paints only as they take part in these actions. . . ." And Lessing demonstrates this fundamental truth with an example from Homer, an example so striking and conclusive that we find it useful to quote this entire section from the *Laocoön* dealing with the scepters of Agamemnon and Achilles respectively:

What is it then that Homer does if he wants us to have a fuller, more precise picture of this important scepter? Does he paint for us not only the golden nails, but also the wood, the carved head? He might have done so had the description been meant for a book of heraldry from which at a later date an exact copy of the scepter were to be made. And yet I am sure that many a recent writer would have given such a heraldic description in the honest belief that he was really painting a picture merely because a picture could be painted from his description. But why should Homer care how far he leaves the painter behind? Instead of a reproduction he gives us the history of the scepter: First it is in the workshop of Hephaestus: then it glitters in the hands of Zeus; then it betokens the dignity of Hermes; now it is the baton of warlike Pelops; now the shepherd's staff of peace-loving Atreus, etc. . . . And again when Achilles swears by *his* scepter to avenge the scorn shown him by Agamemnon, Homer gives us the history of this scepter. We see it still in leaf upon the mountains, the axe severs it from the trunk, pares it of leaves and bark and readies it to serve the judges of the people as token of their god-like office. . . . Homer's concern was not so much to describe two sticks of different shape and material, as to give us a vivid picture of the different kinds of power which these staffs symbolized. One the work of Hephaestus; the other cut in the mountains by an unknown hand. One the old possession of a noble house; the other merely destined for the first fist that seizes it. The one extended by a monarch over many islands and over all Argos; the other borne by a man from among the Greeks, who, together with others, had been entrusted with the duty of upholding the laws. This, in fact, was the distance which separated Agamemnon and Achilles; a distance which Achilles himself, even in the blindness of his anger, could not but admit.

Here we have the precise exposition of that in epic poetry which makes objects really alive, truly poetic. And when we recall the examples from Scott, Balzac, and Tolstoy cited previously, then we must affirm that these writers—*mutatis mutandi*—have worked according to the same principle which Lessing detected in Homer. We say *mutatis mutandi,* for we have already pointed out that the greater complexity of social relations demands of modern literature new literary tools.

Description as the dominant method, however, is an entirely different matter and merely points to the fruitless rivalry of literature with the visual arts. Describing man in order to represent him can only transform him into a dead still-life. Only the art of painting itself possesses the means to express the deepest elements of human nature directly through man's bodily characteristics. Nor is it accidental that in the same historical period in which the visualistic aspirations of naturalism reduced human beings to component parts of still-lives, painting also lost its capacity for heightened sensuous expression. The portraits of Cézanne are as mere still-lives compared with the human, spiritual totality of the portraits of Titian or Rembrandt, as are the characters of Goncourt or Zola in comparison to those of Balzac or Tolstoy.

Man's bodily being as well becomes poetically alive only in the context of human interaction, only in its effect on other human beings. This too is clearly recognized by Lessing in his correct analysis of the way Homer creates and conveys Helen's beauty. We can see also how the classic writers of realism fulfill these demands of the true epic. Tolstoy articulated the beauty of Anna Karenina exclusively through the effect of that beauty on the action of the story, through the tragedies it brings about in the life of others and in her own.

Nearing Again the Legendary Isle

by C. Day Lewis

Nearing again the legendary isle
Where sirens sang and mariners were skinned,
We wonder now what was there to beguile
That such stout fellows left their bones behind.

Those chorus-girls are surely past their prime,
Voices grow shrill and paint is wearing thin,
Lips that sealed up the sense from gnawing time
Now beg the favor with a graveyard grin.

We have no flesh to spare and they can't bite,
Hunger and sweat have stripped us to the bone;
A skeleton crew we toil upon the tide
And mock the theme-song meant to lure us on:

No need to stop the ears, avert the eyes
From purple rhetoric of evening skies.

The Sirens and the Temptation of Knowledge

by Gabriel Germain

As in the case of all the episodes that come after the stay with Circe, the adventure of the Sirens is first foretold to the hero and fulfilled shortly thereafter. Nevertheless it remains sketchy. Set between the prominent episode of the descent into the Underworld and the sanguinary tales of how the Achaeans come to total ruin, it arrests our attention only slightly; one passes by as swiftly as the vessel itself passes the flowery mead of the Sirens. Yet this incident contains a meaning worth clarifying and which distinguishes it from a simple mariner's yarn.

The first thing that needs saying is precisely the fact that the Sirens of the *Odyssey* have no trait in common with the mermaids that dwell in the brine; to the modern reader the name of the Sirens evokes the image of mermaids but the latter are a recent invention. As is shown by the dual number applied to them grammatically, there are two Sirens, and they inhabit an island or, more precisely, a field sown with flowers. This isle cannot be very far from the land of Circe; it appears that the ship reaches it shortly after setting sail.

The isle of the Sirens is marked by "a shoreline of rotting human bones and flayed skins shrivelling around the spot." These are the remains of mariners whom the voice of the Sirens has entranced and held back from their voyage, aided by an unearthly calm which a *daimon,* a supernatural power, casts designedly on the waves. The epic tells us nothing further regarding the isle and its inhabitants. Though he is within earshot, Odysseus doubtless passes too far off-shore to get a close look. For him, as for us, the Sirens remain voices, at once "piercing" as is Circe's, and dulcet as honey.

Thus the nature of the Sirens remains ill defined. The most plausible conjecture is that the poet conceived of them in human guise; he never bestows speech on bestial shapes. Their habitation is already fairly remote from Death's shore; along the axis of Odysseus' travels the Siren

"The Sirens and the Temptation of Knowledge." From *Genèse de l'Odyssée* by Gabriel Germain. Translated by George Steiner.

isle lies in the latitudes of life. Yet plainly it is a place of destruction. But how did those men perish whose bones can be seen rotting? All guesses are possible: starvation after shipwreck or, as the ancients claimed, a sudden death such as poison brings. We may extend the list: drowning, the fang-mark of these ogres of the sea, the direct impact of their spell. On the evidence of their parched skin and of the sea-calm of the blazing Noon—the hour of the Dead—it has even been argued that the mariners died of sunstroke. In fact, the text of the *Odyssey* gives no more support to one guess than to another.

It is natural that one should think of the Sirens as winged spirits of the Dead, such as we find them frequently depicted on graves or placed inside tombs in the form of terra cotta figurines since the very dawn of Greek art. But if the Sirens of the *Odyssey* had wings, why should they not use them to assail their intended victims or, at least, to engage them at closer quarter? It is evident, on the contrary, that they endeavor to draw their prey to themselves. In their sea-girt lair, they remind one also of the Nereids who often act as "conveyors of souls to the Blessed Isles." But these are benevolent deities and one of them, Thetis, has bestowed immortality on Peleus. Moreover, being at home in the water, Nereids would presumably swim toward Odysseus. Again, one could imagine that the Sirens resemble the fabled Sphinx, that they are "spirits avid of blood and sensual lust." But one cannot assert that any such traits are clearly discernible in the account given by the *Odyssey*. On the whole, therefore, the text, with its narration of a complete stillness of wind, might accord best with the notion of rather anonymous and shapeless Demons of High Noon. This takes us back to our starting point: the Homeric Sirens have no exact mythological shape or nature.

What remains certain is that they embody a mortal danger to Odysseus and his crew, and that this danger is conveyed by means of their song. Does this song affect only the senses or does it seek direct access to the mind? To judge by the case of Odysseus, it would seem that the Sirens are not magicians whose power would lie in the exact pronouncement of a magic spell, but that they are *tempters*. Their temptation has a root meaning which must be put into right focus; little attention has been paid to it.

The Sirens promise knowledge; *who has heard them leaves "knowing more."* To Odysseus, whose name they know without having questioned him, they would speak willingly of the heroes of Troy, but they also have knowledge "of all that comes to pass on the fruitful earth." Thus the bait they hold out to a circumspect mind is that dread fruit of knowledge for the sake of which our first parents lost Eden. Whatever the blandishments to which the Sirens may resort when dealing with mariners of a coarser breed, *it is this alone by which they seek to ensnare Odysseus.* In restoring its full significance to this temptation *through knowledge,* we remove this brief narrative from the sphere of naive parables and relate it to a body of myths of which we have just cited the clearest and best known.

The temptation of a hero by some evil power which seeks to make him betray his essential destiny, seems to be an ancient Sumerian theme. We find it twice in the epic of Gilgamesh. Istar had wanted to make of Gilgamesh her lover, but he had scorned her, knowing that he would otherwise be degraded and finally destroyed. Lacking self-mastery, the uncouth Enkidu yields to the wiles of a courtesan and loses the privilege of living in brotherhood with the creatures of field and forest. In both instances, however, the snare is as brutal and palpable as it can be.

The more subtle theme of temptation through knowledge has come down to us only via *Genesis*. Owing to Christian theology, it has become a pillar of religious faith for a significant portion of mankind. Here, however, we must examine the Biblical story in its historical context.

We must note first that the "tree of knowledge of good and evil" is set in Eden next to "the tree of life." Prototypes of the latter can be found in Sumerian tales of remote antiquity. Gilgamesh, notably, has gone seeking out in the depths of the sea "a plant with a flower similar to the hawthorn and whose needles sting like a viper." This plant is called "the old man grows young." Whoever possesses it would be assured of eternal youth. The grass of generation which appears in the myth of Etana is no doubt also a tree of life, "aiding birth and rebirth."

It seems more and more certain, furthermore, that in the clay tablet of Nippur, first published by Langdon and re-examined lately by S. N. Kramer, the disobedience of Uttu to the orders of Enkidu is of the same nature as that of Eve. There can be no doubt as to the place of origin of the entire story. And it is certain that the text contains a list of plants whose fruit Uttu is allowed to eat, and that he is damned for having eaten others.

In the first chapter of this section we have already noted, among Egyptian beliefs, "the lofty sycamore beneath which sit the gods, the tree of life from which they draw their sustenance." The dead shall light on it in the guise of a bird and he too shall eat of its fruit. That is what is enjoined to him by the *Book of the Dead* in one of the chapters thought to be most ancient. Moreover, this chapter is entitled with striking clarity: "that which gives to the dead divine knowledge." The trees of life and of knowledge are conjoined as in *Genesis*.

To explain *Genesis* one is led to look much further into the past than the date at which the Pentateuch was set down, toward myths widespread in the classic Orient.

Finally, one must attempt to be precise about what kind of knowledge the Biblical tree bears in its fruit. This problem has given rise to subtle argument. Are we dealing solely with moral discernment, of which Adam and Eve would, at one stroke, receive the gift? Despite the literal meaning of the text, this is implausible. Verse 22 of Chapter III shows plainly that after his first disobedience man can become godlike by merely tasting of the fruit of life and thus conquering immortality. What knowledge, unless it be a capacity for *absolute* knowledge, could be set beside immortality as attribute of God?

Doubtless this is what the text says. Every object, every deed, every living being can be easily labelled as good or evil in a vision of the world at once simple and rigorous. To know good and evil—whether by knowing individually all good and all evil things, or whether by having a touchstone of ethical judgment which identifies the nature of all things as they arise—is, in the last analysis, to have complete knowledge of a universe in which everything must be either good or evil.

Certain turns of phrase in *Genesis* suggest not so much a detailed mode of knowledge but rather a sovereign intuition, transforming at one stroke Adam's and Eve's vision of the world: "then your eyes shall be opened"; "And the eyes of them both were opened"; "the woman saw . . . a tree to be desired to make one wise." The sights of the world had no *meaning* as yet for Adam and Eve. Suddenly, they are illumined and the mind ascends from brute sensation to an organized, articulate vision of things. This, at least, is what is implied in modern terms by this brusque "opening up" of intelligence.

The Sirens do not indulge in metaphysical speculations; but they also "know *everything* that comes to pass on the fruitful earth," and it is no less than a large bestowal of that universal knowledge that they declare themselves ready to give.

By yet another way these mysterious beings lead us toward a remote past.

Many etymologies have been proposed for the name: *Siren*. On the Greek side, the word has been linked to σείριος: burning. This would suit them well in so far as they are demons of a southern latitude. The actual shape of the word has suggested the name of a people, or in any event makes one think of a term belonging to "an ancient Mediterranean wordstock" rather than to the Hellenic foundations of Greek.

It seems difficult to separate this word from the common name σειρήν which signifies in Aristotle a species of wild bee. Moreover, a semitic scholar, Mr. Marcel Cohen, has suggested that the name of the Sirens can be explained by the Biblical word *sir'â* which the Septuagint renders as σφηκία: wasp, swarm of wasps (wasps' nest in classical Greek), and which Syriac translates to mean: bee. At three places in the Bible, God declares to His people that He will send or has sent these wasps or bees against His foes to put them to rout. "Even if we have here only a metaphor signifying panic, this metaphor presupposes a popular belief in the daemonic power of these insects." The relevant passages give a distinct impression that the terror of a broken, fleeing host is embodied in the insect.

A semantic fact can help us see the popular imagination at work. The Latin words *vespa, vespula, vespillo* meaning "undertaker" (with a slang, morbid overtone of "body-snatching"), are obviously of popular derivation. Mr. Benveniste has very plausibly related these words to *vespa,* the wasp, "by virtue of the carnivorous nature of this insect." Similar observations and interpretations may elsewhere have transformed the wasp into a ravening monster.

The entire pre-Hellenic eastern Mediterranean, furthermore, yields discernible traces of the veneration—if not always of the formal cult—accorded to the bee. In Egypt the bee is a symbol of the Pharaoh. In Sumerian writing it also furnishes a symbol of royalty. The most famous of Hittite myths, that of the disappearance of the god Telepinu, confides to the bee the task of finding the deity once the eagle has failed. The Great Goddess instructs her messenger thus: "Take wax and cleanse him. Make him pure, make him holy, and bring him unto me." From this it would appear that the bee possesses powers of purification in addition to that "piercing spirit" attributed to it by the God of the Storm. The bee also is represented on Phoenician religious monuments. Hence one can suppose that it is not by mere chance that the prophetess Deborah carries a name signifying "bee."

Whether in the form of a bee with furled wings or of a woman whose body tapers into that of a bee, a sacred figurine gives evidence that some such bee-cult existed in the Aegean from the time of pre-Hellenic Crete, that it existed throughout the Cyclades (VIth century jewel found at Thera) and in Rhodes (Camiros pendant). At Ephesus, sacred bees are depicted in the foundations of the archaic Artemis shrines and the insect adorns the coinage of the city; it appears again on the vestment of the statue of Artemis in the Hellenistic period.

It is possible that the priestesses cloistered in the temple of Artemis and wearing the ritual garb of a bee-goddess may have borne the title μέλισσαι ("bee" or "wild bee"). What is known for certain, at this same shrine, is the name Ἐσσῆνες, derived from the noun meaning "king" (we would say "queen") "of the bees." Likewise, the name μέλισσα was used to describe the priestesses of Demeter and Persephone. The priestess of the oracle was called by Pindar Δελφὶς μέλισσα, a name analogous to that of Deborah. And though the actual word is not used, it is to bees that the *Hymn to Hermes* compares the prophetic Fates, the Three Daughters of Zeus who dwell on Parnassus. According to Philostrates, "the Muses guide mariners in the shape of bees."

The association of this insect with priestesses—derived perhaps from an idea that both are diligent and pure—must be very ancient as the name Melissa is borne by the mythical votaries of diverse gods: it applies to a Cretan, the first priestess of the Earth Goddess, Rhea; to a Corinthian woman initiated into the mysteries by Demeter herself and slain by her compatriots for not having revealed the secret rites; to a sister of Amaltheia, who was also a Cretan and daughter of king Melisseus, and who helped nourish the young Zeus by giving him honey while Amaltheia brought milk. Bees allegedly repulsed from Zeus' grotto on Mount Ida a party of marauders who were then changed into birds. All these traditions point toward the Aegean. The Artemis of Epheseus, on the other hand, leads back to the Asiatic world.

In Greece lastly, in speculative writings which may, to be sure, be of a late date, the bee passes for a symbol of the renascent soul.

It is understandable that, to those who observed them, the habits of the bee should have conveyed a lofty notion of its supernatural "powers" —an ambiguous notion which can induce fear as well as admiration. The association of bees with the spirits of the dead can be found equally in northern India, among the Mordves—a Finnish people of the Volga basin—and among the Angami of Burma for whom bees incarnate wicked souls. In China, an ancient text, the *Chanhaï King,* "notes the existence of a bird similar to a bee: if this bird stings an animal, the latter dies; if it stings a plant or a tree, these wither."

One should like to conjecture that in inheriting from some Mediterranean language the word σειρήν, the Greek world preserved an archaic double meaning: "bee" (applied to some savage people) and "supernatural being" conceived originally as having the shape of a bee. Here also μέλισσα would have acquired favourable connotations, making one forget the primitive links between Sirens and insects. Need we underline the fact that the Master of the *Odyssey* was no longer cognizant of these links, for it is evident that he gives to his tempters a human visage? Nevertheless, it is noteworthy that on every hand a study of the Sirens leads outside the confines of the classic world.

We can judge that the very spirit of the Homeric episode points to an alien provenance. Its root meaning, as we have sought to bring it to light, does not seem in accord with the consistent tendencies of the Greek spirit. In the *Odyssey* itself, it is curiosity which impels the Acheans to taste of the lotus plant, which draws Odysseus into the cavern of the Cyclops and makes his companions enter the dwelling of Circe. Such is, indeed, the normal attitude of the race. A truly Greek hero, in some poem of a purely local origin, would have landed among the Sirens at the risk of perishing.

To abstain in the face of divine temptation is the mark either of a man of primitive mistrust, such as Adapa who refuses the food of immortality, or of a superhuman sage. Thus, the Buddha will soon reject the empire of the world and the three daughters of Mara—Concupiscence, Unquietude and Voluptuousness. Similarly, Zoroaster will reject the temporal realm offered him by Anra Mainyu, while Christ will refuse, in His turn, the gift of universal dominion tendered by Satan. Greek heroes are as remote from Adapa as they are from Christ.

To sum up: though we cannot hope to locate the homeland of the Sirens, it does appear, at the least, that the motif of the *Odyssey*, thus interpreted, is more ancient than a first reading would have led one to suspect. Once again, the Singer seems to transpose into a form which may justly be called "rationalistic"—which we may even find somewhat bleak—a motif much more ancient than himself and doubtless of an alien origin. Seeing how little stress he puts on it, we may ask ourselves whether he grasped its full value.

The Silence of the Sirens

by Franz Kafka

Proof that inadequate, even childish measures, may serve to rescue one from peril.

To protect himself from the Sirens Ulysses stopped his ears with wax and had himself bound to the mast of his ship. Naturally any and every traveler before him could have done the same, except those whom the Sirens allured even from a great distance; but it was known to all the world that such things were of no help whatever. The song of the Sirens could pierce through everything, and the longing of those they seduced would have broken far stronger bonds than chains and masts. But Ulysses did not think of that, although he had probably heard of it. He trusted absolutely to his handful of wax and his fathom of chain, and in innocent elation over his little stratagem sailed out to meet the Sirens.

Now the Sirens have a still more fatal weapon than their song, namely their silence. And though admittedly such a thing has never happened, still it is conceivable that someone might possibly have escaped from their singing; but from their silence certainly never. Against the feeling of having triumphed over them by one's own strength, and the consequent exaltation that bears down everything before it, no earthly powers could have remained intact.

And when Ulysses approached them the potent songstresses actually did not sing, whether because they thought that this enemy could be vanquished only by their silence, or because the look of bliss on the face of Ulysses, who was thinking of nothing but his wax and his chains, made them forget their singing.

But Ulysses, if one may so express it, did not hear their silence; he thought they were singing and that he alone did not hear them. For a fleeting moment he saw their throats rising and falling, their breasts lifting, their eyes filled with tears, their lips half-parted, but believed that these were accompaniments to the airs which died unheard around him. Soon, however, all this faded from his sight as he fixed his gaze on the distance, the Sirens literally vanished before his resolution, and at the very moment when they were nearest to him he knew of them no longer.

But they—lovelier than ever—stretched their necks and turned, let their cold hair flutter free in the wind, and forgetting everything clung with their claws to the rocks. They no longer had any desire to allure; all that they wanted was to hold as long as they could the radiance that fell from Ulysses' great eyes.

If the Sirens had possessed consciousness they would have been annihilated at that moment. But they remained as they had been; all that had happened was that Ulysses had escaped them.

A codicil to the foregoing has also been handed down. Ulysses, it is said, was so full of guile, was such a fox, that not even the goddess of fate could pierce his armor. Perhaps he had really noticed, although here the human understanding is beyond its depths, that the Sirens were silent, and opposed the afore-mentioned pretense to them and the gods merely as a sort of shield.

Helen

by Rachel Bespaloff

Of all the figures in the poem she is the severest, the most austere. Shrouded in her long white veils, Helen walks across the *Iliad* like a penitent; misfortune and beauty are consummate in her and lend majesty to her step. For this royal recluse freedom does not exist; the very slave who numbers the days of oppression on some calendar of hope is freer than she. What has Helen to hope for? Nothing short of the death of the Immortals would restore her freedom, since it is the gods, not her fellow men, who have dared to put her in bondage. Her fate does not depend on the outcome of the war; Paris or Menelaus may get her, but for her nothing can really change. She is the prisoner of the passions her beauty excited, and her passivity is, so to speak, their underside. Aphrodite rules her despotically; the goddess commands and Helen bows, whatever her private repugnance. Pleasure is extorted from her; this merely makes her humiliation the more cruel. Her only resource is to turn against herself a wrath too weak to spite the gods. She seems to live in horror of herself. "Why did I not die before?" is the lament that keeps rising to her lips. Homer is as implacable toward Helen as Tolstoy is toward Anna. Both women have run away from home thinking that they could abolish the past and capture the future in some unchanging essence of love. They awake in exile and feel nothing but a dull disgust for the shrivelled ecstasy that has outlived their hope. The promise of freedom has been sloughed off in servitude; love does not obey the rules of love but yields to some more ancient and ruder law. Beauty and death have become neighbors and from their alliance springs a necessity akin to that of force. When Helen and Anna come to and face their deteriorated dream, they can blame only themselves for having been the dupes of harsh Aphrodite. Everything they squandered comes back on them; everything they touch turns to dust or stone. In driving his heroine to suicide, Tolstoy goes beyond Christianity and rejoins Homer and the tragic poets. To them the hero's flaw is indistinguishable from the misery that arises from it. The sufferer bears it; he pays for it, but he cannot redeem it any more than he can live his life over. Clytemnestra, Orestes, and Oedipus are their crimes; they have no existence outside them. Later on, the philosophers, heirs of Odysseus, introduce the Trojan horse of dialectic into the realm of tragedy. Error takes the place of the tragic fault, and the responsibility for it rests with the individual alone. With Homer, punishment and expiation have the opposite effect; far from fixing responsibility, they dissolve it in the vast sea of human suffering and the diffuse guilt of the life-process itself. A flaw in a defective universe is not quite the same thing as a sin; remorse and grace have not yet made their appearance. But it is nonetheless true that this Greek idea of a diffuse guilt represents for Homer and the tragic poets the equivalent of the Christian idea of original sin. Fed on the same reality, charged with the same weight of experience, it contains the same appraisal of existence. It too acknowledges a fall, but a fall that has no date and has been preceded by no state of innocence and will be followed by no redemption; the fall, here, is a continuous one as the life-process itself which heads forever downward into death and the absurd. In proclaiming the innocence of Becoming, Nietzsche is as far from the ancients as he is from Christianity. Where Nietzsche wants to justify, Homer simply contemplates, and the only sound that he lets ring through his lines is the plaint of the hero. If the final responsibility for the tragic guilt rests on the mischievous gods, this does not mean that guilt is nonexistent. On the contrary, there is not a page in the *Iliad* that does not emphasize its irreducible character. So fully does Helen assume it that she does not even permit herself the comfort of self-defense. In Helen, purity and guilt mingle confusedly as they do in the vast heart of the warrior herd spread out on the plain at her feet.

Thus Helen, at Ilion, drags her ill luck along with a kind of somber humility that still makes no truce with the gods.[1] But is it really Aphrodite? Is it not rather the Asiatic Astarte who has trapped her? In a certain way, Helen's destiny prefigures that of Greece which, from the Trojan War to Alexander's conquests, was alternately submitting to and repelling the tremendous attraction of the Orient. What the exile misses in Paris' high dwelling is not the blond Achaean, arrogant Menelaus, son of a wild race of Northern barbarians, but the rude, pure homeland—the familiar city, the child she used to fondle.

How tired she gets of the soft, weak ways of Aphrodite's protégé; he is a humiliation and a wound to her. "If the gods have decreed these evils for us, why could not I have had a husband who was capable of a feeling of revolt?" Here in hostile Troy, where boredom makes her despondent, Helen has no one to cling to but Hector, the least oriental of Priam's sons, the most manly, the most Greek. There is a feeling of

[1] And possibly this royal humility, in Helen and Oedipus, is what distinguishes the antique style from the Christian.

tenderness between them. Helen's presence is odious to everyone, and Hector is her only defender from the hatred she excites. Nobody can forgive the stranger for being the embodiment of the fatality that pursues the city. Innocent though she is, Helen feels the weight of these rebukes; she even seems to invite them, as though courting a just punishment for a crime she did not commit. She is all the more grateful, therefore, to the one person who shows her compassion without importuning her with lust. When Hector comes to scold Paris, Helen is worried about the dangers that threaten her brother-in-law. He is the only one to whom she speaks gently: "Meanwhile, come in, brother, and take this seat. Care assails your heart more than anyone else's, and that because of me, bitch that I am, and the folly of Alexander. Zeus has given us a hard lot, that later on we may be the subject of a song for men to come." These words weave a complicity between Hector and Helen that is something more than fraternal. With an unequalled insight, Homer hears in their talk an accent of intimacy which is attuned to the truth of human relationships. This affection, on Helen's part at least, shields a deeper feeling, which Homer, listening, does not betray.

The exile's lament is the last to echo over Hector's remains; it bathes the end of the *Iliad* in the pure, desolate light of compassion. "This is now the twentieth year from the time I came away and left my native land; yet I have never heard a bad or a harsh word from you. So I weep for you and for my unhappy self too, with grief at heart. I have nobody else now in wide Troy to be kind or gentle to me; everybody shudders away from me." This, however, is not the moan of some humiliated creature at the mercy of her tormentors; it is the grief of a mortal at the mercy of gods who have laden her with dazzling graces, the better to balk her of the joy these gifts seemed to promise. No matter who wins in the end, Helen, unlike Andromache and the Trojan princesses, does not have to fear a life of slavery and forced labor "under the eyes of a harsh master." After twenty years, she is still the stake the war is being fought for, and the reward the winner will carry off. In the depths of her wretchedness, Helen still wears an air of majesty that keeps the world at a distance and flouts old age and death. The most beautiful of women seemed born for a radiant destiny; everything pointed that way; everything appeared to contribute to it. But, as it turns out, the gods only chose her to work misfortune on herself and on the two nations. Beauty is not a promise of happiness here; it is a burden and a curse. At the same time, it isolates and elevates; it has something preservative in it that wards off outrage and shame. Hence its sacred character—to use the word in its original, ambiguous sense—on the one hand, lifegiving, exalting; on the other, accursed and dread. The Helen the two armies are contending for will never be Paris' any more than she has been Menelaus'; the Trojans cannot own her any more than the Greeks could. Beauty, captured, remains elusive. It deserts alike those who beget, or contemplate, or desire it. Homer endows it with the inexorability of force or fate. Like force, it subjugates and destroys—exalts and releases. It is not by some chance, arising out of her life's vicissitudes, that Helen has come to be the cause of the war and its stake; a deeper necessity has brought her there to join the apparition of beauty with the unleashing of rage. Beside the warriors and above them, Helen is the calm and the bitterness that spring up in the thick of battle, casting their cool shadow over victories and defeats alike, over the living and the thousands of dead. For, if force degrades itself in the insignificance of Becoming (one arrow from Paris' bow puts an end to the might of Achilles), beauty alone transcends all contingencies, including those that brought it to flower. The origins of Leda's daughter are lost in fable, her end in legend. In immortal appearance the world of Being is maintained and protected.

Homer carefully abstains from the description of beauty, as though this might constitute a forbidden anticipation of bliss. The shade of Helen's eyes, of Thetis' tresses, the line of Andromache's shoulders—these details are kept from us. No singularity, no particularity is brought to our notice; yet we see these women; we would recognize them. One wonders by what impalpable means Homer manages to give us such a sense of the plastic reality of his characters. Incorruptible, Helen's beauty passes from life into the poem, from flesh into marble, its pulse still throbbing. The statue's mouth utters a human cry, and from the empty eyes gush "tender tears." When Helen climbs the ramparts of Troy to watch the fight between Paris and Menelaus, one can almost feel the loftiness of her step. By the Scaean gates, the Trojan elders are holding council. At the sight of her, "the good orators" fall silent, struck to the heart. They cannot help finding her beautiful. And this beauty frightens them like a bad omen, a warning of death. "She has terribly the look, close-up, of the immortal goddesses. . . . But even so, whatever she may be, let her set sail and go away. Let her not be left here to be a scourge to us and our sons hereafter." Here—and this is unusual—the poet himself, speaking through Priam, lifts his voice to exonerate beauty and proclaim it innocent of man's misfortunes. "I do not blame you. I blame the gods, who launched this Achaean war, full of tears, upon me." The real culprits, and the only ones, are the gods, who live "exempt from care," while men are consumed with sorrow. The curse which turns beauty into destructive fatality does not originate in the human heart. The diffuse guilt of Becoming pools into a single sin, the one sin condemned and explicitly stigmatized by Homer: the happy carelessness of the Immortals.

There follows a scene of starry serenity in which the human accent, however, is still audible. Priam asks Helen to tell him the names of the most famous of the Achaean warriors that he can see in the enemy camp. The battlefield is quiet; a few steps away from each other, the two armies stand face to face awaiting the single combat that will decide the outcome of the war. Here, at the very peak of the *Iliad,* is one of those pauses, those moments of contemplation, when the spell of Becoming is broken, and the world of action, with all its fury, dips into peace. The plain where the warrior herd was raging is no more than a tranquil mirage to Helen and the old king.

No doubt this is where Nietzsche listened to the dialogue between Beauty and Wisdom, set above life but very close to it. "Pushed, pressed, constrained, tracked down by torment," come at length to the place where, around him, everything "turned strange and solitary," he had a vision of Helen (or Ariadne), high and inaccessible against the blue sky.

Meanwhile Helen stands helplessly watching the men who are going to do battle for her. She is there still, since nations that brave each other for markets, for raw materials, rich lands, and their treasures, are fighting, first and forever, for Helen.

Hellas

by Robert Fitzgerald

The young blind fellow saw the wind
Ruffle that pacing loveliness,
The sun of Asia on her shoulder.

Unsmiling in his great humored song
He glanced toward her: western her love
Over the long years' lapping water
Lay in her dear land, Lacedaemon.

At the west gate the gaffers wheezed
Their cricket whispers after her.

The Name of Odysseus

by George E. Dimock, Jr.

There is no way to stand firm on both feet and escape trouble.
Odyssey V, 413-4

In a way, the whole problem of the *Odyssey* is for Odysseus to establish his identity. "After all, who knows who his father is?" says Telemachus in the first book. "My son, if he really ever existed," says Laertes in the last. To establish his identity Odysseus must live up to his name.

This is not a new idea. A nameless ancient commentator has puzzled editors by glossing *hēbēsas* in line 410 of the nineteenth book with *odyssamenos*. *Hēbēsas* means "when he has grown up," a meaning with which *odyssamenos* has nothing to do; but as we shall see, the scholiast means that for Odysseus to grow up, to achieve his full stature, will be for him to "odysseus"—to live up to the meaning of his name, whatever that may be.

"To odysseus" (*odyssasthai* in Greek) is usually said to mean "be wroth against," "hate," and to be connected with Latin *odisse*. Historically speaking, this may be true. For the *Odyssey*'s poetical purposes, however, the verb denotes a more general sort of hostility, which Homer is at pains to define. In the fifth book the nymph Ino explains it as "planting evils," without specifying what sort of hostility is in the mind of the planter. It is true that Poseidon, who happens to be the planter in this case, is angry; but Zeus, who also odysseuses Odysseus, is not. In the nineteenth book Odysseus' grandfather Autolycus indicates that it is not a question of anger; asked to name the baby, he replies,

> "I have odysseused many in my time, up and down the wide world, men and women both; therefore let his name be Odysseus."

Now, all we know from the *Odyssey* about Autolycus' career is that he was the foremost liar and thief of his day. Most naturally, by "odysseusing many" he means that he has been the bane of many people's existence. The secret of his palpable success would seem to be that he has never given a sucker an even break, and he wants his grandson to be like him. In the career of Autolycus, and in the attitude which it implies, we are much closer to the *polytropon* "crafty" of the *Odyssey*'s first line, than to the *mēnin* "wrath" of the *Iliad*'s. So let us think no more of "wrath," which implies provocation and mental perturbation, but rather of a hand and mind against every man, by nature, or as a matter of policy. Autolycus' own name does not suggest "Lone Wolf" for nothing. These considerations, and others, lead me to think that in the *Odyssey odyssasthai* means essentially "to cause pain (*odynē*), and to be willing to do so." We need not draw the line between subjective and objective here, any more than we need do so in the case of the word "suffer." Where did Odysseus "suffer" the "woes" of the *Odyssey*'s fourth line: "on the high seas," or "in his heart"? Just as "suffer" brings to mind both the external and internal aspects of being a victim, so "odysseus" implies subjectively and objectively what it is to persecute. For what it is worth, the seven-odd instances of the verb outside the *Odyssey* show nothing inconsistent with this meaning.

Autolycus, then, we discover in the nineteenth book, intended Odysseus to be a causer of pain. He has been one all along, of course. Perhaps the most prominent fact about him is that more than any other man he was responsible for taking Troy; and what it means to sack a city, we know from the simile at the end of Book VIII. Odysseus

> wept as a woman weeps when she throws her arms around the body of her beloved husband, fallen in battle before his city and his comrades, fighting to save his town and his children from disaster. She has found him gasping in the throes of death; she clings to him and lifts her voice in lamentation. But the enemy come up and belabor her back and shoulders with spears, as they lead her off into slavery and a life of miserable toil, with her cheeks wasted by her pitiful grief.[1]

Less than a hundred lines later, at the beginning of his tale, Odysseus will say,

> The same wind as wafted me from Ilium brought me to Ismarus, the city of the Cicones; I sacked the place and killed the men; their wives, together with much booty, we took out of the city and divided up.

As has been well observed, the Sack of Ismarus is the Sack of Troy in its predatory essentials, with the glamor stripped off. This attitude Odysseus

[1] This quotation is from E. V. Rieu's excellent translation. So, in whole or in part, are many of the passages which follow.

will maintain to the end. "The cattle which the suitors have consumed," he says in the twenty-third book, "I will for the most part make up by raiding on my own; the Achaeans will give others." Perhaps worse than this, Odysseus' going to Troy caused Telemachus grievous mental suffering, wasted Penelope's nights in tears, and reduced Laertes, his father, to misery and squalor; his absence killed his mother, Anticleia.

So conceived, Odysseus is not an attractive character. In fact that poem implies a good deal of criticism of the Autolycan attitude. As Mr. H. N. Porter once pointed out to me, one of the first things we hear about the hero is his predilection for poisoned arrows. Athene, disguised as Mentes, tells Telemachus,

> He was on his way from Ephyre, where he had stayed with Ilus Mermerides —he went there in his fast ship to get a mortal poison to smear his bronze-tipped arrows with. Ilus wouldn't give it to him in fear of the eternal gods. But my father [Zeus?] gave him some. He was terribly fond of him.

Much better, one would think, for Autolycus to have adopted Eurycleia's suggestion of Polyaretus as a name for the baby: "He's our 'Answer to Prayer (*polyarētos*)," she remarked as she put the child on his grandfather's lap. But Autolycus preferred a name that most would regard as ill-omened.

For in spite of the fact that Odysseus is so obviously a causer of pain, the name which Autolycus wished on him strikes one as ironical. Up to the nineteenth book, Odysseus has been referred to as odysseused rather than odysseusing: "Why do you odysseus him so, Zeus?" Athene asks, before the poem is well under way; Ino and Odysseus both say that Poseidon is odysseusing him; finally, as we read the Autolycus passage, we are aware that Odysseus has just told Penelope that Zeus and the Sun-god odysseused her husband. In the *Odyssey*'s proem itself, the hero seems essentially the sufferer: he is the *polytropos* man, the Autolycan rogue who treats the world as his enemy, but who sacks Troy only to be driven far astray thereafter, and take a beating. In the process, we are told, he is to win his *psychē,* which means loosely his life, and more properly the image of life after the liver is gone—in other words something very like identity—but the whole business seems unpleasant, to say the least.

To understand the satisfaction involved in injuring and suffering and the connection between them, we must return to the nineteenth book and the scholiast's note. The giving of the name is coupled with the adventure in which Odysseus first lives up to it. *Hēbēsas* is in fact *odyssamenos.* "When he has grown up," the hero, as though undergoing an initiation, wins Autolycus' favor and recognition by going on a boar hunt; as causer of pain he kills the boar; as sufferer he is slashed by it, thus acquiring the scar important in identifying him later. The pain given and received results in joy:

> Autolycus and the sons of Autolycus
> Efficiently healed him and loaded him with presents;
> Rejoicing they dispatched him rejoicing to his beloved
> Ithaca. His father and his good mother
> Rejoiced at his return, and asked for each particular
> Of how he got his scar.

The suffering results from the doing, and is inseparable from it in the recognition and satisfaction produced by this exploit. Not simply "how he killed the boar" but "how he got his scar," is for Odysseus' parents the measure of their son.

To be Odysseus, then, is to adopt the attitude of the hunter of dangerous game: to deliberately expose one's self, but thereafter to take every advantage that the exposed position admits; the immediate purpose is injury, but the ultimate purpose is recognition and the sense of a great exploit. Odysseus killed a boar to win his name; he went to Troy to enlarge it; in order to keep it, he will presently kill 108 suitors in as cold blood as he can manage.

In the adventure with the Cyclops, Odysseus inflicts pain in order to identify himself, and in so doing challenges the hostility of the universe. Polyphemus' pain is obvious. Even Euripides could not have dwelt more explicitly than Homer on the boring of the red-hot stake into the great eyeball, the sizzling of the eye's fluid, and the crackling of its roots. By virtue of this deed of horror, Odysseus, until now *Outis* "nobody" as far as Polyphemus is concerned, puts himself in a position where he can tell the monster who he is, can cry his name aloud to the Cyclops' face. This cry of defiance is thought to be foolish of the wily Odysseus, no less by his crew than by the critics, but it is in reality, like the boar hunt, a case of deliberate self-exposure for the purpose of being somebody rather than nobody.

To blind the son of Poseidon, and then to defy him, is both to challenge nature to do her worst, and to demonstrate her ultimate impotence to crush human identity. It is challenging nature in the sense that the sailor does, every time he goes to sea. The hero's colonizing eye as he approaches the Cyclopes' island, the remark that they have no ships or shipwrights, the shipbuilding technique employed in blinding Polyphemus and the mention of axe, adze and auger, the tools which enabled Odysseus to leave Calypso and set sail on his raft, all this sounds very much as though Odysseus' crime against Poseidon were the crime of all those who go down to the sea in ships. But Poseidon will not get his revenge. In the *Odyssey* navigation is a practical possibility; the elements are conquered. So to blind Polyphemus is to convict savage nature of impotence and blindness. She is indiscriminate in her blows. Her most hostile efforts, like the rocks thrown by Polyphemus, are as likely to wash the hero to safety as they are to drive him into danger. Thus the power of the elements does not render Odysseus' identity meaningless. Rather he makes sense, and the elements do not. This, I think, is the significance of the general assumption in the *Odyssey* that Poseidon will give Odysseus his bellyful of trouble before he reaches his home, but will not kill him.

Polyphemus and Poseidon, however, are more than the hostility of inanimate nature. There is no "inanimate nature" in Homer anyway. They prefigure all the overt savagery which the universe presents, human and divine. This savagery is as able to breach the conventions, hospitality and the rest, among the civilized suitors in Ithaca, or the hypercivilized Phaeacians (remember Euryalus), as it is among the cannibal Laestrygons, or among the Cyclopes. If Poseidon and Polyphemus are the hostile aspects of this world, it is not foolish for Odysseus to cry his name in defiance of them, and so be subject to Polyphemus' rock-slinging and his curse; or rather, the foolishness or good sense of the action is not the point. To pass from the darkness of the cave into the light, to pass from being "nobody" to having a name, is to be born. But to be born is to cast one's name in the teeth of a hostile universe; it is to incur the enmity of Poseidon. In such a world, what better name could be found than Odysseus, "Trouble"? ("Trouble" is perhaps as good a translation of Odysseus' name as any. When a character in a western movie says, "Just call me Trouble, stranger," we take him to be a hostile type who makes trouble for other people, and so presumably for himself also.)

That braving Polyphemus is being born is not my metaphor; it is Homer's. In the nineteenth book Odysseus hints to Penelope that her husband has undergone a birth somewhere overseas:

> He put in at Amnisus, where the cave of Eileithuia is, in a difficult harbor;
> he barely escaped the gales.

Eileithuia is goddess of childbirth. But in the nineteenth book this is merely a way of reminding us of the Polyphemus adventure and possibly of Calypso as well. In the ninth book, as Polyphemus is in the act of rolling the stone from the mouth of the cave, we are told of his anguish for the second time. We already know how his eye hurts, but this time we hear that he is "travailing in pain"; *ōdinōn odynēsi* are the words used. Whether or not we hear in them the name of Odysseus, we should not fail to reflect that *ōdinō* means essentially "to be in labor of childbirth." We are born for trouble, the adventure of the Cyclops implies, yet to stay in the womb is to remain nobody. There is security of a sort in being nobody, but as the Cyclops promises, Nobody will be devoured in the end, though last of all.

For there are more insidious threats to identity in the *Odyssey* than those which Polyphemus represents, the dangers and sufferings consequent upon taking on the world as one's enemy. Trouble is difficult and dangerous, but it can lead to identity. Security, on the other hand, is inevitable oblivion. The narrative proper of the *Odyssey* begins as follows:

> By now all the others, as many as had escaped sheer destruction, were at home. Odysseus, alone of all, wanting his home and his wife, a queenly nymph held prisoner, Calypso, divine goddess, in her hollow cave, begging him to be her husband.

This is the state of affairs which the fifth book will develop. He wants home and a wife. He has a cave and a goddess. Why do all the gods but one pity him for this? Odysseus has realized the tired soldier's or sailor's dream, an immortality of comfort and physical satisfaction, with no troubles. But Odysseus would rather die, as Athene says. Everybody sees this paradox and understands the flaw in this paradise: such an existence has no meaning. But it adds something, I think, to see life on Ogygia in terms of identity and nonentity. Calypso is oblivion. Her name suggests cover and concealment, or engulfing; she lives "in the midst of the sea"—the middle of nowhere, as Hermes almost remarks—and the whole struggle of the fifth book, indeed of the entire poem, is not to be engulfed by that sea. When the third great wave of Book V breaks over Odysseus' head, Homer's words are: *ton de mega kyma kalypsen*—"and the great wave engulfed him." If this wave had drowned him, it would have been a "vile death," surely, as Odysseus remarks at the beginning of the storm. Much better, he says, to have died where "the spears flew thickest" at Troy; then he would have had "recognition," *kleos.* People would know about him and his death. Odysseus does not wish he were back with Calypso. Though she offered immortality, not death—and immortality of security and satisfaction in a charming cave—it is still an immortality of oblivion, of no *kleos,* of nonentity. Leaving Calypso is very like leaving the perfect security and satisfaction of the womb; but, as the Cyclops reminds us, the womb is after all a deadly place. In the womb one has no identity, no existence worthy of a name. Nonentity and identity are in fact the poles between which the actors in the poem move. It is a choice between Scylla and Charybdis—to face deliberately certain trouble from the jaws of the six-headed goddess, or to be engulfed entirely by the maelstrom. One must odysseus and be odysseused, or else be calypsoed.

Odysseus did not always live up to his name. There was one occasion when oblivion seemed almost preferable to trouble. His name seemed to have lost its magic. Hence his failure with the Laestrygonians, and the necessity of winning back his identity in the Circe episode.

While we remember Polyphemus ("Much-fame") in connection with Odysseus, we are very apt to forget Antiphates ("Against-renown"), the Laestrygonian king. In the Laestrygonian affair Odysseus himself avoids the encounter, and loses his whole fleet. In this, his least creditable adventure, he never makes his identity felt. The Laestrygonians don't know who he is, or care. Yet Odysseus survives. With poetic rather than nautical logic, he escapes by virtue of having left his ship in an exposed position, while the rest of the fleet trusts itself to the security of the fiord and is lost.

Odysseus in the land of the Laestrygonians is not the Odysseus whom we saw with the Cyclops, though in both cases he has to do with cannibal giants. Avoiding the encounter here is perhaps as sensible as avoiding the Planctae, but there are other reasons why Odysseus is not up to it. In the interim, as we have said, his name has lost its magic. "Trouble," intended to mean success, has seemed to be failure. Aeolus has listened with interest to the tale of prowess at Troy and has sent Odysseus on his way, insuring that he will have, for once, a remarkably painless trip. But in sight of the goal, trouble strikes. Aeolus, seeing in this a sign that heaven is inveterately hostile to Odysseus, banishes him from his sight. Such trouble means to Aeolus not identity, but oblivion. Odysseus himself has nearly reached a similar conclusion. Since leaving Troy he has sacked Ismarus in characteristically ruthless fashion and rejected the passive peace of Lotus-land. By handling the situation in a manner worthy of Autolycus, he has been able to cry his name in defiance of Polyphemus. He has come within sight of his home. He has done all this only to find his achievement undone at the first relaxation of his mistrustful watchfulness. Small wonder that success on these terms should seem impossible. As the winds sped Odysseus out of sight of Ithaca, "I debated," he says, "whether to leap from my ship and end it all in the sea" (embracing thus the "vile death" of the Calypso episode), "or whether to bear my misery and remain among the living." He adopts a sort of compromise: "I endured and I remained; *kalypsamenos* I lay in my ship," he puts it, meaning that he had wrapped his head in his cloak. This is the Odysseus who fails to confront Antiphates.

After the discouragement of the Aeolus episode, it is natural that life's difficulties should appear as insuperable as the Laestrygonians; but Odysseus will find the courage to go on. After the Laestrygonian experience his depression is shared by his men. Two days they all lie in weariness and woe on Circe's beach. But against this sea of troubles Odysseus takes arms, a spear and a sword. As he once killed a boar, he now kills a stag. This puts heart in Odysseus' men: "dis-calypsoed" (*ek de kalypsamenoi)* they revive. Odysseus now makes a remarkable speech:

> Friends, we don't know where the darkness is, or where the dawn; where the sun that shines for mortals rises, or where it sets. Still let us quickly consider whether any resource can still be found. I for one don't think so.

The point, as Odysseus goes on to suggest, is whether they must indeed make themselves known and ask the inhabitants of the island for their route, perilous though it has proved to confront Polyphemus and Antiphates. In other words, shall they turn their backs on the comparative security of their present oblivion? Characteristically, this wider implication is stressed by a pun—a blatant pun which has been used before, in the Cyclops passage. "Whether any resource can still be found," sounds in Greek almost precisely like "Whether any of us is going to go on being nobody." "I for one don't think so," is Odysseus' comment. They have been "nobody" for some time, in fact ever since Aeolus refused to recognize their claims as human beings. This cannot go on, as the pun implies. The time has come when Odysseus must stand and be recognized.

Without taking account of the pun, critics have interpreted this passage as Odysseus at the end of his human resources, about to apply for divine aid. The moly plant, soon to be granted, becomes for them almost a symbol of grace. This is fair enough in its way. Identity in the *Odyssey* is in some sense a gift of the gods. But "from the gods who sit in grandeur, grace comes somehow violent." [2] Odysseus doesn't pray for grace; he exacts it, first by killing the stag and then by threatening Circe and forcing her to swear to do him no harm. Hermes, Autolycus' patron, puts him up to the threatening, but it is quite in accord with Odysseus' name and nature anyhow. We remember the oaths exacted from Helen and Calypso. In the present instance Odysseus remains nobody, a denatured wolf or lion like Circe's other victims, until, sword to throat, he makes her recognize him and speak his name. Prior to this, despite the introductory formula "he took my hand and spoke my name," Hermes had not named the hero; he only named his passive aspect, *O dystēne* "poor wretch." But with the gift of moly, "black at the root, but with a flower like milk," Hermes seems to restore the magic of the name of Odysseus. However black its first effects, it will ultimately flower with balm and solace. Though she "struck [him] with her rod and named" him, Circe gives Odysseus no name at all until the hero seems "like one eager to kill her"; once having recognized him as "Odysseus *polytropos*" however, she uses his name every chance she gets, four times with full titles: "Zeus-sprung son of Laertes, expedient Odysseus." By choosing to live

[2] Aeschylus, *Agamemnon* 182-3; Lattimore's translation.

up to his name with Circe, Odysseus restored its magic; he had to in order to get anywhere, and so to be anybody, at all.

For Odysseus to choose to pursue the path of his painful identity as he did on Circe's beach, is to win power over, and recognition from, that ambiguous daughter of Sun, the life-giver, and Ocean, the all-engulfing. It is also to accept pain as the only real basis of meaning in this life or the next. This is the secret of Tiresias.

To achieve the goal of recognition and identity, and to learn the secrets of the abyss, are equally to row upon the sea of trouble. This is the meaning of the apparently witless question, "What ship brought you to Ithaca, for I do not think you came on foot," and of Anticleia's first words to her son in the underworld:

> My child, how did you come beneath the misty dark, alive as you are? It is hard for the living to get a sight of all this. For in between are great rivers and dreadful streams, first Ocean, which there is no way to cross on foot, if one does not have a well-built ship.

But with Aeolus the question arose, is such sea-faring endurable? To ask this question is "to enquire of Tiresias" (*Teiresiēs* in Homer); for Tiresias' name is the weariness of rowing. *"TEIReto d' andrōn thymos hyp' EIRESIÉS alegeinēs,"* Odysseus says of his crew after Aeolus denied them: "*Worn* was my men's spirit by the woeful *rowing*." To enquire of Tiresias is to ask the meaning of trouble.

This is why Odysseus is not so much interested in what the prophet has to say of the troubled future—"You seek homecoming sweet as honey, noble Odysseus; heaven will make it hard for you"—as he is in recognition, in the meaning of his own painful and pain-producing existence:

> Doubtless the gods had all that in store for me. But tell me: I see here the shade of my dead mother; she sits in silence near the blood, and has not the strength to look her son in the face or speak to him. Tell me, lord, how might she recognize the man I am?

His mother's recognition contains a blow. It was Odysseus' sweet nature, she says, that killed her. Thus it appears that even in his gentlest aspect, Odysseus gives pain. He is, after all, soft as well as hard. The predatory brooch, dog throttling fawn, pinned on him by Penelope as he left for Troy, is coupled with a second mark of identification, equally important: the shirt which gleamed on his body

> like the skin of a dried onion—so gentle it was to the touch, and at the same time bright, like the sun; many were the women who admired it.

Yet Odysseus' soft side can be as painful, or as fatal, as his hardness. The love, not the hate he inspired, killed the dog Argus and wasted Penelope's nights in tears. Anticleia recognized at least part of her son's nature by dying for the love of him.

Agamemnon, dead by no sweet nature, but rather by the treacherous hand of his wife, also recognizes Odysseus; despite Penelope's virtue, he had better not, Agamemnon thinks in contrast to Anticleia, tell his wife everything. Neither of these recognitions, neither the first, evoking the hero's sweetness, nor the second, calling upon his guile, can bring Odysseus much comfort as to the value of life as Trouble. Achilles on the other hand makes it clear that it is something to be alive at all, and furthermore his concern for his son's prowess reminds us that Telemachus too, promises to become a credit to his father. Still, neither simple existence, nor existence continued through a worthy son, is of the essence. Ajax' silence, though eloquently expressive of the power of Odysseus as injurer, is discouraging; but the climax of recognition is reached when Heracles, whose "seeming" is hell's own picture of hostile ferocity, but whose reality "dwells in bliss among the immortals," equates Odysseus to himself:

> One look was enough to tell Heracles who I was, and he greeted me in mournful tones. "Zeus-sprung son of Laertes, expedient Odysseus—unhappy man! So you too are working out some such miserable doom as I was slave to when the sun shone over my head. Son of Zeus though I was, unending troubles came my way. . . . a master far beneath my rank . . . sent me down here to bring away the Hound of Hell. And under the guiding hands of Hermes and bright-eyed Athene, I did succeed in capturing him and I dragged him out of Hades realm."

Not just Heracles, but all these people (except Ajax) explicitly recognize Odysseus; still excepting Ajax, all but Anticleia, who appropriately calls him "my child," use Odysseus' full titles. Each sees him differently, and to a greater or less degree, truly. To all of them he means, in one way or another, pain. To Anticleia he is the pain of a lost child; Agamemnon connects him with the pain and betrayal that marriage may bring; Achilles is reminded of the ultimate pain of being dead, Ajax of wounded honor. Heracles sees in him the "unending troubles" of life under the sun. For the secret of life which Odysseus has come to the realms of the dead to discover is the necessity of pain, and its value. The generations of woman ("and each proclaimed her bringing-forth") may be for good or ill, involving Zeus or Poseidon indifferently. Man's fate may seem to be Tantalus' endless craving, never satisfied; or Sisyphus' endless striving, never successful: life's basis may even be Tityus' vultures, a great gnawing in a great belly, as Odysseus several times suggests (VII, 216-21; XV, 343-4; XVII, 286-9; XVIII, 53-4). Yet Minos continues to pass his judgments, and Orion to pursue his quarry. Heracles has his heavenly, as well as his hellish aspect—and so does Odysseus, "Trouble."

Ajax feels only Odysseus' hellish side, but Heracles implies that a life of pain, given and received, snatches something from Death himself. This is the secret of Tiresias, the answer to the weariness of rowing. To know himself as Trouble, and to be so known by others, is the only way for Odysseus to possess his identity.

There is no human identity in other terms than pain. To escape Calypso, Odysseus needs a ship (IV,559-60; V,16-7), and so must accept the weariness of rowing. To see life in any other way is to live in a dream-world, as the Cyclopes do, and the Phaeacians. To avoid trouble, the Phaeacians withdrew, we are told, from their ancestral conflict with the Cyclopes. The conflict is indeed ancestral, for the Cyclopes are as savage as the Phaeacians are civilized; but both are out of touch with reality. Polyphemus thinks he can act with impunity, "for we are much mightier than the gods," but he succumbs to Trouble in the shape of a clever "weakling" and a skin of wine. The Phaeacians on the contrary trust in their piety. Nausicaa thinks that no one could possibly come "bringing enmity, for we are dear to the gods." This she says of Odysseus, Enmity himself. To her, he is either an object of pity or a dream come true:

> Doubtless she has picked up some castaway from his ship [she thinks of someone as remarking of her], a foreign man, since there is nobody like that nearby [or "those nearby are nobodies"], or else in answer to her hopes a god, long prayed-for (*polyarētos*), has come down from heaven to keep her all her days.

Eurycleia's "Polyaretus" fits Odysseus in the sense that his return to Ithaca in his hostile might is something to pray for, but he is not what Nausicaa would pray that he be. Nausicaa is victimized by her too trusting love for him, and his visit is ultimately disastrous for her people. The *Odyssey* has its dream-worlds, and, "near to gods," Scheria is one of them. Its queen, "whose name is Prayed-for" (*Arētē d'onom' estin epōnymon*), suggests her antonym, Odysseus, who, the poem later tells us, might have been Polyaretus, but was not. "So let his name be Trouble" (*to d' Odysseus onom' estin epōnymon*), Autolycus will say in the nineteenth book.

Odysseus no more can exist in the dream-world of Alcinous and Arete, where woman rules man and rowing is no trouble, than he can with Calypso. In a world without trouble love must be as little serious as the affair of Ares and Aphrodite. With Nausicaa there is no scope for the relationship which Odysseus describes to her:

> There is nothing nobler or more admirable than when two people who see eye to eye keep house as man and wife, *confounding their enemies* and delighting their friends, as they themselves know better than anyone.

How can love be really felt, without pain? Therefore, after arriving exhausted, naked, and unknown on Scheria, Odysseus must somehow so impress the inhabitants that they will send him on his way, neither killing him as enemy nor overmuch befriending him and settling him down with Nausicaa. This he accomplishes primarily by means of his well-advertised Tale of Woe. It is received with mingled horror and fascination. Avid for its miseries the Phaeacians certainly are. This supports our impression that their dream-world, lacking pain, is human life *manqué*. On the other hand, after the simile of the woman led into captivity, it is easy to assume Phaeacian feelings of horror at Odysseus' brutal account of the Sack of Ismarus. The recognition accorded the tale is equivocal: "Phaeacians," Arete asks during the intermission, "what do you think of this man, his size and strength and wit?" A dubious answer is implied in Alcinous' polite comment:

> O Odysseus, when we look at you we don't find you a bit like a liar and thief, [or "your *Outis* looks to us like a liar and thief"] such as the black earth produces in such far-flung numbers—thieves piling lie on lie, and where they get them all from nobody knows; your words are charming, there is good sense in them, and you tell your story as skillfully as a bard, the grim sufferings of yourself and all the Argives.

After all Odysseus has shown himself to be a pirate, and it is worth noting that Alcinous' remarks occur half-way through the story of the underworld, before the value of pain is established. But for the Phaeacians this is never established. Their rowing is without drudgery, for all their sea-faring. At the end of the tale Alcinous will tell the guest he once thought of as a son-in-law that he is sure he will never come back. One doesn't quite know whether the Phaeacians are bestowing on Odysseus more wealth than he won at Troy in recognition of his exploits, or as an invitation to leave the country; for it was Odysseus' stated willingness to stay a year that brought forth Alcinous' remarks about liars and thieves. In Odysseus the Phaeacians enjoy Trouble vicariously, but ultimately dismiss him. We may be pretty sure that, for their "painless escorting of strangers," Poseidon's threat to "surround (*amphikalypsai*) their city with mountains" will come off. Just as he turned their ship to stone, he will bar them from the sea, and therefore from any chance of future identity. The price of no trouble is oblivion.

Tiresias implies three modes of pain: first, pain administered, like the slaying of the boar and stag, or the blinding of Polyphemus. Odysseus, Tiresias predicts, will kill the suitors. Second, there is the pain of the resisted impulse. Odysseus must restrain his predatory impulses when he comes upon the Cattle of the Sun. Third, to plant the oar, the symbol of the weariness of rowing, among those "who do not know the sea, nor eat their food mixed with salt, nor know of red-prowed ships, nor balanced oars, which are a vessel's wings" is to introduce the idea of trouble to those who, like the Phaeacians, are not sufficiently aware of it. In establishing his identity, Odysseus must use these three modes of pain.

It is sufficiently clear how administering pain by killing the suitors and threatening their kinsmen with annihilation serves to establish Odysseus in Ithaca. The second mode is subtler. It would seem a denial of Odysseus' name for him to boggle at a little cattle-rustling. That he does so leads some to suppose that his adventures are intended to purge him of the brutalizing effects of the Trojan campaign and bring him home readjusted to civilian life. But the temptation of the Cattle of the Sun is more like the temptation of the Lotus than like the Sack of Ismarus. It is a temptation not to crime but to oblivion. To fall for it is the typical weakness of the "innocent" crew, as the proem suggests. Faced with the Planctae, the Reefs of Hard Knocks, they drop their oars. Knowing the mortal danger in eating the Sun's cattle, they do not know it thoroughly enough to forego the immediate satisfaction of eating when they are hungry. Forgetful of homecoming and identity itself, they eat. Of all that band only Odysseus can resist such impulses and hang on interminably, as he does clinging to the fig tree above Charybdis, refusing to drop and be comfortably engulfed.

Odysseus is a master of the delayed response, of the long way round, of the resisted impulse. That is the reason he is able to keep his identity intact. It is courting oblivion to rush blindly into love, as Nausicaa did, and as Penelope, even when reunited with her husband, did not. In Circe's bed, Odysseus would have become just another denatured wolf or lion, if he had not first with a show of hostility made sure of his integrity. As in love, so with eating. Man is a predatory animal; to eat he must kill; but he must know what he is doing. He must not, like the crew and the suitors, take life as a table spread before him, insufficiently aware of the presence of enemies.

He must not even take life as a song, though the episode of the Sirens suggests that this is the most irresistible of impulses. The Phaeacians are certainly not proof against it. Alcinous may think that the meaning of life's pain is that

> the gods were responsible for that, weaving catastrophe into the pattern of events to make a song for future generations,

but pain must be experienced, not just enjoyed as after-dinner entertainment. Therefore the Phaeacians are victimized by Odysseus' Tale of Woe. Odysseus on the other hand is proof against the Sirens and their singing of "all things that happen on this fruitful earth," just as he is against the Lotus and against Circe. He is steadfast in enduring Tiresias' second mode of pain, the pain of the resisted impulse.

"The steadfast," says a priest in *Murder in the Cathedral,* "can manipulate the greed and lust of others, the feeble is devoured by his own." This leads us from the second mode of pain to the third—introducing the idea of trouble to those insufficiently aware of it. Odysseus in his steadfastness knows the pain of the thirst for life, the danger it leads to, and the trouble involved in successfully gratifying it. He knows it so well ("he saw the cities of many men, and knew their mind"), that he can use this knowledge in manipulating others, for the purpose of getting himself recognized as Trouble. One picture of this is Odysseus in the underworld, sword in hand, controlling the access of the ghosts to the blood. Manipulating the Phaeacians chiefly through their itching ears, he introduces himself to them as Trouble, and wins survival and homecoming. In the second half of the poem, using his lying tales, his wife, and the good things of his house as bait, he maneuvers the upholders and the defilers of his household alike into a position where, bow in hand and arrow on string, like Heracles in the underworld, he can make himself really felt.

For Odysseus to establish his identity at home, manipulation is necessary, manipulation even of those who favor him. It is difficult to get people to accept pain. Even the suitors do not dispute that he was a good king; unfortunately this is not enough to maintain his position in Ithaca. He must get both his pleasant and his hostile aspect recognized at the same time. When they finally are, near the end of the last book, this is signalized by the curious salutation of Dolius, the last to join forces with him: *oule te kai mala chaire,* he says, "hail and rejoice!" But *oule* is an exceedingly rare word, and its auditory suggestions of *oulos* "baneful," and *oulē,* the famous scar, will be felt—something like "Bane and Weal!" For the scar which the boar gave him is in particular the mark of Odysseus as Trouble. Anticleia ("Opposed-to-fame"), in her recognition of her son in the underworld, did not seem to understand the scar's full meaning, but it is easy for Eurycleia ("Far-fame") to accept it. After touching the scar as she washed his feet,

> joy and pain seized upon Eurycleia at the same time; her eyes filled with tears, and the voice caught in her throat. Touching his chin she said to Odysseus: "Surely you are Odysseus, dear child—and I didn't know my master until I had felt all of him!"

Eurycleia knows both aspects. It is she who has to be restrained from howling in triumph over the dead suitors. Telemachus is not much of a problem either. "I am no god;" Odysseus says, "Why do you think I am an immortal? No, I am your father, for whom you groan and suffer so much pain, accepting the insults of your fellows." Telemachus' difficulty is to determine whether Trouble is a miserable wretch in filthy rags or a very god for splendor. We have met this ambiguity before in the double nature of Heracles.

Penelope's recognition is harder to win. She knows Odysseus' soft garment, and her own hands pinned on him the badge of the dog and fawn; but the predatory side of him she cannot accept. Troy is to her not a great and necessary exploit, but something he merely "went to see," and for this she cannot forgive him. To her Troy is not a source of renown, but "Evil Ilium, not to be named." If Odysseus' manipulation, or his knowledge of the mind of man ever fails, it is with her. In their false-recognition scene, his riddle-name is *Aithōn,* the "blaze" which melts her (XIX,204-9) but which she cannot face (XIX,478). In spite of all the help her disguised husband can give her, she reacts to her dream of the eagle, Odysseus, killing her geese, the suitors, not by preparing for his "return," but by deciding, at last, to give him up for good. After the suitors are dead, and Odysseus has had his bath, she still holds out. Even the appeal to her desire as a woman, effective though it was with Calypso, Nausicaa, and Circe, doesn't work; Odysseus, it appears, will have to sleep alone. In exasperation he asks who moved his bed. In spite of all he has done to make permanent their marriage and the symbol of it, he still cannot tell, he admits, "whether it still stands or whether by now someone has moved it elsewhere, and cut through the trunk of the olive." By this bed and by this exasperation she knows him; flinging her arms around his neck, "Odysseus, don't scold me," she cries, giving him his true name at last. Later, she will accept trouble in more detail. The "immeasurable toil" still to come, none other than the planting of Tiresias' oar, she elects to hear of immediately, though in the first book, after ten years, she could not bear to hear the bard singing of the return from Troy. In the end she takes delight in hearing "all the woes Zeus-sprung Odysseus inflicted on others, and all he himself toiled and suffered." She has accepted the meaning of the name of Odysseus.

Tiresias implied that to win identity one must administer pain, resist all impulses to ignore it, and plant the idea of it in the minds of others. Hence the curious behavior of the hero in making himself known to Laertes. Checking his own tears and resisting the impulse to "kiss his father and embrace him, and tell him all, how he had come and was back at home," Odysseus instead teases the suffering old man with the pain of the loss of his son. This is the pain which killed Anticleia, but it now serves to make clear to Laertes and Odysseus what they mean to each other.

Laertes knows Odysseus by his scar, but also by some fruit trees, given to Odysseus as a boy, which the old man is still tending for him. There is something obviously fruitful in the pain of this relationship between father and son, and the sense of the boar-hunt exploit is there too, especially when later the old man delights to see "son and grandson vying in prowess" in the fight with the suitors' kinsmen. The fruitfulness of trouble has been hinted all along, particularly by the image of the olive. There is the double olive thicket which shelters the hero, naked and alone on Scheria; the green olive stake which puts out Polyphemus' eye; and notably the great olive trunk which makes one corner of Odysseus' bed. The recurrent phrase, *kaka phyteuein* "to plant evils," points to the same fruitfulness. Therefore we can be sure that the life of pain contemplated in the *Odyssey* is fruitful, not sadistic. The ultimate object is recognition and the sense of one's own existence, not the pain itself. The pain necessary to win recognition may be as slight as the show of anger to Penelope, or as great as the blinding of Polyphemus, but in some degree pain will be necessary. Nothing less than the death of 108 suitors (to say nothing of the faithless maids), and the readiness to kill the suitors' kinsmen, will get Odysseus recognized in Ithaca. Once recognition is achieved, however, pain is pointless. At the very end of the poem, Odysseus "swooping like an eagle" on the fleeing ranks of the suitors' adherents, "might have killed them all." Then, "Zeus-sprung son of Laertes, expedient Odysseus, stop!" Athene cries, ". . . lest Zeus be angry at you." The daughter of Zeus herself, as Circe and others have done before her, now hails Odysseus with the rolling epithets of his full titles. Killing beyond the point of this recognition would anger Zeus, would violate the nature of things. But has Zeus not been angry all along at the hero "who received so many buffets, once he had sacked the sacred citadel of Troy?" No. The universe is full of hostility, it includes Poseidon, but it is not ultimately hostile. Zeus has been showing Odysseus not anger, but a terrible fondness, to echo Athene's words quoted early in this paper.

It is thus that the *Odyssey* solves the problem of evil, which it raised at line 62 of the first book. "Excessive suffering," says Zeus, or words to that effect, "is due to folly." "So it is," replies Athene; "but what about Odysseus? Why do you odysseus him so, Zeus?" It is a good question; Zeus admits that Odysseus is the wisest of mankind; yet he permits Poseidon to persecute him. It is a good question, and it contains its own answer. In exposing Odysseus to Poseidon, in allowing him to do and suffer, Zeus is odysseusing Odysseus, giving him his identity. In accepting the implications of his name, Trouble, Odysseus establishes his identity in harmony with the nature of things. In the ultimate sense he is "Zeus-sprung," one whose existence is rooted in life itself.

The Untypical Hero

by W. B. Stanford

There is nothing freakish about Odysseus' personality in the Homeric poems. In the *Iliad* Homer endows him with the normal qualities of an Achaean hero—princely birth, good physique, strength, skill in athletics and battle, courage, energy, and eloquence.[1] But in most of these Odysseus is surpassed or equalled by some of his colleagues at Troy. The Atridae and Aeacids are of more illustrious lineage. Agamemnon and Menelaus are of more impressive stature. Achilles and Ajax surpass him in strength and force of arms. Diomedes is more gallant and dashing in battle. Even in oratory he is not unrivalled.

The fact is, of course, that Odysseus is not the chief hero of the *Iliad*. Achilles, and after him Ajax, Hector, Diomedes, and the Atridae, are

[1] For studies of Odysseus' general characteristics in Homer see especially Alexander Shewan, *The Lay of Dolon* (London, 1911), chapter twenty (containing a survey of older views); W. D. Geddes, *The Problem of the Homeric Poems* (London, 1878) (subject to Shewan's corrections); and A. Lang, *Homer and the Epic* (London, 1893), chapter eight; besides the less discursive surveys in Pauly, Wissowa, Kroll, *Real-Encyclopädie der classischen Altertumswissenshaft* (Stuttgart), and W. H. Roscher, *Ausführliches Lexicon der Griechischen und Römischen Mythologie*, vol. iii (Leipzig, 1897-1902), s.v. *Odysseus* (by J. Schmidt). Shewan, p. 150, quoting Wolf and Mure, argues effectively against Wilamowitz's early view that it is foolish to talk of a single Homeric Odysseus. Mure remarks elsewhere (*Critical History of the Language and Literature of Ancient Greece* [London, 1854-67] I, 412) "Like the fabulous Lycian sphinx, which combined the nature of the lion and serpent with its own proper body of Chimaera, Ulysses, whether the king, the beggar, the warrior, or the traveler, is still in word and deed Ulysses": cf. R. Hole, *An Essay on the Character of Ulysses as Delineated by Homer* (London, 1807), pp. 143-4: "the more minutely it [Ulysses' character] is examined, the more evidently we find that the design, however bold, is exceeded by the happiness of the execution."

Since this was written I have seen two other notable discussions of Homer's conception of Odysseus: Hubert Schrade, *Götter und Menschen Homers* (Stuttgart, 1952), pp. 225-59, in which Odysseus is characterized as the first *uomo universale*, a prototype in some respects of the Sophists, but differing from them in his all-pervading piety; and E. Beaujon, *Acte et passion du héros* (Geneva, 1948), in which some new symbolical interpretations of Odysseus are examined.

more prominent.[2] Not that the *Iliad* presents Odysseus as a minor hero: he has his triumphs in the council and in the assembly, on the field of battle and in the athletic contests. But his unique personality is not allowed to divert attention from the *Iliad*'s main themes, the wrath of Achilles and the death of Hector. On the other hand, in the *Odyssey* he, "the man of many turns," is the main theme, and his personal qualities become specially luminous against the sordidness of his environment, as he makes his way among foolish shipmates, ruthless monsters, and greedy usurpers. Yet here, too, Odysseus meets his equals at times. Eumaeus the swineherd shows a loyalty and gentle courtesy quite as fine as his, and Penelope is wily enough to outwit him in their final recognition scene.

By endowing Odysseus with a share of the normal heroic qualities Homer avoided any suggestion that he was an eccentric figure or a narrowly limited type. But at the same time Homer, especially in the *Iliad*, skilfully succeeded in distinguishing Odysseus by slight deviations from the norm in almost every heroic feature. In his ancestry there was the unique Autolycan element. In physique he had the unusually short legs and long torso described by Antenor and Helen in *Il.* III, 190ff. He reminded Helen of a sturdy ram, she said, as he marshalled the Achaean ranks. Any hint of the ludicrous in this comparison is removed by Antenor's subsequent description of Odysseus' imposing presence. But there is something a little unaristocratic, or at least non-Achaean, in this portrait, contrasting with the tall, long-limbed stature of the other heroes.[3]

[2] Odysseus admits inferiority in martial valor to Achilles (*Iliad* XIX, 217ff.) while claiming superiority in intelligence, which he tactfully attributes to his greater age. (See additional note below.) The common soldiers rated Ajax, Diomedes, and Agamemnon as fighters next to Achilles (*Il.* VII, 179-80). Hyginus, 114, gives statistics of the "kills" recorded by the Greek champions: Achilles leads with 72, followed by Teucer (30) and Ajax (28). Odysseus is second last with 12 to Menelaus' 8. Lang (*Anthropology and the Classics* [Oxford, 1908], pp. 60-61; cf. *The World of Homer* [London, 1910], p. 250) holds that it "would not be hard to show that Odysseus is really the hero of the *Iliad*, as well as of the *Odyssey*, the man whom the poet admires most . . ." (one may admit the second view without agreeing with the first: a poet's hero is not necessarily the same as his poem's hero). Against this see also Werner Jaeger, *Paideia*, English edn., vol. i (Oxford, 1939), p. 7, where Achilles is viewed as the golden mean between the rigid Ajax and the slippery Odysseus, and M. H. van der Valk on "Ajax and Diomede in the *Iliad*," *Mnemosyne* v (1952), 269-86. But taking the two poems together Homer certainly merits the title φιλοδυσσεύς, which Eustathius (on *Odyssey* XIX, 583) gives him.

[3] Athene's other great favorite, Tydeus, was also a low-sized man (*Il.* V, 801). Other details of Odysseus' appearance in Homer: he had the normal fair or auburn (ξάνθος) hair of an Achaean hero, but possibly with a dark beard (see Eustathius on *Od.* VI, 230, and XVI, 176, and my note on *Od.* XVI, 175-6), darting, lively eyes (*Od.* IV, 150), expressive eyebrows (*Od.* IX, 468; XII, 194; XXI, 431), large, fine thighs, broad shoulders and chest, powerful arms (*Od.* XVIII, 67-9). See additional note below. Roscher, col. 639, gives details of post-Homeric descriptions. Many of them present a despicable conception of a hero, e.g. suggestions by Tzetzes and Isaac Porphyrogennetos that he was pot-bellied and Philostratus' that he was snub-nosed: but we can probably attribute carica-

Napoleon would have looked like that beside Wellington; or Cuchulain, that "short, dark man," among the taller champions of the Red Branch Knights. Possibly Homer meant to imply something more than a personal peculiarity here. It may be intended as an indication of some racial difference between Odysseus and the other Achaeans. Perhaps—but it is a pure guess—Homer regarded Odysseus as being partly a survival of the pre-Greek stock in Greece, an "Aegean" or "Mediterranean" type.[4] At any rate, the physical difference serves to mark Odysseus out as exceptional, without giving an impression of ugliness, oddity, or deformity.[5]

One finds the same distinction in a quite different kind of trait—in Odysseus' unusually frank and realistic remarks on the importance of food in human life. All the Homeric heroes were hearty eaters and drinkers. But, whether by accident or convention, none of them except Odysseus had anything notable to say about eating. Perhaps it was regarded as a plebeian subject, unfit for high-born Achaeans; or perhaps they simply were not interested in it as a subject for conversation. It was typical of the average Homeric hero that he was prepared on occasion to ignore the need for food, both for himself and for others. The contrast with Odysseus' attitude is well illustrated in a scene between him and Achilles in *Iliad* XIX. Achilles, now equipped with new armor and ready for battle, is impatient to launch a general attack against the Trojans to take vengeance for Patroclus' death. Odysseus objects. The Greek soldiers have been kept awake all night in lamenting Patroclus and in preparing his body for burial. The Trojans, on the contrary, have been able to enjoy a quiet supper and a night's rest. Odysseus, not being blinded by personal feeling like Achilles, knows that unless soldiers get a good meal first they will not be able to fight all day: even if they are eager to continue the battle, "yet their limbs are treacherously weighed down as hunger and thirst overtake them, and their knees fail them as they go." There is both compassionate understanding and Napoleonic common sense here: the spirit may be willing, but the flesh is weak; an army marches on its stomach. Odysseus adds some further remarks on the strengthening and cheering effect of food and wine, and ends by demanding that the army should have a full meal before being ordered to attack.

Achilles' reply to Odysseus' reasonable objection is characteristic: "*You* go and busy yourselves with food: *I* shall not touch a morsel until Patroclus is avenged. And, let me tell you, if I were in supreme command,

---

tures like this to general anti-Ulyssean prejudice. Lycophron's description of him as "the dwarf" (*Alexandra,* 1242ff.) is a good example of propagandist distortion of a Homeric description. See also Tzetzes, *Homerica* 382-3, 626-30, 672-3.

[4] As in Patroni's elaborate but insubstantial theories on Odysseus before Homer. Patroni believes that there is even some surreptitious anti-Achaean propaganda in the Homeric poems, Homer, too, being of Mediterranean race.

[5] Contrast Homer's indication of the positive ugliness of Thersites (*Il.* II, 216-19) and Dolon (*Il.* X, 316).

the whole army would have to fight fasting, too, till sunset. Then, with vengeance achieved, we should have a great supper." What is one to call such arrogant confidence as this—with no thought of fatigue or death, no consideration for himself or for others? Is it heroic, or is it schoolboyish? Is it superb singleness of purpose or callow rashness? Odysseus in his reply deftly and gently suggests that youthful heedlessness is partly, at least, to blame. Addressing Achilles with great deference as "Much the mightiest of the Achaeans" he admits his own inferiority to him in martial valor. But he claims definite superiority in thinking things out. Then after an appeal to Achilles to listen patiently for a moment (Odysseus clearly wants to avoid provoking Achilles' wrath again in any way: but he insists on making his point about the need for food), he emphasizes the danger of fatigue in war, and mildly ridicules Achilles' notion that fasting is a good way for warriors to mourn those slain in battle. Bury the dead with pitiless heart, bewail them for a day, yes—but those who survive must eat to get energy for punishing the enemy. Odysseus is trying to persuade Achilles to eat with the others. If Achilles fights fasting against a well-fed Hector, even Achilles may be conquered. Odysseus' arguments fail, as in the Embassy scene, to overcome Achilles' passionate resolve. But, significantly, Athene intervenes later, at Zeus' request, and feeds Achilles with nectar and ambrosia "so that," the poet remarks, "joyless hunger should not reach his knees." Thus obliquely Homer, Athene, and Zeus agree with Odysseus' advice.

But the typical Homeric hero would probably have admired Achilles' intransigence more than Odysseus' more practical policy. One does in fact find an indication elsewhere in the *Iliad* that Odysseus had already got a reputation for being too much interested in the pleasures of eating. In *Iliad* IV, 343-6, Agamemnon accuses Odysseus and the Athenian Menestheus of being quick to hear invitations to a feast, but slow to answer the call to arms. Odysseus emphatically denies any reluctance to join the fight, but he passes over the accusation of unusual alacrity in coming to feasts. Probably he thought it beneath contempt. Yet, as in Agamemnon's accompanying accusation of evil deceitfulness, it may well be that Homer intends us to catch a glimpse here of a general tendency to regard Odysseus as rather more partial to good fare than a hero should have been.

This is uncertain. But there is no uncertainty about the attitude of post-Homeric writers. Attic comedians, fourth-century philosophers, Alexandrian critics, late classical chroniclers, agree in accusing Odysseus of greed and gluttony.[6] They based their slanders chiefly on some of his

[6] For references to Odysseus' appetite in Attic comedy see Johannes Schmidt, "Ulixes Comicus," *Jahrbücher für Class. Phil.* Suppl. vol. 1888, 361ff. For philosophical criticism see n. 7 below. Alexandrian depreciations will be discussed in chapter nine. Among late writers Athenaeus accuses him bluntly of gluttony and greed (*Deipnosophists* 412 b-d

actions and remarks in the *Odyssey* which, considered out of their contexts, certainly do give a bad impression. Thus in *Od.* VI, 250, Odysseus eats "greedily." In *Od.* VII, 215-18 he asks Alcinous to let him go on with his supper without interruption, remarking that there is no more shameful compulsion than that of "the abominable belly" which compels even a mourner to eat and forget his grief for a while. In *Od.* IX, 1ff., after the Phaeacians have given him a splendid banquet, Odysseus pronounces that he knows of no more beautiful consummation in life than a feast with good food, good wine, good song, and general good cheer. Later, after his arrival in Ithaca, when still in his beggar's disguise, Odysseus returns to the theme of hunger and appetite. He tells Eumaeus that it is for the sake of "the accursed belly" that vagabonds are compelled to suffer all the hardships of wandering from place to place (*Od.* XV, 344-5). Later he tells Eumaeus again (*Od.* XVII, 286-9) that in his opinion it is impossible to conceal the "accursed belly" when it is in its full fury: it brings many evils to men, and for its sake men sail the barren seas to attack their enemies. Soon afterwards (vv. 473-4) he attributes a violent assault by Antinous to the promptings of his "baneful accursed belly." In the following book he pretends that he wants to attack the rival beggar, Irus, at the behest of "the evil-working belly" (XVIII, 53-4), but repudiates a suggestion by a suitor (XVIII, 362-4) that he was good for nothing but gross eating (XVIII, 376-81).

If one remembers that no other hero in the *Iliad,* nor any Homeric heroine in either poem, even uses the word for "belly" and still less discusses its effects, it is clear that Odysseus is an untypical hero in this respect. And it is obvious how easy it was for comic writers to portray him as a glutton, courtly critics as a crudely indelicate eater, and philosophers as a confirmed voluptuary, by concentrating on a few passages out of their contexts. Thus Plato was shocked at Odysseus' praise of banquets, as being one of the finest "consummations" in life.[7] But surely

---

and 513 a-d), alleging that even Sardanapalus would not have made Odysseus' remark in *Od.* VII, 219ff., "But my belly ever bids me eat and drink and makes me forget what I have suffered and bids me fill it up." Athenaeus ignores that fact that Odysseus is speaking of the effect of extreme hunger, not of any Sardanapalan cravings. Lucian (*Tragodopodagra* v, 261-2) alleges that Odysseus died of gout as the result of over indulgence. Cf. Eustathius on *Od.* XVIII, 55, and the scholia on *Od.* VII, 216.

[7] *Republic* 390B. Probably what most provoked philosophers in Odysseus' praise of banquets was his use of the word τέλος which later came to mean something like the *summum bonum*. Even Heracleitus Ponticus, that staunch champion of Homer against Platonic carpings, felt that Odysseus' remark could only be justified on the grounds that he was not himself but only "the remnant (λείψανον) of Poseidon's wrath" when he said it (*Homeric Allegories,* 79). With Plato's view cf. Lucian, *De parasit.* 10, where he takes Odysseus' remarks as praise of the parasite's life. According to Athenaeus 513a, Odysseus' remarks were explained by Megacleides, the fourth century Homeric critic, as a venial piece of opportunistic flattery based on Alcinous' earlier remark on the Phaeacians' love of music and feasting (*Od.* VIII, 248)—which is the most sensible explanation, cf. VIII, 382-4, where Odysseus praises the Phaeacians' skill in dancing.

the effusive remarks of an after-dinner speaker at a royal banquet are not to be judged as a solemn philosophical pronouncement. Besides, should not Odysseus' more sober aphorisms on the harmful effects of appetite in human life be weighed against this? And should it not have been remembered to Odysseus' credit how he had rejected the temptation of the Lotus-fruit and had resolutely held out against eating the Cattle of the Sun? When he eats "greedily" after his reception in Alcinous' palace, should we not bear in mind that (apart from a snack from the remains of Nausicaa's picnic in Book VI) he had not eaten for three days and had suffered terrible physical and mental agonies in Poseidon's long storm? [8] Indeed, he had shown supreme self-control during his first supplication to Nausicaa: he had never mentioned food, but modestly asked only for a scrap of clothing and for information about the city. One almost loses patience with armchair critics who censure the conduct of a ravenous shipwrecked mariner for not conforming with the court etiquette of Alexandria or Versailles, and with moralists who demand the scruples of the confessional in the speeches of the banqueting-hall.

Odysseus' remarks on food in the second half of the *Odyssey* were less criticized, because he was obviously playing up to his role as a beggar in all of them. Further, as the Cynics noticed, he was a philosophical beggar. He showed that he understood the effects of appetite on men in general: how it drives men to war as well as to trade; how it moves the languid fingers of the courtier as well as the clutching fists of the starveling outcast. Yet he never suggested, as the more cynical Cynics did, that the belly was lord of all, and that he and his dog Argos were equally its slaves. He simply accepted it as one of the inescapable elemental forces in human life. Heroes like Agamemnon, Ajax, and Achilles, who had, as far as we know, never been compulsorily deprived of food in their lives, could nonchalantly disregard its demands. But Odysseus, by the time of his return to Ithaca, had become painfully familiar with the effects of involuntary hunger. Homer himself, if he was a bard wandering from audience to audience "for the sake of the accursed belly," may well have made Odysseus his own spokesman here. He, too, if we can deduce his personal feelings from the vivid description of the blind bard Demodocus in *Od.* VIII, 62ff., appreciated the comfort of having a basket of food and a cup of wine within reach to take "whenever his spirit prompted him."

The contrast here between the conventional hero's insouciance, or reticence, on the subject of food and Odysseus' frequent attention to it is one of the best illustrations of Odysseus' unconventionality as a hero.

[8] There is a choice modern example of this out-of-context criticism in a recent (1948) study of the Homeric poems: Odysseus' voracity in *Od.* VI and VII is explained as a "propitiatory rite." Is it unreasonable to insist, in the light of both common experience and Odysseus' own reiterated statements, on a simpler explanation—that extreme hunger compels men to eat grossly?

But Homer, perhaps for fear that his less philosophical hearers might fail to appreciate this kind of example, also exemplified Odysseus' uniqueness in a small matter that all warriors would notice. It is frequently emphasized in the *Odyssey* (and also mentioned in *Iliad* X) that Odysseus had unusual skill as an archer. His triumph over the Suitors at the end of the *Odyssey* depended on this. But only a few, and those not the most illustrious, of the other heroes at Troy show any interest in the use of the bow. Indeed, there are some indications that archery was despised as plebeian or unmanly,[9] much as a medieval knight of the sword and lance scorned to assail another knight with arrows. Perhaps Odysseus was merely old fashioned in his military technique. Or perhaps it was because the plot of the *Odyssey* demanded a triumph by means of the bow. But the trait does also serve to distinguish him from the other chief heroes. Another feature is far more peculiar. It is once mentioned in the *Odyssey* that Odysseus possessed, and so he presumably used, poisoned arrows.[10] This, however, like his Autolycan ancestry, is never referred to in the *Iliad.*

Though Odysseus' Homeric speeches were the admiration of every age of classical rhetoric, their excellence is not that of an orator among tongue-tied men. Oratory was a recognized part of heroic training. Thus in the Embassy scene Achilles' reply is fully as powerful and eloquent as Odysseus' pleadings. At times, too, Nestor's speeches in council are as wise and as cogent as Odysseus'. The difference is not one of skill. It lies more in the fact that, when the other heroes speak, their minds are obsessed with conventions and prerogatives or weakened by passion and self-concern. Achilles' wrath and Nestor's tendency to garrulous reminiscences tend to make their orations more effective as expressions of prejudices and personal feelings than as instruments of policy. In contrast, Odysseus' speeches are strictly functional,[11] as a rule. When he shows passion or introduces a personal touch it is almost always because it will help to achieve his aim—to quell Thersites and to rebuke the wavering Agamemnon or an insolent prince of Phaeacia. Those who

[9] This is the view of D. B. Monro, ed., *Homer's Odyssey,* Bks. XIII-XXIV (Oxford, 1901), p. 305, and others. Shewan (pp. 168-9) questions it, citing Teucer, Philoctetes, Meriones, and Apollo, as reputable bowmen and concluding, "That the bow was in common use as an auxiliary weapon is certain . . . and that it was held in contempt is not proved." Wilamowitz suggested that *Telemachus* (Far-fighter) was named from Odysseus' skill in archery. For the use of the bow by Homeric heroes see H. L. Lorimer, *Homer and the Monuments* (London, 1950), pp. 299ff.

[10] Odysseus' poisoned arrows are referred to in *Od.* I, 260-1. Eustathius and a scholiast on *Od.* I, 259ff. suggest that they were necessary for the ultimate slaying of the suitors, to make every wound fatal (as Heracles killed Nessus with an arrow dipped in the blood of the Hydra). Or they may have been intended for hunting. Gilbert Murray, in *The Rise of the Greek Epic* (Oxford, 1934), p. 130, claims to find traces of the use of poisoned arrows in war in some phrases of the *Iliad.*

[11] Cf. Eustathius on *Il.* II, 157 and 337.

consider passionate self-esteem an essential quality of the genuine heroic type may find this kind of self-possession mean or machiavellian. But, as Sophocles indicates in his *Ajax,* it is the faculty that maintains justice and humanity among passionate men.

Besides this functional difference between Odysseus' speeches and those of other heroes, Homer signalizes his oratory by a peculiar personal trait. In Antenor's speech, as already mentioned, there is a description of Odysseus' curious habitual pose before beginning an important speech. He would stand with his eyes fixed on the ground, his body and gestures stiff "like an ignorant fellow's." His voice, Antenor adds, was of great power. But he seems to have controlled this Gladstonian organ with the deftness of a Disraeli: his words came smoothly, lightly, continuously, flake after flake like falling snow—perhaps in the quiet, level tone characteristic of adepts in the art of plausibility. The general effect, we are told, was overwhelming. Homer corroborates this impression in several scenes in the *Odyssey,* where he describes how Odysseus could hold an audience spellbound "like a skilled bard." Homer could hardly have paid a higher tribute to his oratory.[12] Once again he identifies Odysseus' powers with his own.

In the later tradition Odysseus was often accused of cowardice. The charge was based less on incidents mentioned by Homer than on others first recorded in the post-Homeric tradition, Odysseus' attempt to evade conscription, for example, and in later versions of his conduct with Palamedes and Philoctetes. There is nothing of that kind in the Homeric poems. But one ambiguous incident in *Iliad* VIII [13] left a shadow on his reputation for courage. The circumstances are these. A general rout of the Achaeans has begun. Agamemnon, the two Ajaxes, and Idomeneus retreat rapidly. Nestor is left behind in grave danger. Hector rushes forward to cut him down. Diomedes sees the danger and calls to Odysseus for help in rescuing the old king. "But," Homer records, "Odysseus did not hear (or listen to) his call, and sped on to the Achaean ships." The crucial verb is capable of two interpretations. It was left open to Odysseus' defenders in post-Homeric controversies to argue that Odysseus had

[12] See on *Il.* III, 216ff., in chapter two, and Leaf and Bayfield for the "level tone." "Habitual" is implied by Homer's use of the frequentative or iterative forms στάσκεν, ἴδεσκε, ἔχεσκεν. Odysseus' power of holding an audience is emphasized in *Od.* XVII, 518-21; XI, 334; XIII, 2. Tributes to Odysseus' oratorical powers by later rhetoricians are very frequent, see Roscher, col. 640. The BT scholia on *Il.* III, 216, note that Odysseus' oratory was "firm" or "robust" (πυκνός), the ideal kind, resembling that of Demosthenes, while the styles of Menelaus and Nestor are compared to those of Lysias and Isocrates respectively.

[13] Shewan, pp. 165-7, has refuted the allegations of Geddes and others that Odysseus is deliberately vilified here and in *Il.* XI, 414ff., by the poet of "the Achilleid"; cf. J. A. Houben, *Qualem Homerus in Iliade finxerit Ulixem* (Trier, 1869), pp. 3ff. Note also Odysseus' firm and effective opposition to Agamemnon's proposal to retreat in *Il.* XIV, 64ff. For post-Homeric tributes to his courage see Roscher, col. 639.

simply not heard Diomedes' cry in the confusion of the general retreat. But his detractors could take it as a deliberate ignoring of a comrade's cry for help. Homer's own intention is hidden in the ambiguity. However, no matter what he meant here, he soon makes it clear that none of his heroes attached any blame to Odysseus for his conduct. On the contrary, Odysseus' prestige is at its highest in the next three books.

If one considers the whole of Odysseus' career, a general accusation of cowardice is plainly absurd. In *Iliad* XI, 395ff., he stands valorously alone against the whole Trojan host. His bravery in the Doloneia is incontestable. Similarly it took the highest courage to vanquish the Cyclops, to resist Scylla, to overthrow the horde of suitors. Yet Homer does seem to hint occasionally, not at cowardice, but at a kind of tension between prudence and boldness. Thus in Odysseus' brief spell as supreme champion of the Greeks in *Iliad* XI, he pauses for a moment to wonder whether it would not be wiser to retreat with the rest. He immediately reminds himself of his heroic duty, and, with a touch of fatalism, unusual in him, fights on. There is obviously no cowardice in this. On the contrary, the man who fully foresees danger and then goes on to meet it is more truly courageous than an insensate Ajax or a furious Achilles. The best illustration of this tension between prudence and heroic valor is found in Odysseus' attempt to avoid conscription by feigning madness, to be discussed in a later chapter. Unfortunately it is not certain that Homer knew the legend.

A commentator on Euripides' version of the Cyclops incident has seen something of a Hamletesque figure in Odysseus as portrayed there. This was possible in the atmosphere of the late fifth century. But Homer's Odysseus is obviously no indecisive princeling "sicklied o'er with the pale cast of thought." His decisive boldness is made clear both at the beginning of the *Iliad* in his handling of the Thersites affair, and at the outset of his Odyssean adventures when he sacks Ismarus like any Elizabethan buccaneer or Spanish conquistador. He is "the great-hearted," "the sacker of cities," as well as the prudent and resourceful Odysseus. Yet in both these bold deeds his prudence is not entirely in abeyance. While he faces Thersites uncompromisingly, he coaxes, amuses, and flatters the other Greeks. Again in the sack of Ismarus he orders a withdrawal as soon as a counter-attack seems likely. His comrades refuse, with disastrous results. Odysseus calls them "great fools" for not obeying his prudent command. But when he first gave it, they, for their part, may well have thought his prudence was mere timidity.

The fact is that, even though no real cowardice was involved, Odysseus' gift for anticipating dangers and his readiness to avoid them when it best served his purpose, did separate him from the normal hero of his time. Whether one admires it or not, a certain mulish stubbornness in the manner of Ajax, a reckless *élan* like that of Diomedes, a readiness to let everything be turned upside down for the sake of some point of honor in the manner of Achilles, was more characteristic of the early heroic temperament than a prudent resourcefulness. When the typical hero found his path to fame and glory blocked, his instinct was to batter his own or someone else's head against the obstacle until something broke. The gentle Hector and the tough Ajax were alike in this intransigence. Odysseus was no less determined to gain his purpose; but he was far less intransigent. He was prepared to undermine an obstacle or to look for another path, to imitate the mole or the fox rather than the rhinoceros.

In the later tradition, admirers of the simpler, prouder kind of hero will despise this quality, calling it cowardly or opportunistic. Homer suggests no such disapproval. On the contrary the *Odyssey* implies that some such resourcefulness is necessary to overcome the trials of human life in general. Almost all Homer's more intransigent heroes die unhappily, Agamemnon murdered by his wife, Ajax killed by his own hand, Achilles slain by a cowardly arrow. Odysseus, like Nestor and Menelaus, returns home at last to live in peace and prosperity.

Odysseus was also the "much-enduring" man. Among the other Homeric heroes only Nestor, whose life had extended over three normal generations, shared this epithet with him. Why? After all, many of the rest showed great endurance in battle. The answer seems to lie in a special implication in Homer's use of epithets in *poly-* meaning "much." As has been suggested elsewhere,[14] it seems to imply variety rather than degree, especially in its active compounds. The other heroes were "much-enduring" in their own special forte, namely, fighting. But Odysseus and Nestor were men who had shown their endurance in an unusual variety of circumstances: Nestor because of his abnormally long life, Odysseus because of his enterprising nature. Here once again a clash between Odysseus' qualities and the typical heroic temperament emerges. Ajax or Achilles would never have been willing to undergo some of Odysseus' experiences—his three adventures in beggar's disguise, for instance, and his ignominious escape from the Cyclops' cave by hanging under a ram's belly (which was a kind of Trojan Horse stratagem in reverse). In the later tradition Odysseus is accused of ignobleness, even cowardice, for his readiness to employ disguise or stealth when necessary to achieve his purpose. Undoubtedly one can detect an element of Autolycanism here. But what was often forgotten was that these various examples of combined resourcefulness and endurance were generally used *pro bono publico*.

We shall see all this argued out in the later tradition. Here it need only be emphasized that without this quality Odysseus could never have been so serviceable to the Greek cause. This serviceability varied from

[14] See the article cited in n. 2 to chapter two. The A scholia on Odysseus' epithet πολυμήχανος in *Il.* VIII, 93, give a long list of his various accomplishments as ploughman, shipwright, carpenter, hunter, steersman, and so on. Homer clearly admires this kind of versatility.

such an ordinary task as that of pacifying the indignant Chryses in *Iliad* I to the final triumph of Ulyssean cleverness in the ruse of the Wooden Horse. But it is the common fate of serviceable men to be despised by their more self-centered associates.

All these deviations from the heroic norm are exemplified in the *Iliad* as well as in the *Odyssey*. The next quality to be considered has little or no scope in the restricted Iliadic *milieu*. It needs the more expansive background of the *Odyssey*. It is a quality that points away from the older Heroic Age with its code of static conventions and prerogatives, and on to a coming era, the era of Ionian exploration and speculation.[15] This is Odysseus' desire for fresh knowledge. Homer does not emphasize it. But it can be seen plainly at work in two of the most famous of Odysseus' Odyssean exploits. It becomes the master passion of his whole personality in the post-classical tradition, notably in Dante, Tennyson, Arturo Graf, and Kazantzakis.

This eagerness to learn more about God, man, and nature is the most characteristic feature of the whole Greek tradition. To quote a recent commentator[16] on Dante's conception of Ulysses:

> To be a Greek was to seek to know; to know the primordial substance of matter, to know the meaning of number, to know the world as a rational whole. In no spirit of paradox one may say that Euclid is the most typical Greek: he would fain know to the bottom, and know as a rational system, the laws of the measurement of the earth. . . . No doubt the Greek genius means many things. To one school . . . it means an aesthetic ideal. . . . To others, however, it means an austere thing, which delights in logic and mathematics; which continually wondering and always inquisitive, is driven by its wonder into philosophy, and into inquiry about the why and wherefore, the whence and whither, of tragedy, of the State, indeed, of all things.

This eagerness to learn is not, of course, entirely a Greek quality. Every child, scholar, and scientist, shares it. But it can hardly be denied that the Greeks were endowed more richly with intellectual curiosity than any other ancient people. More conservative cultures like the Egyptian and the Roman judged the Greek spirit of experiment and inquiry either childlike or dangerous. But, for good and ill, it has been the strongest force in the development of modern European civilization and science.

Odysseus is alone among Homer's heroes in displaying this intellectual curiosity strongly. There is an obvious reason for this. A spirit of inquiry would naturally get more stimulus from the unexplored territories of Odysseus' fabulous wanderings than from the conventional environment

[15] Jaeger, p. 98, describes Odysseus as "not so much a knightly warrior as the embodiment of the adventurous spirit, the explorer's energy, and the clever practical wisdom of the Ionian," and cf. p. 20, "the cunning storm-tossed adventurer Odysseus is the creation of the age when Ionian sailors wandered the seas far and wide."

[16] Sir Ernest Barker, *Traditions of Civility* (Cambridge, 1948), p. 6.

of the *Iliad*. But it was hardly accidental that Odysseus should have had these special opportunities for acquiring fresh knowledge. To him that hath shall be given: adventures are to the adventurous. One may well doubt whether an Ajax or a Nestor would have shown as much alert curiosity even in the cave of the Cyclops or near the island of the Sirens if they had been there instead of Odysseus. Odysseus' personality and exploits are indivisible: he has curious adventures because he is Odysseus, and he is Odysseus because he has curious adventures. Set another hero in Circe's palace or in Phaeacia and you may have some story like *Innocents Abroad*, or a *Childe Harold's Pilgrimage*, or an *Aeneid*, but not an *Odyssey*.

Odysseus' desire to know is most clearly illustrated in the episodes with the Cyclops and the Sirens. He himself asserts that his original motive for landing on the Cyclops' island was to see whether its unknown inhabitants were "violent, savage and lawless, or else hospitable men with god-fearing mind"—almost as if, in modern terms, he wanted to do some anthropological research. It is more the motive of a Malinowski approaching the Trobriand Islands,[17] than of a pirate or a conquistador. But his crew did not share this zeal for knowledge. When they entered the Cyclops' cave, the Companions felt a presentiment of danger and begged him to withdraw. Odysseus refused, still eager to see what the giant was like. In describing the consequences Odysseus admits his folly here in the strongest words of self-denunciation that he ever uses (*Od.* IX, 228-30). As a result of his imprudence six of his companions were eaten. It becomes clear later, in the Sirens incident, when Odysseus meets a similar temptation to dangerous knowledge, that he had learned a lesson from his rash curiosity, for he takes great care to prevent any danger to his companions from hearing their deadly song.

But Odysseus' motives in the Cyclops episode were not unmixed. He admits that his second reason for wanting to meet the ogre was a hope of extracting some guest-gifts from him—acquisitiveness as well as inquisitiveness. The post-Homeric tradition was inclined to censure Odysseus for unheroic cupidity here and elsewhere. But other Homeric heroes were quite as eager to receive gifts as he.[18] It was a normal part of heroic

[17] A friend has asked me to reconsider this view, claiming that Odysseus' motive for visiting the island of the Cyclops was simply a desire to get information on his whereabouts (as in *Od.* X, 190ff.). But the phrasing of *Od.* IX, 174-6 still seems to me to imply a special kind of curiosity.

[18] See the Homeric lexicons at δῶρον. Aelian, *Var. Hist.* 4, 20, observes that both Menelaus and Odysseus resembled Phoenician merchants in the way they acquired wealth on their travels: cf. the young Phaeacian's taunt against Odysseus in *Od.* VIII, 161-4. Comments on Odysseus' love of gifts will be found in the scholia on *Od.* VII, 225; XIII, 103; and in Eustathius on *Od.* X, 571. Plutarch, in *How to study poetry*, 27, explains why Odysseus need not necessarily be convicted of avariciousness in checking his Phaeacian gifts so carefully on his arrival in Ithaca (*Od.* XIII, 215ff.): he may simply have wished to see if the Phaeacians were honest and truthful men; or for rejoicing at

etiquette; and in general the Greeks always had a flair for trade as well as for science. Odysseus' fault lay not in his hope of getting gifts but in his allowing that hope (combined with curiosity) to endanger the lives of his companions. Homer left it to others to draw a moral.

But there is a deeper difficulty in this incident. To anyone who has followed Odysseus' career from the beginning of the *Iliad* up to his encounter with the Cyclops, Odysseus' general lack of prudence and self-control in it must seem quite uncharacteristic of his usual conduct, especially his foolhardy boastfulness[19] after his escape from the Cyclops' clutches (*Od.* IX, 490ff.). By this last imprudence, despite his companions' entreaties, he nearly brought disaster on them all from the monster's missiles. Perhaps the explanation is that this particular episode retains much of its pre-Homeric shape and ethos. It may have been fairly fully worked out before Homer incorporated it into his poem.[20] Its outline is almost pure folklore. Homer's additions seem to consist mainly of vivid descriptions of scenery and the motivation of Odysseus' conduct. In order to fit Odysseus into the traditional plot, and also in order to make him incur the wrath of Poseidon, Homer may have had to strain his own conception of Odysseus' character more than elsewhere. So while in one way the victory over the Cyclops was Odysseus' greatest Autolycan triumph—especially in the typically Autolycan equivocation of his No-man formula—it was also his greatest failure as the favorite of Athene. And, significantly, by provoking Poseidon's enmity it was the main cause of his losing Athene's personal protection for nine years. In other words, in this episode Odysseus relapses for a while nearer to his original character as the Wily Lad than anywhere else in the Homeric poems.

To return to Odysseus' intellectual curiosity: it is presented in a much purer light in his encounter with the Sirens. Here no greed for gain, or indifference to his companions' safety, intrudes. Circe (who in Athene's absence takes her place for a while in advising Odysseus) has warned Odysseus of the Sirens' fatal attractions, telling him of "the great heap of men rotting on their bones" which lies in the flowery meadow beside

---

Penelope's receiving of gifts (*Od.* XVIII, 281-2): he may merely have been glad at the suitors' over-confidence. But both excuses are rather weak. It is better to admit that Odysseus, like the other heroes of his time, delighted in acquiring wealth: see A.-Ed. Chaignet, *Les Héros et les Héroines d'Homère* (Paris, 1894), pp. 271-4, and Bruno Snell, *The Discovery of the Mind,* Eng. trs. T. C. Rosenmeyer (Oxford, 1953), pp. 156-7.

[19] The scholiast ad loc. admits that this was "over quarrelsome" (φιλονεικότερον) but adds that it would give some consolation to the injured feelings of the Greeks.

[20] A far-reaching problem opens up here; and a greater emphasis on Homer's debt to his predecessors would demand a quite different view of the characterization of Odysseus in *Od.* IX-XII. But I must leave it to the others to explore this line of interpretation. See D. L. Page, "Odysseus and Polyphemus," *Latin Teaching,* 1949, 8-26, and, more generally, D. Muelder in *Hermes* xxxviii (1903), for possible signs of imperfectly digested material in the Cyclops incident. C. C. van Essen in *Mnemosyne* lviii (1930), 302-8, suggests an Etruscan origin for the Cyclops and Odysseus.

them. Better not to hear their seductive song at all; but if he, Odysseus cannot resist a desire to hear it—and Circe knows Odysseus well enough to expect that he cannot resist it—he must fill his comrades' ears with wax and have himself bound tightly to the mast.

What happens in the actual encounter became one of the most famous stories in European literature and a rich source of allegorical and symbolical interpretations. Its significance for the present study lies in the nature of the Sirens' temptation. This was not based on any amorous enticements. Instead the Sirens offered information about the Trojan war and knowledge of "whatever has happened on the wide, fertile earth." To put it in modern jargon, the Sirens guaranteed to supply a global news-service[21] to their clients, an almost irresistible attraction to the typical Greek whose chief delight, as observed in the Acts of the Apostles (xvii. 21) was "to tell or to hear some new thing."

As Homer describes the incident, the attractions of the Sirens were primarily intellectual. Merely sensual pleasures would not, Homer implies (and Cicero[22] later insists), have allured him so strongly. He had resisted the temptation to taste of the fruit of the Lotus. But one must not overlook, with Cicero, the effect of their melodious song and their unrivalled voices. Music for the Greeks was the most moving of the arts. Besides, as Montaigne observes in his essay on *Glory*, there was a subtle touch of flattery in their first words:

> Deca vers nous, deca, O treslouable Ulysse,
> Et le plus grand honneur dont la Grece fleurisse.

And perhaps their subtlest flattery was in recognizing Odysseus' caliber at once and in appealing only to his intellect. If an Agamemnon or a Menelaus had been in his place, they might have changed their tune.

For some reason Odysseus' intellectual curiosity, as displayed in his encounter with the Sirens, was not much emphasized in the earlier classical tradition. Presumably so typical a quality of the early Greeks (as distinct from the Achaean heroes) was taken for granted. But the later allegorists, both pagan and Christian, made it a favorite theme for imaginative moralization, as will be described in a later chapter.

It might rashly be concluded from the preceding analysis that Homer's Odysseus was a man distracted by psychological conflicts and distressed by social tensions. The general impression derived from the Homeric poems suggests nothing of the kind. The inner and outer tensions are skilfully

[21] For the Sirens as a kind of "poetical gazette" see T. W. Allen, *Homer, the Origins and Transmission* (Oxford, 1924), p. 142, n. 1, who quotes Sextus Empiricus, *Adv. math.* 1, 11.

[22] Cicero, *De finibus* 5, 18: see further in chapter nine. For the view that the Sirens appealed especially to those ambitious for ἀρετή see Xenophon, *Memorabilia,* 2, 6, 11.

implied, but the total portrait is that of a man well integrated both in his own temperament and with his environment. As Athene emphasized, he was essentially "self-possessed," fully able to control conflicting passions and motives. His psychological tensions never reach a breaking-point. They serve rather to give him his dynamic force. As a result his purposefulness is like an arrow shot from a well-strung bow, and his energy has the tirelessness of coiled springs. Resilience, elasticity, concentration, these are the qualities that maintain his temperamental balance. In contrast the Ajax-like hero was superficially firm and strong. His code of conduct and his heroic pride encased his heart like archaic armor. Once this psychological carapace was pierced by some violent shock the inner parts were as soft as any crustacean's. Odysseus' strength and self-possession did not depend on any outer armor. He could be as firm and enduring in the role of a beggar or in the cave of a Cyclops as in full battle-dress at Troy. This was the quality that the Cynic and Stoic philosophers were most to admire later.

Such was his inner harmony and strength. His conduct in matters of major importance shows a similar purposeful integrity. He had a remarkable power of taking the long view, of seeing actions in their widest context, of disciplining himself to the main purpose in hand.[23] Thus while other heroes at Troy are squabbling like children over questions of honor and precedence, Odysseus presses on steadily towards victory. And why? Not, Homer implies, for the sake of triumph and plunder, but in order to return to his beloved Ithaca as soon as possible. Here Odysseus' efforts for the Greek cause are integrated with his fundamental love

[23] Cf. H. Fraenkel, *Dichtung und Philosophie des frühen Griechentums* (New York, 1951), pp. 123-4. Chaignet, p. 193, sums up his impression of Odysseus in the Homeric poems thus: *au fond Ulysse est un idéal de la vie morale en même temps qu'un représentant de toutes les qualités de sa race. C'est le type non pas le plus sympathique, le plus noble, mais le plus complet du héros grec.*

Additional Note: The evidence for Odysseus' age in the Homeric poems is inconclusive. Antilochus, in *Il.* XXIII, 790-91, describes him as being "of an earlier generation and of earlier men" and also as ὠμογέρων. The last term is ambiguous: it could denote a person in the early stages of old age, or an active old man, or one who is prematurely aged. Considering that Odysseus' only son was then barely ten years old and that Laertes was still active ten years later, he can hardly have been far advanced in years. Antilochus was a very young man and to such even the moderately middle-aged often seem old. If Odysseus was in his late thirties and Antilochus was eighteen or nineteen, he might loosely be described as "belonging to an earlier generation." This would place him in the late twenties when he left Ithaca and in the late forties on his return home, which seems to fit the general implications of the poems best. On the other hand, the flagrant inconsistency in the implied ages of Neoptolemus (see commentators on *Il.* XIX, 326ff.) warns against assuming chronological consistency in matters of this kind. If ὠμογέρων meant having a prematurely aged look, as some ancient commentators held, it would be in character for a man like Odysseus: and Idomeneus (whose brother Odysseus pretends to be in *Od.* XIX, 181) is described as "half-gray" in *Il.* XIII, 361. But the description of Odysseus in *Od.* XIII, 430-34, seems to preclude any premature ageing in his appearance.

of home; *pro bono publico* is ultimately *pro domo sua*. Similarly his loyalty to the Companions during the fabulous voyages, and his patience with their infuriating alternations of rashness and timidity, were part of the same enlightened egotism: he needed a crew to sail his ship home. His love for Penelope, too, was, as has been suggested already, not based entirely on *eros* or *agape,* but also contained that *philia,* that attachment to one's normal and natural social environment which underlies so much of Greek happiness. And his piety is the piety of one who wishes to keep on good terms with the gods.

Such mixed motives may seem impure or ignoble to those who take their ideals from self-sacrificing patriotism, or from self-effacing saintliness, or from self-forgetting romanticism. But these are post-Homeric concepts. Within the context of the Heroic Age and perhaps of the Homeric Age, too, this identification of one's own best interests with the general welfare of one's kith, kin, and comrades, with one's *philoi* in fact, was a saving grace for both the individual and society. All the Homeric heroes are egotists; but Odysseus' egotism has sent its roots out more widely into his personal environment than that of Agamemnon, Achilles, or Ajax.

One other aspect of Odysseus' Homeric character needs to be kept in mind at the last. In a way it is the most important of all for the development of the tradition. This is the fundamental ambiguity of his essential qualities. We have seen how prudence may decline towards timidity, tactfulness towards a blameworthy *suppressio veri,* serviceability towards servility, and so on. The ambiguity lies both in the qualities themselves and in the attitudes of others towards them. Throughout the later tradition this ambiguity in Odysseus' nature and in his reputation will vacillate between good and bad, between credit and infamy. Odysseus' personality and reputation at best are poised, as it were, on a narrow edge between Aristotelian faults of excess and deficiency. Poised between rashness and timorousness, he is prudently brave; poised between rudeness and obsequiousness he is "civilized"; poised between stupidity and overcleverness he, at his best, is wise.

Homer was large-minded enough to comprehend a unity in apparent diversity, a structural consistency within an external changefulness, in the character of Ulysses. But few later authors were as comprehending. Instead, in the post-Homeric tradition, Odysseus' complex personality becomes broken up into various simple types—the *politique,* the romantic amorist, the sophisticated villain, the sensualist, the philosophic traveler, and others. Not till James Joyce wrote his *Ulysses* was a successful effort made to recreate Homer's polytropic hero in full. Similarly after Homer judgments on Odysseus' ethical status became narrower and sharper. Moralists grew angry in disputing whether he was a "good" man or not—good, that is to say, according to the varying principles of Athens, or

Alexandria, or Rome, or Florence, or Versailles, or Madrid, or Weimar. Here is another long Odyssey for Odysseus to endure. But Homer, the unmoved mover in this chaotic cosmos of tradition, does not vex his own or his hero's mind with any such problems in split personality or ambivalent ethics. He is content to portray a man of many turns.

Ulysses

by Robert Graves

To the much-tossed Ulysses, never done
With woman whether gowned as wife or whore,
Penelope and Circe seemed as one:
She like a whore made his lewd fancies run,
And wifely she a hero to him bore.

Their counter-changings terrified his way:
They were the clashing rocks, Symplegades,
Scylla and Charybdis too were they;
Now they were storms frosting the sea with spray
And now the lotus island's drunken ease.

They multiplied into the Sirens' throng,
Forewarned by fear of whom he stood bound fast
Hand and foot helpless to the vessel's mast,
Yet would not stop his ears: daring their song
He groaned and sweated till that shore was past.

One, two, and many: flesh had made him blind,
Flesh had one pleasure only in the act,
Flesh set one purpose only in the mind—
Triumphs of flesh and afterwards to find
Still those same terrors wherewith flesh was racked.

His wiles were witty and his fame far known,
Every king's daughter sought him for her own,
Yet he was nothing to be won or lost.
All lands to him were Ithaca: love-tossed
He loathed the fraud, yet would not bed alone.

Preface to *Homer and the Aether*

by John Cowper Powys

It is not necessary, as I think of the youthful readers I am particularly anxious to persuade to read this book, to enter here upon such questions as to what Greek city gave birth to Homer, or how many centuries elapsed between the *Iliad* and the *Odyssey*. Sufficient it is to say I feel it grows clearer and clearer the more familiar you become with both *Iliad* and *Odyssey* that these two poems had different authors or originals and that there is an historic gap of three or four hundred years between them.

If a youthful mind, whether a masculine or feminine one, were to ask me *point-blank* the question I am presently going to ask you all—and how much more expressive and full of meaning those two words "point-blank" are than this vaporously-vague grandiloquent expression full of vaunting pomposity that many of us are tempted these days to use, namely "by and large"; and what actually does "by and large" mean? I always see it accompanied by that particular gesture in a speaker that implies "I am too grand an orator to descend to silly details"—the question "In what respect does Homer's *Iliad* surpass Dante and Shakespeare and Milton and Goethe?" I would answer at once: It is not nearly as imaginative as Dante. It is not nearly as dramatic as Shakespeare. It is not nearly as eloquent as Milton. It is not nearly as philosophical as *Faust*. And yet it is a greater poem than the *Inferno* or *King Lear* or *Paradise Lost* or *Faust*! Why is this? In what way can it possibly surpass these masterpieces?

I will tell you at once. By being more realistic and more natural. In other words, it is more like what has happened, is happening, and will happen to us all, from the very beginning, in our history in this world until the end of human life upon this earth. Of course we use different weapons against each other and against the various subhuman living creatures who surround us than they used in the *Iliad*. So they did in the earliest cave-men times, twenty thousand years ago. So they will do in future times when many of us will have successfully invaded our planetary neighbors in space. But I tell you, my dear young questioner, it isn't the instrument we use in our quarrels with one another that counts. Some of us may simply use our tongues. Others among us may simply use our silences. Others may—O! there is no end to our weapons against each other! There may even come a day when by means of repeated concentrated thought applied for a certain length of time we shall be able so strongly and intensely to wish Mr. So-and-So or Mrs. So-and-So dead that the particular person *will* die and not a soul will be able to accuse the killer.

No, we must get out of our heads that because the Homeric people use swords and spears and arrows against each other that the whole of the *Iliad* is just an old-fashioned fairy-tale like *Jack the Giant Killer* or *Cinderella.* It is much more than that! It has the varieties of character, the mysterious intricacies of character, the inexplicable vagaries of character, the confounding leaps and plunges of character that we get in Hardy and Dostoevsky and Dickens and Victor Hugo and Thomas Mann; and it has also got the romantic surprises of Sir Walter Scott, as when we find the beautiful Briseïs tearing her hair on the ground by the dead body of Patroclus.

No, let me repeat once again, what has made Homer for three thousand years the greatest poet in the world is his *naturalness.* We love each other as in Homer. We hate each other as in Homer. We are perpetually being interfered with as in Homer by chance and fate and necessity, by invisible influences for good and by invisible influences for evil, and we see the unconquerable power that Homer calls *keer* leading our parents, leading our uncles and aunts, leading our grandparents to a particular death; and there do exist among us those who even feel this implacable destiny propelling themselves to a definite end, actually indicated as inescapable when some particular date in the calendar is reached or when some particular event has occurred. Thus Achilles assures his horse Xanthus, who is dragging his chariot, and who turns his head to remind him that if he kills Hector his own end will shortly follow, that he needs no reminding of this *keer,* for he knows it well, but "all the same for that"—*alla kai empees,* as Homer puts it—he intends to drive on to the end.

What is so particularly natural about the *Iliad* and what is such a daily inspiration to me in my ordinary life is the place he gives to women. First of all are the beautiful mistresses of the houses and halls of Homer's warriors, such as Argive Helen, carried off from Menelaus by Paris, *alias* Alexander; such as Hector's mother, Hecabe, and his wife, Andromache, and his half-sister, the beautiful prophetess Cassandra, whom Agamemnon takes captive and conveys to his home. Then there are the women who are taken captive by the conquerors who have slain their parents, husbands and sons. These women are treated at first as if they are slaves. In fact we are told in one place that their value is equal to the value of four oxen. But when once they enter the dwelling of their conqueror and take up their abode there, they very quickly dominate the whole house.

The beautiful Lady of the House may go off on her own and leave her lord as Helen did Menelaus, but these women brought into the Homeric hall as "worth four oxen" very quickly by their wisdom, beauty, tact and competence became either the housekeeper, whom Homer calls "the *Tamiee*" and who always is praised by the guests for the delicious things to eat and drink "which she brings out of her store," or, if the Lord is an old man, as Nestor was, without any Lady, become in that old man's dwelling a beautiful handmaid like Hecamede, daughter of Arsinoös of Tenedos. Homer certainly describes with reverential relish the lovely meal she once arranged upon old Nestor's table, and how ready she would be, as Nestor told them himself, to give Doctor Machaon, the son of the greatest of all doctors, Asclepius, a beautiful cleansing and healing warm bath. I sometimes wonder whether other commentators on Homer share my reluctance to transliterate the vowel "Eeta" into a repetition of our letter "e," which is really the Greek letter "Epsilon." But this double "e" looks so unpleasing that I have thought it better to rely on the notes about pronunciation made by my friend J. Redwood-Anderson, for thus I can insure that a name like that of the girl from Tenedos called Hecamede should not be changed from a name of four syllables to a name of three.

There are many scenes in the *Iliad* where we touch the reality of our life as it is today when it is transformed for us by our own private thoughts; as for example when we struggle with certain forces of nature. Consider, for instance, the passage in Book XXI, line 308, where the River Scamander calls upon his brother, the River Simoïs, to help him in his battle with Achilles. Here we have a perfect example of that element in life where the subhuman wrestles with the human and they both are compelled in some strange way to appeal to the superhuman to decide their strife. Here the burden of our oldest ballads seems anticipated by Homer, and all those ancient market-town quips and proverbs and all those immemorial fairy-tales and roadside legends reaching us from forests long ago cut down, and from moorlands long ago built over, find their parallel. There is something about the rhythm of the Homeric hexameter that is more able to catch and absorb into its current, as it rolls along, these familiar human situations that are always recurring, than any other form of poetic rhythm except the simplest of our best-known old ballads.

There is an authentic echo of Homer's hexameters in those of that great and unfairly neglected poet, Longfellow, an echo such as none of our cleverest modern poetasters are able to catch, or, indeed, have any wish to catch. Take the first lines of "Evangeline" for example:

This is the forest primeval. The murmuring pines and the hemlocks
Bearded with moss, and in garments green, undisturbed in the twilight
Stand like Druids of old, with voices sad and prophetic,
Stand like harpers hoar, with beards that rest on their bosoms.

Loud from its rocky caverns the deep-voiced neighboring ocean
Speaks and in accents discordant answers the wail of the forest.

Many of the most appealing passages in the *Iliad* consist of prayers; and it is impossible sometimes not to associate these prayers, such as "O Sun that beholdest all things and hearest all things, O Rivers, O Earth, O all ye lost ones of our race, who, weary of life, rest forever in peace below it all," with the calm, majestic resignation of so many of the Collects in the Book of Common Prayer of the Church of England "as by Law established."

My own favorite book in the whole of the *Iliad* is Book XXI, wherein the gods and goddesses fight among themselves, some taking the side of the Greeks and some the side of the Trojans; and nothing is more perfectly characteristic of Homer as a poet than the fact that the chief of all the immortals, the great Zeus himself, Heavenly Father of both gods and men, regards this fighting among the gods with humorous amusement. I implore all those among Homer's readers who may be following me, as I have been following my imaginary thought-reader, the immortal Aether, to ask themselves whether they can imagine the author of *Hamlet* and *Macbeth* and *Othello* and *King Lear* and *The Tempest,* however shrewdly he may hint that the Power above us all laughs at lovers' quarrels, going so far as to suggest that the behavior of angels and devils, as they contend for the victory in our hearts, is to that great Power a matter for hilarious amusement. Does the Deity in Dante's *Divine Comedy* even for a moment look down upon it all as if it were a comedy in *our* sense of the word? Can we imagine for a moment Milton's "Heavenly Muse," who "with mighty wings outspread dove-like satst brooding on the vast Abyss and mad'st it pregnant," chuckling with ribald amusement at the silly quarrels going on in both Heaven and Earth?

What we get as we follow Homer through the *Iliad* is not at all the feeling that "all the world's a stage and all the men and women merely players," nor is it the feeling that there is what Wordsworth, my own favorite poet, calls

. . . something far more deeply interfused,
Whose dwelling is the light of setting suns,
And the round ocean and the living air,
And the blue sky, and in the mind of man:

A motion and a spirit, that impels
All thinking things, all objects of all thought,
And rolls through all things.

Without any of these exalted emotions, derived from the contact of our human souls with the colors and forms and substances of our planetary Earth, dominated by Sun and Moon, as it swings through infinite Space —yes, without any of these emotions, we who love Homer in the way the immortal Aether loved him may find ourselves by degrees learning, without effort, without any particular concentration of will, to enjoy the natural, ordinary course of our daily life with all its shocks, stresses, quarrels, rivalries, frustrations, surprises, desperations and heavenly quiescences, just in the sort of way Keats felt when he wrote that perfect fragment of an ode which begins:

Mother of Hermes! and still youthful Maia!
May I sing to thee
As thou wast hymned on the shores of Baiae?

and which breaks off with the words:

Rounded by thee, my song should die away
Content as theirs,
Rich in the simple worship of a day.

I am tempted to go so far as to say that we Britishers have appreciated Homer more than any other race in the world; and I think a person has only to read a little of Chaucer and Spenser to see why. The truth is we are the most unphilosophical race in the world. We are also, second only to the Saxons and Bavarians of Germany, the fondest of fairy tales in the world. We are certainly the fondest of old ballads and old popular sayings for their own sake. We are the most obstinate in hanging on to old local traditions for their own sake; and finally we are the least cultivated, the least concerned with what is called intellectuality, of all the races in the world. Then again we have appreciated the Jews, and done justice to the Jews, beyond all other western peoples; and if, compared with the Germans, our lack of metaphysical and psychological power is deplorable, and compared with the French, our lack of civilized receptivity and subtle appreciation of the nuances of human life is almost comical, no Europeans have given themselves up with a more impassioned and, I might say, a more childlike abandonment to delight in simple beauty for its own sake than English travelers have done when visiting Italy or Greece.

All these qualities, both positive and negative, when joined together, tend to strengthen my conviction, quite apart from the number of famous translations of the *Iliad* that have been made in this country, both in prose and verse, that there is something about our attitude to Homer that comes nearer to the attitude of the immortal Aether, to whom I have presumed to give a human consciousness, than that of any other nation. This is no theory; for again and again in watching my friends talking together, and watching men's attitude to their wives and children, and watching the attitude of their wives and children to them—especially when the ladies, as is now often the case, have to play the part of a Homeric housekeeper and handmaid, as well as that of the beautiful Cassandra, who speaks out so freely, and of the unequalled Helen who may so easily be beguiled—I have been swept away by a fascinating wave of excitement in observing how this stupendous poem, that may easily have been recited by some reciter with my own mania for it three thousand years ago, still embodies the life of men, women, and children as it is lived upon this earth. And the exciting thing is that Homer treats his Divine Beings in exactly the same way that he treats us ourselves, his Human Beings. Over and over again, we find ourselves awed and hushed in the presence of his Divine Beings and aware of a natural feeling that their ancient altars must be respected and their legendary ritual upheld; but at the same time there is absolutely nothing of that peculiar atmosphere of unctuous solemnity and oily gloom that some of us find so hard not to associate with our Christian Sunday.

How interesting it is that the peculiar shiver of terrified awe which our great religious prophets and teachers and preachers and saints have, by degrees, ever since the year one of our calendar, forced us to associate with the word God, doesn't enter for a moment into Homer's conception of Zeus, any more than its does into Virgil's conception of Jupiter or Jove. How satisfactory it is to be able to worship Zeus or his daughter Pallas Athene or his sister-wife Hera, without having to think of a God that we have been taught for nearly two thousand years to associate with the "bowing and scraping" of a Hush-a-bye Heaven and the infernal cruelties of a diabolical Spanish Inquisition Hell, not to speak of the Predestination doctrines of Knox and Calvin and the fiery stakes of Bloody Mary.

The essential thing with Homer—and most especially is this true of the *Iliad*—is the magical, bewitching, irresistible, intoxicating sweep of music of his meter. There is no meter in the world, there never has been, that can equal the hexameter of Homer. No doubt the "blank verse," as I was brought up to call it, of Milton or of Shakespeare—though it's not a very suggestive name—contains, as my friend Redwood-Anderson, our greatest authority on meter, would soon point out, rhythmic subtleties that do not appear in the hexameter at all; but I am sure he will agree with me when I say that no poetical sound in the world carries with it quite the same evocation of sonorous echoes, that rise and fall like the waves of an ocean over rocky promontories, as these transporting "oio" sounds with which Homer's hexameters are perpetually closing.

Every lover of Homer will I think agree that the most significant and characteristic thing about his gathering, accumulating, enlarging, thickening, expanding, deepening story of human life—of human life as it has been in every age from the beginning and as it will be to the very end—is his emphasis upon the family. He does not, as so many poets since his time have done, talk a great deal about tribes and groups and clans and sects and varieties of idealistic associations, whether pacific or belligerent. What Homer does is to confine himself to the immediate family of the warrior in question. In the speeches they make to each other, in the appeals they make to the people, every single one of them will invariably refer to the father by whom he was begotten; and Homer himself is concerned with this paternal link to such an intense degree that if the two names can possibly be united into one single name he will unite them.

But now let us pause to consider the Homeric attitude to sex love. I think everyone will agree with me that in the passionate love of Achilles for Patroclus there is not a trace of homosexuality. Their love is like the love that existed in historic cases all down the ages between man and man while both men can at the same time have their women. Indeed it is an interesting and remarkable thing that it is impossible to avoid noticing in Homer the complete absence of the least suggestion of homosexuality or of Lesbianism. Considering the emphasis laid upon these erotic eccentricities in this modern age of ours what are we to make of their complete absence in Homer? I would even be inclined to go a little further and to emphasize the absence from the *Iliad* of any mention of those two sexual aberrations connected with cruelty, namely, what we have come to call Sadism and Masochism. There are several familiar historic cases of tyrants obviously addicted to sadism, and several prehistoric myths and legends whose cruelties can easily be connected with these two sexual aberrations. But there is not, as far as I can discern, a trace of either of them in the *Iliad*. Is the reason for this the fact that in the *Iliad* we are dealing with a desperate war, a war that so exhausts everyone's energy that there is no energy left over to indulge in erotic sensations except the most natural and ordinary ones? Or is the reason simply that the lovers of and composers of poetry all the way down human history are so absorbed in the normal current of human life that they instinctively tend to avoid abnormalities, whether erotic or otherwise?

There are those who instinctively prefer the neat Greek tragedians, Aeschylus, Sophocles, and Euripides to Homer. Why, I ask you, do they? The answer is simple. Because they are full of intellectual Ideas and Theories and Interpretations of Life, full of creative Visions and moral Principles as to how human existence upon earth could be improved. Matthew Arnold, one of my own favorite poets, tells us that Sophocles "sees life steadily and sees it whole." O what a pure delight it is to return to Homer after "seeing life whole"! Why, I ask you, *is* it such a relief and such a comfort? Because Homer has the reality of our natural feeling about life, and Sophocles has an intellectual vision of things that may turn out to be, as my brother A.R.P. said of some wild theory of mine or of Llewelyn's, no reality at all, *in fact a lie*. Sophocles may see life as "steadily" and as "wholesale" as he likes, but real life, as all men and women and children soon discover from personal experience, is the extreme opposite of anything you can see "steadily" or as "a whole." It is a wild, chaotic series of exhausting contradictions. When is Shakespeare at his greatest? When his characters are philosophizing? Not a bit of it! All the supreme scenes in Shakespeare are when his people are transported by ecstasies of love and hate.

> And yet I call you servile ministers
> That will with two pernicious daughters join
> Your high-engender'd battles 'gainst a head
> So old and white as this!

> Out, out, brief candle!
> Life's but a walking shadow, . . .
> . . . . . . It is a tale
> Told by an idiot, full of sound and fury,
> Signifying nothing.

But none of the passionate defiances and challenges of Shakespeare's stage, nor any of the pandemoniacal eloquence of Milton's angels and archangels, nor the most contorted twists of Browning's tipsy piety with its belching outbursts of county-council optimism, really expresses, as we all know well, the actual experience of life which we poor mortals from childhood to manhood and womanhood have fled from or endured, have fought against or submitted to, ever since we were born. But Homer does express precisely this. We may be put off by the Greek words or annoyed by the conventional or slangy translations. But now and again, as we go struggling on, there come glimpses and murmurs, as I have sought to make my immortal Aether show, of a natural and wonderful reality that the sweeping tide of these tremendous hexameters has caught up from the simplest human lives. Let us therefore listen to it rolling on with all its multifarious crosscurrents, as it has done from the beginning, if there was a beginning, and will do until the end, if there will be an end, suffering and enjoying at the same time what *"is all,"* as Keats said, "ye *know on earth,* and all ye need to know."

The Authoress of the *Odyssey*

by Robert Graves

When our daily routine was something like normal again, I took Phemius aside. "Phemius," I asked, "what payment are you prepared to make for the new spell of life I gave you?"

"I had been wondering when I should have to answer that question," he said. "The answer is: I accept the price you name, though I fear it will be a high one."

"For so valuable a life it must be exceptionally high. Besides, I might have been killed myself in saving you. Come then, it is as follows. Since you are a Son of Homer and your guild alone is privileged to perform in the courts of Greece, I demand that you shall approve, sing, and circulate an epic poem of my own composition on which I am already working and which, if Athene continues to inspire me, I shall finish within two or three years. It begins with the opening verses of *The Return of Odysseus*, as far as his visit to the Lotus-eaters. After that the story will be different. Probably it will include the adventures of Ulysses (whom some believe to have been Odysseus) and end with the massacre of Penelope's lovers. I have a fair notion now how Odysseus managed it singlehanded. The *Iliad*, which I admire, is devised by a man for men; this epic, *The Odyssey*, will be devised by a woman for women. Understand that I am Homer's latest born child, a daughter; and listen attentively. When I have finished the poem, and written it out in cuttlefish ink on sheepskin, you must memorize it, and (if necessary) improve the language where it halts or flags. One day I shall send you back to Delos and you will carry my poem to all the courts of Asia. When princes and princesses—but especially princesses—praise it and heap gifts on you, asking: 'Phemius, golden-mouthed minstrel, where did you learn that glorious story?' you must answer: 'My ancestor's songs are highly esteemed by the Elymans, who live at the far western fringe of the

The Authoress of the *Odyssey*. From *Homer's Daughter* by Robert Graves (New York: Doubleday & Co., Inc., 1955; London: Cassell & Co., Ltd., 1955).

civilized world; and it was at the Elyman court that I learned this *Odyssey.*' I shall be careful to include nothing that might betray the land of its origin, though immortalizing my own name and Aethon's and yours in the course of the story."

"But if I refuse, Princess?"

"Then you may expect a worse fate than Melantheus. Be wise: take your oath by Athene and by Apollo."

Eventually he swore: perhaps because he thought me incapable of completing the immense labor which I had set myself. As though I ever fail in any of my undertakings!

I must confess that Phemius behaved very well when, a couple of years later, I presented him with a manuscript of more than twelve thousand lines—not written on sheepskin but on scrolls of Egyptian papyrus which Aethon won in his glorious sack of Canopus. After all, Phemius is a professional bard and I am a mere interloper and a woman; and we had several serious tiffs while I was composing it. However, I let him have his way sometimes when he protested that this verse or that was faulty. But not always.

He hated me to borrow passages from the *Iliad* for what he considered improper contexts, and he grew furious to find that Homer's lines about the water being heated to wash Patroclus's dead body were now used to describe the warm bath prepared for Odysseus, and that I had put part of Hector's farewell speech to Andromache into Telemachus' mouth, when he forbids his mother to meddle in men's affairs. Phemius called me heartless to treat any passage so tragic as the first, or so moving as the second, with such disrespect. "I am heartless, eh?" I countered, my eyes blazing. "In that case you had better behave a little more subserviently or you will find yourself sold to an upland farmer. Do you like gruel and skim milk and rags?" He drew in his horns, which are tender, and tears ran down his plump cheeks. It was a ridiculous threat, of course, and if I had made it to a man like Demodocus he would have laughed in my face.

Yet I admire Phemius, who helped me to smooth out incidents in which the Goddess Athene had not been particularly helpful.

For safety's sake, on his advice, I have consigned to oblivion all the names of my living characters, giving them pseudonyms—as I also do here, with only four exceptions. I retain my own as a personal signature; Phemius retains his as a reward for the collaboration; I allow Odysseus to call himself "Aethon son of Castor" and tell Aethon's life story in one of his many fictions; and (as I decided halfway through the poem) Eurycleia deserves to be immortalized for urging Aethon and me to marry. Our most heated argument concerned the preponderance of women in my epic and Athene's ubiquity, and the precedence given to famous women when Odysseus meets the ghosts of the departed. I had mentioned only Tyro, Antiope, Alcmene, Jocasta, Chloris, Leda, Iphimedeia, Phaedra, Procris, Ariadne, Maera, Clymene, and, naturally, Eriphyle and let Odysseus describe them to Alcinous. "My dear Princess," said Phemius, "if you really think that you can pass off this poem as the work of a man, you deceive yourself. A man would give pride of place to the ghosts of Agamemnon, Achilles, Ajax, Odysseus' old comrades, and other more ancient heroes such as Minos, Orion, Tityus, Salmoneus, Tantalus, Sisyphus, and Hercules; and mention their wives and mothers incidentally, if at all; and make at least one god help Odysseus at some stage or other."

I admitted the force of his argument, which explains why, now, Odysseus first meets a comrade who has fallen off a roof at Circe's house —I call him Elpenor—and cracks a mild joke about Elpenor's having come more quickly to the Grove of Persephone by land than he by sea. I also allow Alcinous to ask after Agamemnon, Achilles and the rest, and Odysseus to satisfy his curiosity. For Phemius' sake I have even let Hermes supply the moly in passages adapted from my uncle Mentor's story of Ulysses. In my original version I had given all the credit to Athene.

While altering the saga of *Odysseus' Return* to make my Elyman suitors serve as Penelope's lovers, I had to protect myself against scandal. What if someone recognized the story and supposed that I, Nausicaa the irreproachable, had played the promiscuous harlot in my father's absence? So, according to my poem, Penelope must have remained faithful to Odysseus throughout those twenty years. And because this change meant that Aphrodite had failed to take her traditional revenge, I must make Poseidon, not her, the enemy who delayed him on his homeward voyage after the Fall of Troy. I should therefore have to omit the stories of Penelope's banishment and the oar mistaken for a flail, and Odysseus' death from Telemachus' sting-ray spear. When I told Phemius of these decisions, he pointed out, rather nastily, that since Poseidon had fought for the Greeks against the Trojans, and since Odysseus had never failed to honor him, I must justify this enmity by some anecdote. "Very well," I answered. "Odysseus blinded a Cyclops who, happening to be Poseidon's son, prayed to him for vengeance."

"My dear Princess, every Cyclops in the smithies of Etna was born to Uranus, Poseidon's grandfather, by Mother Earth."

"Mine was an exceptional Cyclops," I snapped. "He claimed Poseidon as his father and kept sheep in a Sican cave, like Conturanus. I shall call him Polyphemus—that is, 'famous'—to make my hearers think him a more important character than he really was."

"Such deceptions tangle the web of poetry."

"But if I offer Penelope as a shining example for wives to follow when their husbands are absent on long journeys, that will excuse the deception."

Admittedly, I made several stupid mistakes which I wish could be amended: for instance, when I composed the story of Odysseus' escape from Polyphemus the Cyclops, I put a rudder at the prow of his ship as well as at the stern. This was because, misled by the equestrian metaphor "turning her head about," frequently used by our sailors, I presumed a prow-rudder, which I had never noticed. And I have since discovered that one cannot cut seasoned timber from a growing tree as Odysseus does in Ogygia, and that hawks do not eat their prey on the wing, even in prodigies, and that it takes more than two or three men to hang a dozen women simultaneously from the same rope. Alas, a verse once sent on its travels can never be overtaken or recalled; nor can I fairly blame Phemius for not pointing out these mistakes to me. They all occur in passages which he criticized on other grounds, and I threatened him with a diet of bread and water if he changed a single word of them.

I also got into difficulties by first calling Eurycleia "Eurynome" and then forgetting and using her real name; so that later on I had to pretend that there were two of her. And I forgot, in my account of the massacre, that Penelope's lovers—whom I make her suitors because the legend, as Phemius used to tell it, disgusts any decent audience—could have armed themselves with the twelve long axes through which Odysseus shot, and used them as maces to hack him and his men in little pieces. But Homer, I am sure, went equally wrong at times, and I flatter myself that my story is interesting enough to blind Phemius' listeners to its faults, even if he has a cold, or the banquet is badly cooked, or the good dark wine runs short.

"μητις. . . .οὐτις"

by W. D. Snodgrass

For R. M. Powell

He fed them generously who were his flocks,
Picked, shatterbrained, for food. Passed as a goat
Among his sheep, I cast off. Though hurled rocks
And prayers deranged by torment tossed our boat,
I could not silence, somehow, this defiant
Mind. From my fist into the frothed wake ran
The white eye's gluten of the living giant
I had escaped, by trickery, as no man.

Unseen where all seem stone blind, pure disguise
Has brought me home alone to No Man's land
To look at nothing I dare recognize.
My dead blind guide, you lead me here to claim
Still waters that will never wash my hand,
To kneel by my old face and know my name.

Translator's Note

by T. E. Shaw (Lawrence of Arabia)

The twenty-eighth English rendering of the *Odyssey* can hardly be a literary event, especially when it aims to be essentially a straightforward translation. Wherever choice offered between a poor and a rich word richness had it, to raise the color. I have transposed: the order of metrical Greek being unlike plain English. Not that my English is plain enough. Wardour-Street Greek like the *Odyssey*'s defies honest rendering. Also I have been free with moods and tenses; allowed myself to interchange adjective and adverb; and dodged our poverty of preposition, limitations of verb, and pronominal vagueness by rearrangement. Still, syntax apart, this is a translation.

It has been made from the Oxford text, uncritically. I have not pored over contested readings, variants, or spurious lines. However scholars may question the text in detail, writers (and even would-be writers) cannot but see in the *Odyssey* a single, authentic, unedited work of art, integrally preserved. Thrice I noted loose ends, openings the author had forgotten: one sentence I would have shifted in time: five or six lines rang false to me: one speech seems to come before its context. These are motes in a book which is neat, close-knit, artful, and various; as nearly word-perfect as midnight oil and pumice can effect.

Crafty, exquisite, homogeneous—whatever great art may be, these are not its attributes. In this tale every big situation is burked and the writing is soft. The shattered *Iliad* yet makes a masterpiece; while the *Odyssey* by its ease and interest remains the oldest book worth reading for its story and the first novel of Europe. Gay, fine, and vivid it is: never huge or terrible. Book XI, the Underworld, verges toward "terribilità"—yet runs instead to the seed of pathos, that feeblest mode of writing. The author misses his every chance of greatness, as must all his faithful translators.

This limitation of the work's scope is apparently conscious. Epic belongs to early man, and this Homer lived too long after the heroic age to feel assured and large. He shows exact knowledge of what he could and could not do. Only through such superb self-criticism can talent rank beside inspiration.

In four years of living with this novel I have tried to deduce the author from his self-betrayal in the work. I found a bookworm, no longer young living from home, a mainlander, city-bred and domestic. Married but not exclusively, a dog-lover, often hungry and thirsty, dark-haired. Fond of poetry, a great if uncritical reader of the *Iliad,* with limited sensuous range but an exact eyesight which gave him all his pictures. A lover of old bric-a-brac, though as muddled an antiquary as Walter Scott—in sympathy with which side of him I have conceded "tenterhooks" but not railway-trains.

It is fun to compare his infuriating male condescension toward inglorious woman with his tender charity of head and heart for serving-men. Though a stickler for the prides of poets and a man who never misses a chance to cocker up their standing, yet he must be (like writers two thousand years after him) the associate of menials, making himself their friend and defender by understanding. Was it a fellow-feeling, or did he forestall time in his view of slavery?

He loved the rural scene as only a citizen can. No farmer, he had learned the points of a good olive tree. He is all adrift when it comes to fighting, and had not seen deaths in battle. He had sailed upon and watched the sea with a palpitant concern, seafaring being not his trade. As a minor sportsman he had seen wild boars at bay and heard tall yarns of lions.

Few men can be sailors, soldiers, and naturalists. Yet this Homer was neither land-lubber nor stay-at-home nor ninny. He wrote for audiences to whom adventures were daily life and the sea their universal neighbor. So he dared not err. That famous doubled line where the Cyclops narrowly misses the ship with his stones only shows how much better a seaman he was than his copyist. Scholiasts have tried to riddle his technical knowledge—and of course he does make a hotch-potch of periods. It is the penalty of being pre-archaeological. His pages are steeped in a queer naïveté; and at our remove of thought and language we cannot guess if he is smiling or not. Yet there is a dignity which compels respect and baffles us, he being neither simple in education nor primitive socially. His generation so rudely admired the *Iliad* that even to misquote it was a virtue. He sprinkles tags of epic across his pages. In this some find humor. Rather I judge that here too the tight lips of archaic art have grown the fixed grin of archaism.

Very bookish, this house-bred man. His work smells of the literary coterie, of a writing tradition. His notebooks were stocked with purple passages and he embedded these in his tale wherever they would more or less fit. He, like William Morris, was driven by his age to legend, where he found men living untrammelled under the God-possessed skies. Only, with more verbal felicity than Morris', he had less poetry. Fashion gave him recurring epithets, like labels: but repetitions tell, in public speaking. For recitation, too, are the swarming speeches. Perhaps the tedious delay of the climax through ten books may be a poor bard's means of prolonging his host's hospitality.

Obviously the tale was the thing; and that explains (without excusing it to our ingrown minds) his thin and accidental characterization. He thumb-nailed well; and afterwards lost heart. Nausicaa, for instance, enters dramatically and shapes, for a few lines, like a woman—then she fades, unused. Eumaeus fared better: but only the central family stands out, consistently and pitilessly drawn—the sly cattish wife, that cold-blooded egotist Odysseus, and the priggish son who yet met his master-prig in Menelaus. It is sorrowful to believe that these were really Homer's heroes and exemplars.

James Joyce: An Encounter with Homer

by Frank Budgen

It was shortly after our meeting at Taylor's *pension* that I again met Joyce, by chance this time, and we strolled through the double avenue of trees on the Utoquai from Bellevue toward Zürich Horn. To the left of us were the solid houses of Zürich burgesses, on our right the lake and on the far shore of the lake the green slopes and elegant contours of the Uetliberg ridge.

"I am now writing a book," said Joyce, "based on the wanderings of Ulysses. The *Odyssey,* that is to say, serves me as a ground plan. Only my time is recent time and all my hero's wanderings take no more than eighteen hours."

A train of vague thoughts arose in my mind, but failed to take shape definite enough for any comment. I drew with them in silence the shape of the Uetliberg-Albis line of hills. The *Odyssey* for me was just a long poem that might at any moment be illustrated by some Royal Academician. I could see his water-color Greek heroes, book-opened, in an Oxford Street bookshop window.

Joyce spoke again more briskly:

"You seem to have read a lot, Mr. Budgen. Do you know of any complete all-round character presented by any writer?"

With quick interest I summoned up a whole population of invented persons. Of the fiction writers Balzac, perhaps, might supply him? No. Flaubert? No. Dostoevsky or Tolstoy then? Their people are exciting, wonderful, but not complete. Shakespeare surely. But no, again. The footlights, the proscenium arch, the fatal curtain are all there to present to us not complete, all-round beings, but only three hours of passionate conflict. I came to rest on Goethe.

"What about Faust?" I said. And then, as a second shot, "Or Hamlet?"

"Faust!" said Joyce. "Far from being a complete man, he isn't a man at all. Is he an old man or a young man? Where are his home and family? We don't know. And he can't be complete because he's never alone. Mephistopheles is always hanging round him at his side or heels. We see a lot of him, that's all."

It was easy to see the answer in Joyce's mind to his own question. "Your complete man in literature is, I suppose, Ulysses?"

"Yes," said Joyce. "No-age Faust isn't a man. But you mentioned Hamlet. Hamlet is a human being, but he is a son only. Ulysses is son to Laertes, but he is father to Telemachus, husband to Penelope, lover of Calypso, companion in arms of the Greek warriors around Troy, and King of Ithaca. He was subjected to many trials, but with wisdom and courage came through them all. Don't forget that he was a war dodger who tried to evade military service by simulating madness. He might never have taken up arms and gone to Troy, but the Greek recruiting sergeant was too clever for him and, while he was ploughing the sands, placed young Telemachus in front of his plough. But once at the war the conscientious objector became a *jusqu' auboutist.* When the others wanted to abandon the siege he insisted on staying till Troy should fall."

I laughed at Ulysses as a leadswinger and Joyce continued:

"Another thing, the history of Ulysses did not come to an end when the Trojan war was over. It began just when the other Greek heroes went back to live the rest of their lives in peace. And then"—Joyce laughed—"he was the first gentleman in Europe. When he advanced, naked, to meet the young princess he hid from her maidenly eyes the parts that mattered of his brine-soaked, barnacle-encrusted body. He was an inventor too. The tank is his creation. Wooden horse or iron box—it doesn't matter. They are both shells containing armed warriors."

History repeats itself. The inventor of the tank also found his Ajax at the War Office in the shape of Lord Kitchener.

It seems to me to be significant that Joyce should talk to me first of the principal character in his book and only later of the manifold devices through which he presented him. If the two elements of character and material can be separated this is the order in which he would put them. On the home stretch back to Bellevue a question grew in my mind.

"What do you mean," I said, "by a complete man? For example, if a sculptor makes a figure of a man then that man is all-round, three-dimensional, but not necessarily complete in the sense of being ideal. All human bodies are imperfect, limited in some way, human beings too. Now your Ulysses. . . ."

"He is both," said Joyce. "I see him from all sides, and therefore he is all-round in the sense of your sculptor's figure. But he is a complete man as well—a good man. At any rate, that is what I intend that he shall be."

Ithaka

by C. P. Cavafy

When you set out for Ithaka
ask that your way be long,
full of adventure, full of instruction.
The Laistrygonians and the Cyclops,
angry Poseidon—do not fear them:
such as these you will never find
as long as your thought is lofty, as long as a rare
emotion touch your spirit and your body.
The Laistrygonians and the Cyclops,
angry Poseidon—you will not meet them
unless you carry them in your soul,
unless your soul raise them up before you.

Ask that your way be long.
At many a summer dawn to enter
—with what gratitude, what joy—
ports seen for the first time;
to stop at Phoenician trading centers,
and to buy good merchandise,
mother of pearl and coral, amber and ebony,
and sensuous perfumes of every kind,
sensuous perfumes as lavishly as you can;
to visit many Egyptian cities,
to gather stores of knowledge from the learnéd.
Have Ithaka always in your mind.
Your arrival there is what you are destined for.
But do not in the least hurry the journey.
Better that it last for years,
so that when you reach the island you are old,
rich with all you have gained on the way,
not expecting Ithaka to give you wealth.

Ithaka gave you the splendid journey.
Without her you would not have set out.
She hasn't anything else to give you.

And if you find her poor, Ithaka has not deceived you.
So wise have you become, of such experience,
that already you will have understood what these Ithakas mean.

Epilogue:
Homer and the Writers

by Robert Fagles

There was a time when an Ideal Homer ruled our writing: a good king in a moated land where the taxes were low, the streets safe, the women willing, and the food and weather incomparable. A delightful land, but not an undemanding one; a good king, but not permissive. He had been cut to the brains by a ten-year siege, as the story goes (in the *Iliad*), and gathering up his helmets and swords and bronze greaves to beat them into ploughshares, had taken a firm resolve to study war no more. And so, readjusted to a saner code of conscience in the postwar decade, he won the peace and regained (in the *Odyssey*) the paradise that his earlier, more headstrong ways had lost. At least we liked to think so, once, and we always put our hopes in the later epic that seemed to correct and even atone for the disastrous fury of the first. We had many hopes: Chapman's hope for the haven that is Heaven, reached at last by Odysseus and his "naked vertue"; Pope's hope for a state where willing nations know their lawful lord, a rather Romanized Ulysses. In other words, we used to think that a hero was a model far above us, that a poem built a perfect world—that Homer stood behind us, always offering what Keats had called "the realms of gold."

We believed in such exalted, "epic" values until we unearthed Troy, reduced the *Iliad* and the *Odyssey* from aspirations of the mind to relics of the real world, and heard Matthew Arnold, in an extended lecture *On Translating Homer,* tell us how to turn those relics into English. Arnold never wanted us to translate the Real Homer; what stirred him was the Ideal Homer who could provide not only an aesthetic norm for Arnold's age of "eccentricity, and arbitrariness" but a moral norm as well, the norm he had given statesmen like Lord Granville who, on the strength of Sarpedon's resolve, struggled up from his deathbed to approve the Treaty of Paris. That scene, recounted so movingly by Arnold, is an emblem of the age he wanted most, "the English aristocracy at its very height of culture, lofty spirit, and greatness, towards the middle of the 18th century." And yet, for all his dedication to neoclassic grandeur, Arnold makes Pope one of his four whipping-boys; he repeats Bentley's judgment—"It was a pretty poem, but must not be called Homer" (according to Arnold's version of that famous anecdote)—and decides "the work was judged." It *was* judged—as a reproduction, not as a poetic recreation of Homer. Arnold's dilemma was also judged: he hungered for ideals, but he hungered more to see a poem "as in itself it really is." Consequently, in his hands Homer became a clump of assessable data, and translation became a drone's search for historical equivalents, a search in which imagination is confusing, and prose more practical than verse.

At least it was for Arnold's disciples, Butcher and Lang, who 'renovated' half of Homer, "the simple truth about the matter of his *Odyssey,*" with the unpromising stuff of an old-fashioned, dilapidated English vocabulary. But they did meet opposition. Despising their "crumbs from Homer's richer table," Samuel Butler went to work on the "spirit" of the *Odyssey,* then asked us to compare his "readable prose" with their "words that are old and plain." And there is a choice here, one that favors Butcher and Lang because their prose gets the better of their purpose: their "old plainness" does give Homer some of the formality he needs, though slogging along through twenty-four books, it becomes mercilessly dull. Butler, however, with all the right intentions, completely misses the "spirit" of the *Odyssey,* and gives us a drab scrap from his bone of contention that its author was a woman. He "enlivens" the poem, not with solid Victorian authority, but a grimy kind of mill-town talk, and maps—elevations and water-ways clearly marked—a floorplan of Odysseus' house, and grainy tin-types of defunct Sicilian saltworks: Homer's "inspiration" for Scheria and parts of Ithaca. Butler, and Butcher and Lang are polar opposites—that have the same results. Whether dead of contemporaneity or old age, Homer falls before The Facts.

Arnold would not have thanked them, but he had facilitated their work. He clung to the faith of an Augustan, pathetically confused by the unruly empirical world that declared war on classical ideals; and his legacy is just as ambiguous. By bringing Homer within the range of shabby prose, he in effect gave Rouse and Rieu the license to commit their own *Odysseys* in prose—the supposed rough-and-tumble campfire yarn of the first, the unctuous chitchat of the second—but the Real Homer that he brought to the fore may reward us at the last. For we may discover what the English epic never really understood: namely, that the *Odyssey* is not the *Aeneid,* and that Homer, far from the lure of visionary missions, is simplicity itself, as Arnold puts it, "the pure lines of an Ionian horizon, the liquid clearness of an Ionian sky." By stripping away the saintly and civic robes that Chapman and Pope had draped around Homer, Arnold reveals the authentic, unpretentious Homer who is the basis of our modern triumphs with the *Odyssey*: the novels of T. E.

Lawrence, Graves, and Joyce, and the epic poems of Robert Fitzgerald and Pound.

I

For Lawrence of Arabia the Real Homer may have his lapses as a writer—more snores than sleepy nods—but Lawrence's burly, combative prose finally gives Homer a compelling stature that he deserves. Of course Lawrence misses Homer's stature, and no one knew it better than he himself. He hated his results because he felt the limits of translation: by lessening the relevance of originality, it muffled his own "inevitable word." He tried for such a word only once, in the invocation that his designer Bruce Rogers printed in capitals so that it engraves the page like a votive tablet. Here Lawrence sets out on Odysseus' "AGONY TO REDEEM HIMSELF" and appeals to "DIVINE POESY GODDESS-DAUGHTER OF ZEUS." A noble introduction—with little bearing on what follows from the Muse of Prose. Lawrence made prose of Homer, however, not only because he was not a poet, but because he found the "business of living . . . too big and too absorbing" for poetry; only prose could take his whole life in. He once wrote, "I aspire most fervently in Homer," and the way he conscripted his own experience in the *Odyssey* shows how radically the poem's meaning has shifted. No longer the metaphor for an all-embracing external order, cosmic or social, Elizabethan or Augustan, the *Odyssey* has penetrated the translator's mind until it reflects his private life. Lawrence said he would rather have written it than *The Seven Pillars of Wisdom,* giving some point to Beerbohm's oily remark, "he confused the *Odyssey,* you know, with his translation of it." Lawrence never confused the quality of his work with Homer's, but he had to confuse Odysseus' experience with his own:

> I have handled the weapons, armor, utensils of those times, explored their houses, planned their cities. I have hunted wild boars and watched wild lions, sailed the Aegean (& sailed ships), bent bows, lived with pastoral peoples, woven textiles, built boats and killed many men.

To lift Homer to life—Lawrence's phrase—he had to lift him from his own life, and his strategy had mixed results. Disillusioned by the Peace Conference and his futile struggles for Feisal, he found Odysseus' public settlement in Ithaca a "drooling" anticlimax that "stinks of unreality." Labor as he would through numerous revisions, his last two books show a marked falling off in intensity. And Lawrence's life left as little room for Homer's gods. He wanted to make them lifeless masks, yet he wanted even more to strengthen his convention, and so he made them personalities. A limitation but no loss: the intonation of his gods—their easy slips into gruff man-talk—reveals them for their old Homeric selves. And for all his hero's pangs of conscience, he suffers no agonies of self-redemption: he is simply a "mad egotist" (as Lawrence promised he would be), and yet his egotism makes him winning in a ruthlessly cut-throat, marvellously Homeric way of self-assertiveness. Lawrence's lasting contribution to the English epic is this irresistible voice that unifies his *Odyssey,* warning us with a jaunty shrewdness, "Look out; I've been there and back with more complex equipment than any of you could manage." There is no high moral commentary in that voice. But there is, I think, a lively novel. And certainly there is a part of Homer that all the earlier English *Odysseys* had ignored or decried: the part that took experience by the scruff and shook it into order, not God's order but the individual order of the self.

II

Robert Fitzgerald has made the *Odyssey* again a poem. He gives the Muse notice not only to tell Odysseus' adventures "in our time" but to "lift the great song again." Whereas Lawrence's opening lines (ironically) exile Homer from an old poetic and moral tradition, Fitzgerald reinstates him with a manifesto as public as Pope's. If Lawrence lifts Homer back to life, Fitzgerald lifts him back to greatness.

Each translator stands in a unique relationship to Homer. For Lawrence art is craft: as his Odysseus puts it in his rather mercantile way, "the Muse cherishes the whole guild of singers and teaches to each one his rules of song." And Lawrence himself serves a fairly dutiful apprenticeship to Homer: 'aspiring most fervently in' a master who allows few liberties, he cobbles close behind him, always writing 'toward' him; rather than take command himself, Lawrence hopes to approximate the Greek. But Fitzgerald's art is a blend of inspiration and craft, so passive that for Phemius "a god shaped all the various ways of life in song," yet so creative that Demodocus himself has "skill to shape with such great style [his] songs of the Akhaians." Approaching the Greek with his own idea of imaginative wholeness fully formed, Fitzgerald always writes 'with' Homer, never 'toward' him; he wants to collaborate and react, not report, explain, and approximate.

The result is a language of unequalled range—chatty, punning, and hard-bitten, but at the same time, handsome, formulaic, and high-flown. Fitzgerald's great achievement may well be to convince a generation brought up on what Auden calls "the wry, the sotto-voce, ironic and monochrome" that once we read Homer we will never be quite the same. From him, as Pound would say, "we can get nearly 'all of it' " (meaning all of poetry): the dense weave of the vowels, the swell and thrust of the strong line, and the memorable image. In his world men are a "drooping dance and dreams," Helen holds out nepenthe, the "mild magic of forgetfulness," and when he sees the famous women, Odysseus exclaims,

"Here was great loveliness of ghosts!" Here, then, is a compelling stylishness, and when it weds a more confiding tone of voice, the work is all Fitzgerald. I remember the wraith of Heracles, that "vast figure" who turns "of a sudden" to give Odysseus a "kindly" salute in Hell:

> "Son of Laërtês and the gods of old,
> Odysseus, master mariner and soldier,
> under a cloud, you too?"

Fitzgerald has made the fabulous realm of Homer long-lost but inescapable. First he raises its incantatory roll of lofty names; then he makes it thrill our wits away with warmth.

And so he amplifies the tone that Lawrence first asserted in his *Odyssey*, the tone of expertise that was at best attractively adept, but at worst full of the arrogance of the insecure. Lawrence could never call a spade a spade; it had to come out an adze or a mattock or an ash-hafted carbon-steel shovel. He was always afraid that some of Homer's life might leave him and his lonely, fervid aspirations in the lurch, and his *Odyssey*, published *entre deux guerres*, is all attrition and combat, a staunch companion in the trenches or the shelters. But Fitzgerald has none of this anxiety. His *Odyssey* makes the wars feel ten years behind us—the public fountains are up, the concert halls refurbished, and once again the presses roll their rich black loam of print. Fitzgerald's tone may also say, "I've been there and back," but he always adds quickly, reassuringly, "Come along with me; here's sensibility enough for both of us." A deep inclusiveness in that voice welcomes us into a world too close to ours to leave us disengaged, yet too impressive not to leave us changed.

Fitzgerald makes Homer new by making him ours. Looking both to the Greek and to this age, he creates a marvellous amphibious *Odyssey*. On one hand, for the first time in an English translation, Homer's poem takes the form of a romance, perhaps the form he gave it from the start. Here is a man—not divine but, like his closest kin, the Ancient Mariner, a target for divine wrath—who wanders through woods where the messenger rhymes and the witch's golden hair is tempting, or more alarmingly, through serial terrors and the dark forces of negation, until he reaches a daylight clearing where happy accidents make his world come right. At the same time, the form of Fitzgerald's *Odyssey* is clearly more modern than Homer's, not as desperately modern as the muzzy stuff of Butler, Rouse, and Rieu, but modern as the post-Homeric epic, the poem of national purpose invigorated by a spirit who would take the hearts of humanists from Virgil to Chapman and Pope. Unlike the wily in-fighter of Homer and Lawrence, Fitzgerald's Odysseus is a hero of "detachment" who persuades us that, far from the martyr's immunity or the king's aloofness or the icy numbness of his excutioner, this best of modern virtues leads to action--swift, unpretentious, sound. If

Lawrence's personal image of Odysseus confines his *Odyssey* and even weakens his last two books, Fitzgerald finds a personal image that is choric, and thus he solves the dilemma of every epic poet after Keats: he makes the narrow limits of biography open into an all-inclusive whole. His Odysseus is very much a man, but by mastering his tugs of passion and indulgence he becomes what most romances lack: earthbound as he is, yet a model for us all, he takes on the aura of a canonical hero.

What he canonizes is a kind of self-expressionism: as much a realm of gold as our contemporary outlook can envision. A good deal lower than Chapman's Heaven, this realm is based upon the drab average and the day-by-day, the bruising arena where Odysseus does his work. He deliberately turns away from the soft luxury of Alcinous' "house of gold" to take his stand amidst another "place of gold" that Fitzgerald has named, elsewhere, "the rational savage city of man." Here paradox routs out what Pope would call "close systems of benevolence." But if we have no state of the world, each of us has his state of mind, and in confirming his, one makes the rigors of experience viable for the moment. Willing to turn us all to "quiet wicks in the wild night," Fitzgerald gives us what Pope gave his Augustans and what Lawrence of Arabia wanted most: a compelling hope, an inevitable word derived from Homer.

III

Our best translators turn the *Odyssey* into a biography, a highly personal one for Lawrence, a universal one for Fitzgerald. Our best adapters, Graves, Joyce, and Pound, turn the *Odyssey* into the biography of a specific sort of man, the artist, but the artists they describe and their goals are worlds apart.

Although Butler had an affair with Nausicaa, the "authoress" of the *Odyssey,* he hid her behind the cranky prose of a long debate, rather than parade her—enticingly—in public. Half a century later, in his novel *Homer's Daughter,* Robert Graves takes Butler's tack and gives it all the energy it needs. Now we have Nausicaa's daring, personal revelation, one that is full of Odyssean events, or rather full of Odyssean parodies that begin in a low key and slowly take on Homer's brilliance. A lovers' quarrel over an amber necklace replaces Poseidon's wrath and gets the story going, but the civil war that sweeps across Nausicaa's island mounts to an Homeric pitch; and although she may be (amusingly) underdeveloped and difficult to marry off, she manages to wed the stranger who straggles up from the underbrush. In other words, here is Homer from a woman's point of view. Graves's novel is less a game of free-associationism than the memoir of a highly engaging individual, and the better we understand her, the better we will understand her art. Graves's Odyssey is the autobiography that explains Homer's epic.

Look at Nausicaa—no more than "religious-minded," scorning Aphrodite with fine fury in a world where *moly,* after all, is garlic, prophets are merely "men of experience," and Odysseus' fabulous adventures—the four books that the English Renaissance had fired with the zeal of a moral exploration—are nursery tales that little girls at last get over. Nevertheless, excitement crowds her world (midnight sailings and darker murders), but it is the excitement of intrigue, not of soul-voyages and the death of self-esteem, and she meets it with unsentimental address: her "tears are rarer even than [her] kisses." When she foments a counter-revolution for her father's partisans, she gives such a swagger of competence to every step that her last taunt to Phemius—"As though I ever fail in any of my undertakings!"—can summarize her life.

But like the *Odyssey,* Graves's Nausicaa always veers away from tragedy and centers on the comic. She looks at the carnage of the rebels and quickly turns it off with, "Well, they were warned—repeatedly," and a gesture somewhat more girlish than heroic: the giggle. In the lists of love, however, she can be unyielding, even merciless at times, but above all "high-spirited" in the way that men find most disarming. She knows too much: "I have always hated a man who, trying to hide crooked intentions behind a honeyed smile, is vain enough to believe that I cannot see through him." And yet, like a Virginia Woolf heroine, she knows that tantalizing measure more: how to give a man the delicious lie of feeling in control. And even her one neurosis—too much mortality on the mind—begs for coddling more than psychotherapy and so endears her still more warmly; in fact, thanks to her level-headedness, it results in her most winning achievement. "This preoccupation of mine with death excuses, or at least explains, the most unusual decision I have recently taken: of securing for myself a posthumous life under the mantle of Homer." She falls to work on her immortalizing epic with just the blend of charm and cool finesse that marks her life—and Homer's *Odyssey.* In other words, Nausicaa's very attitude and tone determine the nature of the Real Homer. She is not a born liar, but she has had to "adapt, disguise, shift, diminish and enlarge incidents to square them with the epic tradition." In particular, she has played it free and easy with an old (and conveniently unavailable) saga called "The Return of Odysseus," fleshing out its old bare bones with her own exuberant relish of life.

Her *Odyssey,* then, the *Odyssey* as we know it, is a maverick like Penelope who (she tells us) was actually notorious for loose-living. In fact the *Odyssey* might have been as immoral as the *Iliad,* but Nausicaa was stopped by a trusty reflex in her conscience: "What if someone recognized the story and supposed that I, Nausicaa the irreproachable, had played the promiscuous harlot in my father's absence? So, according to my poem, Penelope must have remained faithful to Odysseus through those twenty years." And Penelope serves another, less personal purpose that does have a feel of piety about it, the only piety that counts in

Graves's secular world: by making Penelope a sop to moralists Nausicaa can atone for her extravagant sins against poetic license, her shifting and disguising. At the last she even becomes contrite and performs the fine mockpenance of a writer who has seduced the Western world for two millenia: she lists her errata, hands us the keys to her characters, and confesses her most fiendish tricks. Here, as always, she is only spoofing in her expediently "religious-minded" way. She undergoes no saint's life or conversion; she simply carries out her quest for the sheer craft of craftiness essential to her own survival. Phemius may wag an outraged finger and protest, "Such deceptions tangle the web of poetry," but they clear the web of an artist's creative process. Homer sang an epic before which most people have genuflected too much and laughed too little. Con the magic in the web, Graves seems to say, and the finished fabric will delight you more.

IV

Like Lawrence and Fitzgerald, Graves explores the *Odyssey* as a metaphor for biography. While they give us a version of Homer's poem, however, Graves treats it as the index for the subject of his novel: Homer's supposed inner workings revealed in Nausicaa's life and mind. Probing in the same direction, Joyce internalizes Homer still more deeply.

Compare Bloom's voyage to that of Odysseus. He reaches none of Homer's optimistic unions: no binding talks with Stephen, his briefly-adopted son, no intercourse with Molly, and for all the Utopian schemes "flashing through his . . . busy brain," Bloom passes for "the world's greatest reformer" only in the phantasmagoria of Bella Cohen's brothel —where he is no sooner crowned and worshipped as the founder of the New Bloomusalem, than his city crumbles and all Ireland routs him out. But if Bloom falls short of Odysseus' conclusions, he seems to reach some of his resolutions, for he and the Greek hero are "centripetal." Of course the goal that draws him suits the character of a "mixed-middling," not the many-turned, bell-wether Odysseus, and his "voyage round [his] own little world" leads to a fitting loss of ambition that rules out public settlements in Ithaca, and settles down to rest in Flowerville and a snug bourgeois cottage. And yet this very limitation of his goal suggests that Bloom, like Odysseus, has met his own peculiar test of seaworthiness. He is

> that vigilant wanderer, soiled by the dust of travel and combat and stained by the mire of an indelible dishonor, but from whose steadfast and constant heart no lure or peril or threat or degradation could ever efface the image of that voluptuous loveliness which the inspired pencil of Lafayette has limned for ages yet to come.

And when he reaches this "loveliness," Bloom proves himself still more steadfast and constant: he resigns himself to Molly's whims; he decides that her adultery is "more than inevitable," it is "irreparable." This terrible rationalization is Bloom's most positive act, perhaps the very triumph that he builds from defeat, for it marks his arrival at that most secure of current havens: "equanimity."

His journey is Homeric in still another sense. Bloom solves his dilemmas by finding what Odysseus seeks: an ethos. While Bloom's ethos gives him none of Odysseus' self-assertiveness, it insures his survival with such Homeric rigor that it finally 'places' him Homerically. Bloom's ethos relates him—if only in frighteningly negative terms—to those areas of experience that are pertinent to him: not to morality but to "the inanity of extolled virtue," not to the mind but "the lethargy of nescient matter," not to cosmic order but "the apathy of the stars." While he shudders his "lonechill" of alienation from the world, Bloom at least snuggles into touch with all that he had first affirmed in the Hell of Glasnevin Cemetery, the "warm fullblooded life" that floods from Molly and concludes the novel.

As Lenehan says, "There's a touch of the artist about old Bloom," a contemporary artist something like Nausicaa: Bloom manipulates his world only as he manipulates his own imaginings. And yet the mastery he wins, unlike Nausicaa's, does not lead to the art of epic but merely to the art of acceptance, an art confined to Bloom's own rocky Ithaca, the mountains of his mind. Unable to create an image that controls his world, Bloom creates one that controls himself. His work may be Homeric, but it is not Homer's. The *Odyssey* never crossed his mind.

The *Odyssey* obsessed another manipulative mind, however, that of Joyce as he perfects Bloom's art of acceptance and his own of epic. If Bloom's art is not Homeric, Joyce's is, yet only as a parody, and readers and characters do not respond to parodies as the writer does. Parallels depend on sources (like the *Odyssey*) and build them into art; parodies diverge from sources and include them only to diminish them. Parallels are guideposts for readers, parodies are catalysts for writers. As Harry Levin observes, Homer gave Joyce the matrix of order that he needed most: "Utterly unshackled from the usual conventions, Joyce hedged himself in with far more complicated conditions and far more rigorous restrictions than any school of criticism would ever dare to exact." Perhaps, however, Homer's matrix was less limiting than Levin suggests. It seems, in fact, that by parodying Homer, Joyce so channeled his "chapter of accidents" that at last he lifted its miscellany into the liberating realm of myth.

Ulysses is mythic, not in an historical or a theological sense, but in an artistic one. It is neither equal to, nor inescapably demeaned by, the Homeric past. Although the present is remade in the light of the Homeric past, it is self-contained. Like other myths, its order makes a narrative possible, and yet it does not embody a unifying system of beliefs; it merely carries Bloom's final attitude, the one credible attitude in a Land of Phenomenon, the land of "Beer, beef, business, bibles, bull-dogs, battleships, buggery and bishops." In other words, only one aspect of Joyce's myth is truly Homeric: its unpretentiousness. It teaches nothing. It simply displays. It displays so fully, in fact, that all debts to Homer disappear, and at last it stands alone, the myth that Joyce has made:

> What went forth to the ends of the world to traverse not itself. God, the sun, Shakespeare, a commercial traveller, having itself traversed in reality itself, becomes that self.

As Bloom explores Dublin to traverse himself, Joyce explores the *Odyssey* to traverse his art, internalizing Homer to the furthest point. Rather than present Homer's poem, like Lawrence and Fitzgerald, or penetrate into his process, like Graves, Joyce absorbs the *Odyssey* into his own process. Graves causes Nausicaa's autobiography to shape the *Odyssey;* the *Odyssey* excites Joyce's 'autobiography' of Bloom. Graves's novel serves Homer by illuminating him; Homer serves Joyce by informing *Ulysses,* and so (as Stephen might maintain) Homer—"like the God of the Creation . . . refined out of existence"—is the inner rite on which the artist, not his hero or his reader, rests.

V

Pound's idea of his *Cantos* complements his idea of Homer's epic. He told Rouse that the *Odyssey* and all the classics must be placed in a "plenum" of world literary history, and as "the history of the tribe," his own epic is ideally suited for the job. Homer, in recompense, can help the *Cantos*: if they will follow Pound's plan and generate their history "from one man's body"—Pound's apparently—Odysseus' career can guide his growth. Pound collaborates with Homer, writing his own epic and placing Homer's simultaneously. He will have oriented the *Odyssey* in time, as he orients himself around the quest of Homer's hero, the quest for a future ethos that begins in Homer's Underworld, which "shouts aloud that it is *older* than the rest, . . . hintertime that is *not* Praxiteles, not Athens of Pericles, but Odysseus." Here in Hell, Pound like Bloom discovers that "both ends meet," the limit of death and the limit of life, but Pound will make his unions go beyond his single mind. As he tries to bind the poles of time, he will try to bind Homer's epic and his own.

The First Canto forecasts his sweeping intentions. He begins, self-effacingly, by serving Homer as his translator, and gives a rather close version of the start of the descent to Hades. But he ends as a creative adapter of Homer, and sounds out a free imitation of an Homeric hymn that seems in praise of Pound himself. His language reflects his shifting stance toward Homer. The Canto begins in the past, ground down in its data, and its rhythms are based on the blocks of Old English—

> And then went down to the ship,
> Set keel to breakers, forth on the godly sea,

—but by taking on an ornamental Latin, the Canto wells into the even rolling cadence of

> Aphrodite,
> *Cypri munimenta sortita est,* mirthful, *oricalchi,* with golden
> Girdles and breast bands, thou with the dark eyelids
> Bearing the golden bough of Argicida.

a cadence that lifts Pound's language into a celebrational mood that he will try to assign to himself in the later portions of his epic. What seems to evoke these realignments of Homer and his own language is the sequence of figures that he faces, as if at a sacrificial fosse within his mind. They range from Elpenor, the victim of circumstance, "A man of no fortune, and with a name to come," to Tiresias, the seer of circumstance, to the demonic masters of circumstance who ascend in the order of their benevolence: from the Sirens, to Circe, to Aphrodite at the last. These in effect are the roles or "personae" that Pound plans to play throughout his *Cantos,* or in the case of the last three figures, the powers whom he will confront and try to master. The First Canto sets up their order of appearance, hence the full itinerary of Pound's imaginative Odyssey. While he hopes that his world will advance from fact to glorious fantasy, he will attempt to grow from a servant of the past, to a minister for the future, from a victim and an alien to a lord. That much the First Canto would seem to imply, and its closing phrase, "So that," like the Greek *hôste,* makes all the *Cantos* a result clause opening out in what may be the fulfilment of its promises.

The completion of his journey is unique among modern Odysseys. Our versions of Odysseus, like Bloom and Kazantzakis' hero, aspire to cities of their own design, symbols of social unity in the image of themselves, but these cities either disintegrate or collapse into cottages. Pound, on the other hand, would have us believe that his version of Ithaca is firm and spacious; like its laws announced in *Thrones,* its very edifice is claimed to reflect the order of the gods. In other words, Pound designs his Odyssey so that it will complement, not the Real Homer who describes life as it is and who has intrigued our modern writers, but the earlier English Homer who prescribed life as it ought to be. In fact, Pound seems to thread backward through the steps that interpret Homer in the English epic line. Like Arnold he sees the *Odyssey* as an object, but he lets his daring as a free-adapter take command, and so he claims the goal that

Arnold strove for but ironically denied himself; he claims to reconstitute his culture around Homer and grasp again the world of order that was last confirmed by Pope. Like the Augustan *Odyssey,* Pound's celebrates a "Domination of Benevolence"; its "basis is man," its code is "Balance." Pound would have us believe that the *Cantos* make a perfect world, and that he himself becomes its paradigm, like Augustan Ulysses the lawful lord of willing nations. First he translates the Real Homer; at last he tries to transform into a neoclassical ideal.

This might be a noble achievement—if only it were credible. Far from regaining a neoclassical ideal, Pound may have shown its radical impossibility in our age. Perspective is everything in Pope. His epic begins in the kind of ideality that circumstance contributes to, but never threatens. From the start of his epic he distances Odysseus in terms of an objective world order, and this order virtually decrees our belief in the hero's final apotheosis or "lordship" over willing nations. Pound's epic, on the other hand, begins in a welter of circumstance, but rather than absorb its threats, he simply shuts them out and sets up his ideals. What takes over in Pound's world is not order but will-power, and it may seem muscular and exalted—or downright annoying. As it is with Aristotle's young men, Pound's "generalities cannot be born from a sufficient phalanx of particulars"; as he promised his father, he has quite arbitrarily "bust[ed] through from quotidien into 'divine or permanent world.'" The danger here is that we are left with two unattractive extremes: allusions too picayune to be of value—generalities too big to bolt down whole. There is nothing in-between; the *Cantos* are all process or all pattern.

What they need is a steady, mediating perspective. If they must end in a personal apotheosis, they need disciplined selectivity from the start. An "Odyssean" scaffold can be flung up to give the *Cantos* bold outline and support, the sort of scaffold that Forrest Read, Jr. details with such precision; but to many readers this may seem an act of violence—or uncalled-for generosity. The clutter of the poem can easily obscure this sort of framework, and when it does, an objective correlative for Pound's career is gone, and his arrival at thrones and godhead seems implausible. And there is another lack of perspective as well. The *Cantos* need an oblique commentary on their hero's growth, the second voice that will pronounce some agonies of remorse and failure, the kind of voice that makes Pound's perception of order in the Pisan Cantos more compelling than his late, civic "triumphs" which he harps on in the "over-Whitmanated" hymns of *Thrones.* And yet even the awareness won in Pisa is not fully proved; it is stated more than dramatized. In general, then, what we need is an alternative and unbiased vision of Pound as he undergoes his imaginative career, and if it puts an end to his apotheosis, many readers will call this an act of enlightened self-criticism—euthanasia, not murder. One cannot reach Pope's goal with external order. As Lawrence,

Fitzgerald, Graves, and Joyce have shown, one can make a decent pattern from an unruly and often murderous empirical world or process, but one cannot leap to lofty patterns which exclude that process.

So Pound may actually devaluate the currency that others give the *Odyssey*. As the autobiography of a self-expressive man, Homer can lead us to resignation, and resignation works in modern art: it is ironic, circumstantial, generous with possibilities for drama—Bloom's settlement can be intensely *shown*. The images that he and Nausicaa project upon experience have an appealing modesty that makes them plausible: their images control, but never exceed, the world around them. Center Homer on the first person for too long, however, and a writer may become as solipsistic as Tennyson's Ulysses, or like Pound decree himself a god by fiat. But fiats are affairs of faith. As art, they thrive only in an age of one belief, not many, an age not of paradox but of earlier pieties and the big words that seem to have made many people happy centuries ago. As Eliot sees it now, however,

> what there is to conquer
> By strength and submission, has already been discovered
> Once or twice, or several times, by men whom one cannot hope
> To emulate.

Rubbed against our private touchstones, the ways of a model hero high above us—his godhead, his benevolent thrones, his perfect world—all his winnings may prove fool's gold.

But what we have lost in universal authority we have gained in personal freedom, and as our *Odysseys* suggest, that freedom is our obsession, a superior obsession according to Wallace Stevens and one that has set terms: "You are free, but your freedom must be consonant with the freedom of others." Consonant freedom—that is epic material far from Pope's and Chapman's. Keats first found it; Joyce and Graves and Fitzgerald beat it into another world that, hardly perfect, is only an intenser version of our own, a world as terrible as the one where Hector dies and Paris lives, yet also as freshly realistic as the one where Odysseus wins: a modern world as exuberant as Homer's realms of gold.

The Argonauts

by D. H. Lawrence

They are not dead, they are not dead!
Now that the sun, like a lion, licks his paws
and goes slowly down the hill:
now that the moon, who remembers, and only cares
that we should be lovely in the flesh, with bright, crescent feet,
pauses near the crest of the hill, climbing slowly, like a queen
looking down on the lion as he retreats.

Now the sea is the Argonaut's sea, and in the dawn
Odysseus calls the commands, as he steers past those foamy islands
wait, wait, don't bring the coffee yet, nor the *pain grillé*.
The dawn is not off the sea, and Odysseus' ships
have not yet passed the islands. I must watch them still.

Notes on the Editors and Authors

GEORGE STEINER, co-editor of the anthology, is a writer, critic, teacher, and journalist. He has published verse, numerous articles and studies on foreign affairs, and essays, as well as two books: *Tolstoy or Dostoevsky* and *The Death of Tragedy*. He is presently on the editorial board of the *Kenyon Review*.

ROBERT FAGLES, co-editor of the anthology, recently published a translation of Bacchylides and has completed a study of Homer and the English epic. He is contributing to the Twickenham Edition of Pope's *Iliad* and *Odyssey* and is an Assistant Professor of English at Princeton University.

W. H. AUDEN's most recent work includes a translation (with Chester Kallman) of *The Magic Flute* and two volumes of original poetry, *The Shield of Achilles* and *Homage to Clio*.

The late ERICH AUERBACH, professor, philologist, and critic, was among the founders of comparative literature; his works translated into English are the *Introduction to Romance Languages and Literature, Mimesis: The Representation of Reality in Western Literature*, and *Dante, Poet of the Secular World*.

RACHEL BESPALOFF, French philosopher and essayist of Russian origin, has written *Cheminements et carrefours: essais d'art et de philosophie*.

ERNST BLOCH is a German metaphysician, moralist, and master of poetic prose; among his most respected works are *Freiheit und Ordnung, Geist der Utopie*, and *Das Prinzip Hoffnung*.

FRANK BUDGEN, "boozer, bard, and canvas dauber" in Joyce's words, was the author's confidant during the period in Zürich when he wrote the middle part of *Ulysses*.

C. P. CAVAFY, one of the major forces behind the renascence of contemporary Greek verse, considered himself "that best of things, a Hellene: mankind has no quality more precious."

C. DAY LEWIS, Professor of Poetry at Oxford University (1951-56), is the author of *Collected Poems* and distinguished verse translations of Virgil's *Georgics* and *Aeneid*.

GEORGE E. DIMOCK, Jr., teaches Classics at Smith College and is at work on a study of the *Odyssey*.

ROBERT FITZGERALD's translation of the *Odyssey* won the first Bollingen Prize for verse translation in 1961; he has published versions of Sophocles and St. John Perse, as well as a collection of original poems, *In the Rose of Time*.

GABRIEL GERMAIN, the French classicist and anthropologist of North African background, has written *Genèse de l'Odyssée, Le fantastique et le sacré* and *Homère et la mystique des nombres*.

ROBERT GRAVES's rôles as novelist, essayist, and mythologist "have always," in his own words, "been subordinate to an an inveterate profession of poetry"; *The Anger of Achilles,* an adaptation of the *Iliad,* and *Collected Poems* are his most recent productions.

In addition to his more celebrated works, FRANZ KAFKA wrote an intriguing book of Parables on subjects from the Orient, Israel, Hellas, and the Occident.

Novelist and essayist, D. H. LAWRENCE also wrote many books of verse: *Amores* 1916; *Bay* 1919; *Birds, Beasts and Flowers* 1923; and *Last Poems* 1932.

ALBERT B. LORD, Professor of Slavic Languages and Literatures at Harvard University, collected Serbocroatian heroic songs with the late Milman Parry; his study of the oral art of Homer, *The Singer of Tales,* appeared in 1960.

GEORG LUKÁCS, whose *Studies in European Realism* was translated into English in 1950, is perhaps the most eminent of living Marxist philosophers.

The late EDWIN MUIR, translator of Hermann Broch and Franz Kafka, wrote an autobiography and books of verse, *Collected Poems 1921-1951* and *One Foot in Eden* (1956), that are beginning to loom large in the perspective of modern English letters.

EZRA POUND is translating certain plays by Sophocles and continues to build the edifice of his *Cantos. Section: Rock-Drill* (Cantos 85-95) was published in 1955 and *Thrones* (96-109) in 1959.

JOHN COWPER POWYS, novelist, essayist, and necromancer, has made two bold ventures into the Greek world: *Homer and the Aether* and *Atlantis: A Novel of Odysseus.*

T. E. SHAW (LAWRENCE OF ARABIA), soldier of fortune and translator of the *Odyssey,* claimed that he would rather have written Homer's epic than his own monumental *Seven Pillars of Wisdom.*

W. D. SNODGRASS's first volume of poems, *Heart's Needle,* was awarded the 1960 Pulitzer Prize in Poetry.

W. B. STANFORD, Professor of Classics at Trinity College, Dublin, and author of *The Ulysses Theme: A Study in the Adaptability of a Traditional Hero,* has done an annotated edition of the *Odyssey,* as well as studies of ambiguity and metaphor in Greek literature.

CEDRIC H. WHITMAN, of the Department of the Classics at Harvard University, is known for his *Sophocles: A Study of Heroic Humanism* and *Homer and the Heroic Tradition.*

Further Reading

THE SCHOLARS

Bassett, Samuel Eliot. *The Poetry of Homer,* Berkeley, Cal.: University of California Press, 1938.

Bérard, Victor. *Les Navigations d'Ulysse.* Paris: A. Colin, 1927-9.

Bowra, Sir Maurice. *Tradition and Design in the Iliad.* Oxford, Clarendon Press, 1930.

Carpenter, Rhys. *Folk Tale, Fiction and Saga in the Homeric Epics.* Berkeley, Cal.: University of California Press, 1958.

Finley, Moses I. *The World of Odysseus.* London: Chatto & Windus, Ltd., 1956.

Jaeger, Werner. Book One, Sections 1-3, of *Paideia: the Ideals of Greek Culture,* trans. Gilbert Highet. New York: Oxford University Press, 1939.

Lorimer, H. L. *Homer and the Monuments.* London: The Macmillan Company, Ltd., 1950.

Myres, Sir John L. *Homer and his Critics,* ed. Dorothea Gray. London: Routledge & Kegan Paul, Ltd., 1958.

Nilsson, Martin P. *Homer and Mycenae.* London: Methuen & Co., 1933.

Page, Denis L. *History and the Homeric Iliad.* Berkeley, Cal.: University of California Press, 1959.

Rahner, Hugo. "Die Seelenheilende Blume: Moly und Mandragore in antiker und christlicher Symbolik," *Eranos-Jahrbuch,* XII (1945), pp. 117-239.

Scott, John A. *The Unity of Homer.* Berkeley, Cal.: University of California Press, 1921.

Snell, Bruno. Chapter I, of *The Discovery of the Mind,* trans. T. G. Rosenmeyer. Cambridge, Mass.: Harvard University Press, 1953.

Wade-Gery, H. T. *The Poet of the Iliad.* Cambridge, Eng.: Cambridge University Press, 1952.

Webster, T. B. L. *From Mycenae to Homer.* London: Methuen & Co., 1958.

Winterstein, Alfred. "Die Nausikaaepisode in der Odyssee," *Imago,* VI (1920), pp. 349-83.

GREAT ENCOUNTERS

Arnold, Matthew. *On Translating Homer;* three lectures given at Oxford. London: Longman, Green, Longman and Roberts, 1861.

Broch, Hermann. Introduction to *On the Iliad* by Rachel Bespaloff. The Bollingen Series IX, 1947.

Butler, Samuel. *The Authoress of the Odyssey*. London: A. C. Fifield, 1897.

Porter, Katherine Anne. *A Defense of Circe*. New York: Harcourt, Brace & World, Inc., 1954.

Pound, Ezra. Letters to W. H. D. Rouse in *The Letters of Ezra Pound,* ed. D. D. Paige. New York: Harcourt, Brace & World, Inc., 1950.

Shaw, T. E. (Lawrence of Arabia). Letter to Sir William Rothenstein (20.x.32) in *The Letters of T. E. Lawrence,* ed. David Garnett. London: Jonathan Cape Ltd., 1938.

———. *Letters from T. E. Shaw to Bruce Rogers*. 200 copies privately printed, 1933.

Weil, Simone. *The Iliad, or, The Poem of Force,* trans. Mary McCarthy. New York: Politics Pamphlet No. 1.

TRANSLATIONS, IMITATIONS, AND ALLUSIONS

Arrowsmith, W. A. "Helen on the Walls" [*Iliad,* III. 121-242], *Hudson Review,* XIV (1962), pp. 567-70.

Fitzgerald, Robert. Trans. *The Odyssey*. New York: Doubleday & Co., 1961.

Giraudoux, Jean. *Tiger at the Gates* (*La guerre de Troie n'aura pas lieu*), trans. Christopher Fry. New York: Oxford University Press, 1956.

Gunn, Thom. "The Book of the Dead," in *My Sad Captains*. London: Faber & Faber Ltd., 1961.

Hughes, Ted. "Everyman's Odyssey," in *Lupercal*. London: Faber & Faber Ltd., 1960.

Kazantzakis, Nikos. *The Odyssey: a Modern Sequel,* trans. Kimon Friar. New York: Simon and Schuster, 1958.

Lattimore, Richmond. Trans. *The Iliad*. Chicago: University of Chicago Press, 1951.

Lowell, Robert. "The Killing of Lykaon," in *Imitations*. New York: Farrar, Straus & Cudahy, 1961.

MacNeice, Louis. "Circe," in *Collected Poems 1925-1948*. London: Faber and Faber, Ltd., 1949.

Muir, Edwin. "Ballad of Hector in Hades," in *Collected Poems 1921-51*. New York: Grove Press, 1957.

Pound, Ezra. Cantos 1 and 39, in *The Cantos of Ezra Pound*. New York: New Directions, 1948.

Reid, Alastair. "A Homecoming," in *Oddments, Inklings, Omens, Moments*. Boston: Little, Brown and Co., 1959.

Seferis, George. Selections from *Mythical Story,* in *Six Poets of Modern Greece,* trans. Edmund Keeley and Philip Sherrard. New York: Alfred A. Knopf, Inc., 1961.

Stevens, Wallace. "The World as Meditation," in *Collected Poems.* New York: Alfred A. Knopf, Inc., 1955. "The Sail of Ulysses," in *Opus Posthumous.* New York: Alfred A Knopf, Inc., 1957.

Wilbur, Richard. "The Sirens," in *Ceremony and Other Poems.* New York: Harcourt, Brace & World, Inc., 1950.

Yeats, William Butler. "A Woman Homer Sung," "Leda and the Swan," and "No Second Troy," in *The Collected Poems of W. B. Yeats.* New York: The Macmillan Co., 1956.

European Authors in the Twentieth Century Views Series

BAUDELAIRE, edited by Henri Peyre—S-TC-18
BRECHT, edited by Peter Demetz—S-TC-11
CAMUS, edited by Germaine Brée—S-TC-1
DANTE, edited by John Freccero—S-TC-46
DOSTOEVSKY, edited by René Wellek—S-TC-16
FLAUBERT, edited by Raymond Giraud—S-TC-42
HOMER, edited by George Steiner
 and Robert Fagles—S-TC-15
IBSEN, edited by Rolf Fjelde—S-TC-52
KAFKA, edited by Ronald Gray—S-TC-17
LORCA, edited by Manuel Duran—S-TC-14
MALRAUX, edited by R. W. B. Lewis—S-TC-37
THOMAS MANN, edited by Henry Hatfield—S-TC-36
MOLIERE, edited by Jacques Guicharnaud—S-TC-41
PROUST, edited by René Girard—S-TC-4
SARTRE, edited by Edith Kern—S-TC-21
SOPHOCLES, edited by Thomas Woodard—S-TC-54
STENDAHL, edited by Victor Brombert—S-TC-7

British Authors in the Twentieth Century Views Series

Jane Austen, edited by Ian Watt—S-TC-26
Samuel Beckett, edited by Martin Esslin—S-TC-51
Blake, edited by Northrop Frye—S-TC-58
Byron, edited by Paul West—S-TC-31
Conrad, edited by Marvin Mudrick—S-TC-53
John Donne, edited by Helen Gardner—S-TC-19
Dryden, edited by Bernard N. Schilling—S-TC-32
Fielding, edited by Ronald Paulson—S-TC-9
E. M. Forster, edited by Malcolm Bradbury—S-TC-59
Hardy, edited by Albert Guerard—S-TC-25
Hopkins, edited by Geoffrey H. Hartman—S-TC-57
Samuel Johnson, edited by Donald J. Greene—S-TC-48
Ben Jonson, edited by Jonas A. Barish—S-TC-22
Keats, edited by Walter Jackson Bate—S-TC-43
D. H. Lawrence, edited by Mark Spilka—S-TC-24
Marlowe, edited by Clifford Leech—S-TC-44
Milton, edited by Louis L. Martz—S-TC-60
Shakespeare: The Comedies, edited by Kenneth Muir—S-TC-47
Shakespeare: The Histories, edited by Eugene M. Waith—S-TC-45
Shakespeare: The Tragedies, edited by Alfred Harbage—S-TC-40
G. B. Shaw, edited by R. J. Kaufmann—S-TC-50
Shelley, edited by George M. Ridenour—S-TC-49
Swift, edited by Ernest Tuveson—S-TC-35
Dylan Thomas, edited by C. B. Cox—S-TC-56
Yeats, edited by John Unterecker—S-TC-23